Bill Shankly

It's Much More Important Than That

A Biography

Stephen F. Kelly

Bill Shankly

It's Much More Important Than That

A Biography

Stephen F. Kelly

Virgin

First published in Great Britain in 1996 by
Virgin Books
an imprint of Virgin Publishing Ltd
332 Ladbroke Grove
London W10 5AH

A catalogue record for this book is available from the British Library.

ISBN 1 85227 547 2

Typeset by TW Typesetting, Plymouth, Devon
Printed and bound in Great Britain by
Mackays of Chatham, Lordswood, Chatham, Kent

For Nessie Shankly

Contents

Illustrations

Acknowledgements

First and foremost, my deepest gratitude must go to Bill Shankly's widow, Nessie Shankly, and to their daughter Jean, for all their help and kindness. This book is dedicated to them and to the everlasting memory of their father who brought much happiness into the lives of many thousands of ordinary people.

But there have also been many others who have given their time and help in the production of this book. Among them, but in no specific order are Dave Hickson, Philip Pike, Ray Spiller, the Association of Football Statisticians, Eddie Boot, Eddie Brennan, Derek Wynne and the Manchester Institute for Popular Culture, Stan Hey, Steve Hale, Ivan Ponting, Elton Welsby, Phil Thompson, Ian Hargreaves, The *Liverpool Daily Post and Echo*, Alan Driscoll, Keven McHale, Denis Law, Geoff Twentyman, Brian Gibson, the Huddersfield Public Library Local History Section and particularly Allison Larkins, Les Massie, Huddersfield Town Football Club, Manchester Central Library, Peter Hinchcliffe and the *Huddersfield Examiner*, Carlisle United Football Club, Liam Sluyter and Sportspages Manchester, Stuart Brownlee and John Laurenson of the Cumnock and Doon Valley District Council; Muirkirk Public Library, the District History Centre at Cumnock, Peter Gronow, Alan Stevenson and Carlisle Library; Tom Finney, Bob Greaves, the staff at Liverpool Central Library, Jackie Lindsay, Ian St John, Ian Ross, Phil Chisnall, Roger Hunt, Denis Mooney, the late Sydney Moss, John King, George Higham, Liverpool Football Club and staff, Brian Porter, Granada Television and BBC Radio's *Desert Island Discs*. There were also a number of other contributors who, for one reason or another, wished to remain anonymous. My thanks to them and to everyone who gave their assistance.

A special word of thanks should go to football historian David Steele of Carlisle for all his efforts in producing material around Shankly's days in Carlisle. Thanks also to Chris Prior and my colleagues in the Media Division at the University of Huddersfield for their continuing support. A word of appreciation must also go to Jim Gardiner who has patiently read and corrected the manuscript covering the Liverpool years. Any errors that remain are entirely my fault and mine alone. I should also like to thank my publishers Virgin, for their enthusiasm and hard work, particularly Mal Peachey, Hannah MacDonald and Wendy Brown. I am also grateful to my agent John Pawsey for his continuing support and advice.

Finally, a note of appreciation to my family for their encouragement during the time it has taken to compile this book; to my mother Mary Kelly and to my parents-in-law, Anthony Rowe Jones and Marjorie Rowe Jones, a special thanks. And, last but never least, to my wife Judith for her unstinting advice and support as well as help, and to my children Nicholas and Emma who, as ever, have brightened the darker moments of writing with their regular trips up the stairs to my study.

Stephen F. Kelly
Liverpool, December 1995

1 Say It Ain't So, Bill

COULD SWEAR I saw him recently. In the dusk of an autumn evening as menacing clouds rolled in across the Mersey. The last man out of Anfield, switching off the lights, slamming the door shut, then shuffling across the car park towards the Shankly Gates. And before heading off down the Anfield Road, pulling the gates to and locking them securely. Gates almost too heavy for a man of his age. Then off home towards West Derby, a squarish figure in his white mac, the little tough guy, a slight stiffness in his walk, the legacy of 60 years of football.

Connoisseurs of the early Cagney would recognise the style. There goes a satisfied man you might have thought as he disappeared into the blackness of the chill November night, duties done. Tell us you haven't gone, Bill. Tell us you're still there keeping an eye on things.

Maybe it was Shankly, maybe it wasn't. In the half lip of a dull moon, you could never be sure. It was probably just the old memory playing tricks. But others have felt his presence too, stalking the corridors, sitting in the corner of the dressing room or preparing to play five-a-side at Melwood. Shankly is as alive today as he was 30-odd years ago. Make no mistake. Bill Shankly is more than just a legend. He has become a part of the fabric of Liverpool, as unmistakably Liverpudlian as Cilla Black, the Beatles or *Brookside*.

Shankly is everywhere, immortalised in graffiti on the walls, his name etched on Liverpool shirts and still chanted from the Kop. Young kids, born years after he died, have been reared on tales of his exploits; old men who watched and cheered his teams of the sixties and early seventies can never forget the joy and pride he brought to their lives and to the city. His off-the-cuff remarks were immortalised in print. Shankly is a legend never to be forgotten in this part of the land.

'I came to Liverpool because of the people,' he claimed. 'They have a fighting spirit with fighting blood in the veins, but mixed with it is a tremendous kindness. They will threaten your life one minute and give you their last penny the next.'

There may have been more than a smattering of romanticism in his words, but they caught the mood of a city where sentimentality is as thick as the salt in the sea breezes. To understand how Shankly manipulated that sentimentality, you also need to understand Liverpool and its people.

Liverpool was well capable of being just as obsessive, bizarre, emotional and contradictory as Shankly. They were almost one and the same character. He spoke the dreams of those on the Kop. But he was also full of loyalty, as fundamental a Liverpool characteristic as any. Nor could you pigeonhole him. He was anarchic, subversive and always ready to speak his mind. And of course he was witty. He could so easily have been born a scouser.

It was little wonder they soon took him to their hearts. Shankly was charismatic, a spokesman, voicing their thoughts and speaking their language. All that power. In another man, it could have been frightening. It was a good job he had so many likeable qualities. It's hard to think of anyone in British life, let alone a sportsman, who commanded as much affection and respect, and who could manipulate his audience like Shankly.

Talk to any of the older Kopites and they will tell you the same. 'He was one of us, a man of the people, a Kopite. He understood us, and we shared the same passion for football and Liverpool. He wanted the team to win as much as we did. He wasn't like today's managers with their gold medallions, sleek cars and fast women, taking a few back-handers here and there for players. He was a man of principle, who loved the game more than anything.'

The respect was mutual. Said Shankly, 'Occasionally, I would have a walk around the ground before a match, and I went into the Kop one day, before it had filled up. A little chap there said, "Stand here, Bill, you'll get a good view of the game from here!" I couldn't take him up on that offer because I had to look after the team. The encouragement the supporters have given the team has been incredible. When there is a corner kick at the Kop end of the ground, they frighten the ball!'

Shankly was a messiah who arrived at Anfield just as the city was set to burst on to the world map. It's hard to think of anyone else, who so captured the hearts and minds of Liverpool people. The Beatles may have brought international acclaim to the city, but once they had achieved their glory they were off chasing the Yellow Brick Motorway to fame and fortune, preferring the suburban squirearchy of Surrey, or the glens of Scotland, to the chaos of Liverpool. But once he had arrived, Shankly, the man from Ayrshire, was here to stay: he was never embarrassed by his fame, nor did he shirk the responsibilities it brought.

He was the ultimate obsessive: fanatical not just about Liverpool Football Club but about football in general. He'd buttonhole fans in pubs, cross swords with journalists in remote corridors of Anfield, argue with his players in the dressing room and then urge them all on from the bench. All he ever wanted to do was talk football, to be involved with the game.

And no game was less important than any other, whether it was Wembley, the San Siro, or a five-a-side at Huddersfield with the dads. Even before his death, he was an icon, elevated to the loftiest position, a god who couldn't be knocked down. It's hard to find anyone with a sour word to say, or indeed a story that shows Shankly in a harsh light. There are hundreds of anecdotes about him. Anyone who met him has a tale, and the stories are nearly always amusing, bizarre, the stuff of legend.

But of course there was another side. Nobody could be as dedicated without having forfeited something. There's a picture of Shankly taken by Liverpool photographer Steve Hale. It's one of those memorable photographs, instantly recognisable, of a victorious Shankly walking triumphantly around Anfield. There he stands before his beloved Kop, Liverpool scarf tied caringly around his neck, the emperor greeting his subjects. Shankly has an old-fashioned face, grey and seamed, a boxer's jaw, a welterweight's shoulders. But it is his eyes. Look at them. Staring, almost frightening, into the wilderness. The eyes of a man obsessed. There is a mystical messianic quality that cannot easily be explained away.

As a player, Bill Shankly was the archetypal Scottish half back, aggressive, punishing, but always honest. With his short-cropped hair and middle parting, he was a terrifying prospect for any forward, even if it was Matthews or Lawton. He was the leader on the park, motivating his fellow players, urging them on. It was hardly surprising that, when he retired, he should immediately land himself a managerial job.

Bill Shankly

His career took him across the wastelands of English football, from Carlisle to Grimsby, then to Workington and on to Huddersfield before finally he rolled into Liverpool. Shankly spent most of that time in the Third Division North, hardly ideal preparation for his later success. Yet those places shaped his philosophy and style of football management. But none of his achievements could have come without his loyal bootroom lieutenants at Anfield, particularly Bob Paisley, whose wise, unassuming counsel kept Shankly in check.

Shankly was also the last of a dying breed. By the time he came to retire, football had moved on from the thirties. Track-suited managers, agents and sky-high transfer fees had taken over. The old loyalties had all but disappeared.

In Shankly's day, they shook hands over a deal and toasted it with a cup of tea. By the eighties, the lawyers were drafting the contracts, the agents doing the talking, and the champagne corks kept popping. Shankly would have hated it all, though no doubt he would have been every bit as successful. However, the game of the 1990s was not the same honest game that he had played.

As a manager, he will always rank among the best. Only Busby and Stein could compare. They were all out of the same mould, growing up with the same set of values, from backgrounds where adversity bred backbone. But Shankly was a one-off. No other manager in the history of the game has been as idolised by the fans. Busby was loved and respected for all his success, but never idolised. Busby did his talking on the football field. Shankly did it wherever he was. For Shankly, football really was much more important than life or death.

On the last day of the Kop on Saturday 30 April 1994, more than 44,000 fans came to Anfield to celebrate the end of an era. It was an occasion dedicated to Shanklyism. The old banners of the sixties fluttered in the breeze and scarves dating back to the days of Hickson and Yeats had been pulled out from bottom drawers, as the chants and songs of a past era were once again aired.

The Kop, in full cry, belted out choruses of 'She Loves You' or 'Go back to Ital-ee'. Many of its younger inhabitants were not even alive when their fathers had sung the same words in the sixties. Yet the songs have been lovingly passed down over the years, each one learnt by a new generation.

That day, one by one, the great players of the past were introduced to the crowd – Albert Stubbins, Billy Liddell, Phil Thompson, Tommy

Smith, Kenny Dalglish and so on. But they saved the biggest cheer for a woman, Nessie Shankly, widow of Bill. As she tottered across the pitch leaning on the arm of Joe Fagan, a roar erupted from the Kop. 'Shank-lee, Shank-lee, Shank-lee,' they wailed to the tune of 'Amazing Grace'. It was their way of saying thank you to Bill Shankly's widow, after all those years when she had to share him with Liverpool. Twenty years on since he left Anfield, and still they had not forgotten him.

2 The Glenbuck Cherrypickers

NOBODY GOES TO GLENBUCK THESE DAYS. Why should they? Not for the past twenty years has the casual traveller through Ayrshire needed to take a detour from the A74 to visit the lowland village of Glenbuck – though you just might skirt past it on the way to Ayr, Troon or Kilmarnock. It might have been a different story 50, 40 or even 30 years ago. But not any more. The days of Glenbuck as a thriving, attractive community have long gone.

Thirty miles north of Dumfries and twenty miles south of Glasgow, Glenbuck nestles in the Southern Uplands. Today, it's almost disappeared, a mere pinprick on the map of Scotland. A sleepy little hamlet, not even a village, filled with little else but history. It would be nice to report that its future is uncertain. But that would be wrong. Its future is all too certain. It has been consigned to the dustbin of economic history. Everywhere you can see and smell its past, from half-demolished buildings to the grassed-over remains of what were once coal pits.

In the past twenty years, the Scottish mining industry has been decimated. Back at the turn of the century, there were more than 10,000 miners in Ayrshire alone. Today, there are little over a thousand in Scotland itself. But Glenbuck's decline goes back much further. At the time when Bill Shankly was born in September 1913, the village of Glenbuck was shrinking. The population then was little more than 800.

At the turn of the century, it was more than twice that. But after 1908, the pits began to close and the population dropped continuously from then on. When the First World War began in 1914, it was down to 700 as men enlisted and began the trek across Europe. Five would never return: their names are inscribed on a memorial stone that has now been transferred to nearby Muirkirk. There was a brief stay of execution for some pits as the war effort demanded more coal and iron. But it didn't last long and, when the soldiers returned to the 'land fit for heroes', they found 'for sale' notices going up at the pitheads.

Glenbuck's days stretch back to 1659 when the village was first mentioned in the Muirkirk parish records, but little else was heard of it until 1760 when the New Mills Weaving Company of Lanark established a branch there. Prior to that, it had been the favoured hunting ground of the ancient Douglases. Within a couple of years, the population had risen to 580. Thirty years later, English entrepreneurs arrived, hellbent on building a small iron works with a blast furnace and foundry.

The mines soon became a hive of activity and, in the early years of the nineteenth century, further pits were sunk, christened with evocative names such as the Davey, the Lady, Joe and Spireslack. They even tried to build a railway to Glenbuck, but the viaduct that was to carry the line over the River Ayr, east of Muirkirk, proved to be unsafe due to mining subsidence and had to be abandoned. It might have made such a difference.

By the 1870s, Glenbuck was a busy little community, so busy that they had to open a school in 1876 and, six years later, as the population edged towards its peak they built a church. It was a typical Ayrshire pit village. The houses, all owned by the coal company, were mainly long and short rows, many of them with the staircase outside. Few, if any, had baths. There were no gardens either, nor any electricity. The streets were dark with no streetlights and little in the way of pavements. There were of course the usual shops. Sanny Hamilton's butchers shop had been in the family for years; Miss Kerr ran the drapery; there was a co-op, a sub post office, a tailor, a fish and chip shop and of course a public house known as The Royal Arms.

There was also a quoiting green and, on the outskirts of the village, a football pitch. Tom Bone, the famous world champion quoiter, was born and bred in the village. It was said that Bone could toss a 20-pound quoit a distance of 21 yards and ring a gold watch placed on top of the pin.

There was plenty of agricultural activity in the area with the black-faced Glenbuck ram famous throughout the land. But in Glenbuck itself most men worked in the pits. They were a loyal mining community. In the 1926 national coal strike, the Glenbuck miners were solid to the core: there was no danger here that anyone would ever 'blackleg', even though the coal-owners were tempted to evict their tenants from their homes as the strike dragged through its tiresome nine months. If you did 'blackleg', you would automatically be ostracised from this tight-knit community. Keir Hardie, the first leader of the Labour Party, represented the miners of Ayrshire for many years during the 1880s.

Glenbuck had a noble history of trade unionism. The miners were hard men, scarred by their work, believing in fraternity and common decency. If a neighbour or work colleague needed help, they gave it. In Glenbuck, life could only be tolerated if there was a degree of mutual help and unity. The door to every house was always open. You just knocked and walked in. It was the kind of background that rubbed off on you. You could not be a miner in this part of the world and simply forget it all when you moved away. Coal-mining stayed in the blood, along with its traditions and attitudes.

By 1920, Glenbuck was becoming a transient community. Pits were closing fast and men were forced to take the local bus to other pits at Muirkirk or even further afield at Carmacoup. Grasshill was the only pit in the village. Sometimes, families were forced to up sticks and move elsewhere. Glenbuck was beginning to disintegrate. More and more houses were abandoned: it was impossible to sell them or let them out. In the early thirties, the closure of the Grasshill pit all but finished Glenbuck. In 1954, the church held its final service.

Glenbuck may have been known throughout the county for its black-faced rams, its coal pits and its Covenanters, but it was better known throughout Scotland for its football team, the Cherrypickers. Their exploits alone ensured Glenbuck's survival in the history of English and Scottish football.

In a period spanning forty years, the Glenbuck Cherrypickers sent some 50 players into professional football. Seven of them were capped by Scotland and two won English FA Cup medals. It is an astonishing record probably unequalled by any other village team in Britain. Bill Shankly was to be the finest of all the Cherrypickers, though his connection was always tenuous.

The club was founded in the late 1870s by Edward Bone and William Brown, and originally called Glenbuck Athletic. John Shankly, father of Bill, was a prominent committee member. The Cherrypickers were essentially a pit team, playing competitive matches against other pit villages. They played on a couple of pitches before they finally settled on a field alongside the road that was to become known as Burnside Park.

As you glance through the roll of honour, two things strike you. First, the family connections. Brothers, cousins, all of the same name – the Shanklys, the Taits, the Bones, the McKenzies, the Wallaces and so on. The same surnames recur in regular cycles. Secondly, the Cherrypickers were elite. Everyone who ever played for them came from Glenbuck. Unlike other village teams, they never bent the rules to allow some useful inside forward from a neighbouring village to join them. They were the Glenbuck Cherrypickers, and proud of it. Outsiders were not welcome, no matter how talented they might be.

The team changed its name from Glenbuck Athletic to the Cherrypickers some time around the turn of the century. At first, it was just a nickname, but it soon stuck and after a while it became official. Quite how they ever came to be known as the Cherrypickers is open to debate. It certainly had nothing to do with their strip of white shirts and black shorts.

The story that has now been accepted into mythology is that two of the players, Tom Menzies and his brother, used to strut about the streets of Glenbuck in caps like those worn by the Hussars. They claimed that they were 'cherrypickers', the name commonly given to the 11th Hussars following the Peninsula War in Spain. Arriving in a dusty village one burning afternoon, the Hussars cleaned out a cherry orchard to quench their thirst and hunger. From that moment on, they were known as the cherrypickers and wore cherry-coloured breeches.

It's likely that there were men from around Glenbuck who would have served with the 11th Hussars in the Boer War of 1900 and they would have passed on their stories to the likes of Tom Menzies. Whatever the truth of the tale, the name certainly stuck.

The football team were very successful. For three years in succession – 1889, 1890 and 1891 – they won the Ayrshire Junior Challenge Cup. In 1906, they picked up three trophies and in later years added countless honours to their collection. It was an infinite nursery of talent. The cherrypickers fame spread south of the border to England with many players signing straight from Glenbuck to the best English clubs including Everton, Aston Villa, Sheffield Wednesday, Newcastle and Sunderland.

In all, six cherrypickers were to win Scottish honours in some form. They were Bill Shankly, Alec Brown, Willie Muir, George Halley, John

Crosbie and Bill's brother Bob. Two others were capped at junior level, while Alec McConnell was selected but then two days later signed for Everton making him ineligible to play.

A total of fifty-odd players went on to play senior professional football in Scotland and England. The most famous of all was, of course, Bill Shankly but others such as Alec Tait captained Tottenham to the Southern League championship and, a year later, to an FA Cup triumph. Indeed, that FA Cup Final winning side of 1901 boasted two Glenbuck lads, the other being goalscorer Sandy Brown, who hit a record fifteen goals in the competition that season – a record which still stands today. Later that year, Tait and Brown returned to Glenbuck bringing the FA Cup with them for display in a local shop window. It sat there proudly for days as visitors flocked into the village just to see the English cup.

Then there was George Halley, the Burnley half back, who won an FA Cup winners medal in 1914 as Burnley beat Liverpool in the all-Lancashire Cup final at the Crystal Palace. Seven years later, Halley won a league championship medal with Burnley. One other footballing fact connected with Glenbuck ought to be mentioned. It is that Glenbuck footballers were renowned for playing the five-a-side game. Quite where and how the five-a-side game evolved is debatable, but it was undoubtedly being played in Glenbuck at the turn of the century. It was usually played in the summer months, bridging the gap between the end of one season and the beginning of another.

Local fairs and agricultural events would often feature five-a-side tournaments, some of which would last a day or more. Glenbuck was fond of basing teams around families, with the five Knox brothers at one time reckoned to be almost invincible. Years later, local dreamers would imagine a contest between the Knoxes and the Shanklys. It was almost certainly this Glenbuck tradition that gave Shankly his love of the five-a-side game, a love he would take with him around the training pitches of the world and which would lay the foundation for Liverpool's later success.

In September 1913, the nation stood less than a year from a World War that would wreak havoc on Europe and destroy the flowering of the continent's youth. The population of Glenbuck stood at a little over 700. It had been a balmy summer and the autumn nights were beginning to draw in, but the evenings were still warm. Tom Bone would no doubt have been practising his quoits, while the younger men of the village might have been over at Burnside Park playing football.

Glasgow Rangers had just completed a hat-trick of championships, though neither of the big Scottish clubs had reached the final of the Cup. That honour had gone to Falkirk and Raith Rovers, with the former winning 2-0. South of the border, Aston Villa had beaten Sunderland to win the FA Cup. But Sunderland bounced back to pip them to the championship. Had you told anyone that gloriously rich, lazy autumn that they were about to be plunged into the most horrific war mankind had ever known, they would have thought you a fool.

Barbara Shankly had ten children, not uncommon in those days, and Bill, born on 2 September 1913, was her second youngest. In all, she had five sons – Alec, Jimmy, John, Bob and Bill – and five daughters – Netta, Elizabeth, Isobel, Barbara and Jean. The sequence was an astonishing son/daughter/son, all the way through the lineage. All five boys would in time become professional footballers. 'At our peaks,' recalled Bill, 'we could have beaten any five brothers in the world.' It was probably true.

But the toll of ten children showed on Barbara Shankly. By the age of fifty, with her hair well greyed and her shoulders rounded, she looked a good ten years older than she was. But if she had grown old physically, she had certainly weathered the years gracefully in spirit. Always smiling, prepared to do anything for her children, she coped cheerfully and magnificently until she was a month off 80. Sadly, she died shortly before Bill moved to Liverpool and was to miss his phenomenal success as a manager.

Barbara Shankly was born Barbara Gray Blyth. Her brother Robert played for Glasgow Rangers and had then gone on to Portsmouth where he eventually became chairman. Her other brother William turned out for Preston North End and Carlisle where he also became a club director. Football was in the blood. It was little wonder that all her boys became footballers.

Her husband John Shankly was born at Douglas in Lanarkshire, about seven miles from Glenbuck. He was a strong, well-built man with formidable features. In later life, Bill would bear a striking resemblance to his father.

Never a footballer, John Shankly started working life as a postman, but for most of Bill's time at Glenbuck he was a tailor, producing hand-made suits. Those were the days when all suits were hand-made, never 'off the peg'. And, like any good tailor, he could turn his hand to the most basic of tailoring. When times were hard, he would tackle any small jobs in the village, altering clothes as well as making trousers longer or shorter for his own lads. Always well-turned out, it was rare to see John Shankly in anything but a suit, or without a grin on his face. It was another feature that was to rub off on young Bill. Rarely would you spot him in later years in anything other than a well-cut suit, collar and tie, and well-scrubbed shoes, topped off by a grin.

'Sometimes when he did a job for someone,' remembered Bill years later, 'they would ask, "how much is it?" "Two shillings," my father would say. "Oh, I've only got a shilling," they would reply. "Oh, it's alright," he would say. "Pay it some other time." Of course the money was never paid and it was never asked for.'

Although John Shankly was never a footballer, he was always interested in sport, especially fighting, a passion he was to pass on to his son Bill. He was also an athlete, a quarter miler, reckoned to be the best in Glenbuck, and for a time was a committee member of the Glenbuck Cherrypickers. Like most fathers at that time, he was feared and respected by his family. 'Do you want to be punished by me or by your father?' the schoolteacher asked young Bill one day. 'By you,' replied Bill, fearing far worse retribution from his father.

The family lived in the second cottage of Monkey Row. Like most houses in the village, there was no bathroom, no hot water and no inside toilet. Twelve of them – ten children and two parents – squeezed into just a couple of rooms. It was a hard life. 'I don't know how they coped,' says Nessie Shankly. 'There were just a couple of rooms. They even had beds in the wall,' she remembers.

All ten children were born at home, and for a dozen years or more there was never a moment when there was not a baby wailing or nappies hanging to dry on a creel in the warmth of the kitchen. For a family of that size, cooking alone was a mammoth task as well as an expense. It was a typical Scottish household: the women were all expected to lend a hand with cooking, cleaning or washing; the men to bring home the money.

Winters were hard and cold, and it was not uncommon for snow to lie for weeks on end. There was no heating at number 2 Monkey Row except in the kitchen, where a coal fire and the ever-lit cooker provided the household's only warmth. Luxuries were few and far between. Christmas was the only time when presents appeared and even then these were simple: sweets, apples, oranges, maybe a hand-me-down pair of football boots or an altered pullover. Holidays were unheard of. The only break might be a visit to nearby Yoker to see one of the cousins, but that was only ever a daytrip.

Like most lads their age, the Shanklys would help themselves to a few vegetables or pieces of fruit from local farms. If it was in the ground, it was God's own produce. It was never anything serious, but enough to make them run when the farmer appeared.

Raids were usually ordered like some military operation, under cover of darkness and with one or more of the brothers acting as look-out. They even helped themselves to an enormous bunch of bananas from a lorry on one occasion. This was so enormous that it took five of them to carry it home and a month to devour. But somehow you couldn't think of it as stealing. It was more a redistribution of what belonged to the earth.

Alec Shankly, the eldest of the brothers and 20 years Bill's senior, was born in 1893. Before the First World War, he played professionally in the Scottish league with Ayr United and Clyde, then served during the war with the Royal Scottish Fusiliers. After the war, he was troubled with sciatica and had to abandon his football career. He returned instead to the mines, but mining was hardly the occupation for someone with his health problems and he was soon forced into early retirement.

Jimmy was the next eldest son, four years younger than Alec. After Glenbuck, he signed for Carlisle United, then in the North Eastern League, but later joined Sheffield United for £1,000, a not inconsiderable transfer fee in those days. But it never quite worked out at Bramall Lane where an abundance of centre forwards, in particular Jimmy Dunne, limited his appearances.

In 1928, he was transferred to Southend United, where he enjoyed considerably more success, quickly making his mark with 31 goals in 39 matches – Jimmy was leading goalscorer for six seasons. He was a tough, stocky little character and, in all, scored 96 goals for Southend. After that, he went to Barrow, then in the Third Division North, hitting an all-time goalscoring record for the club of 39 goals in one season.

He had a further season with the Holker Street club, then returned briefly to Carlisle before retiring from the game and going back home to set up a coal merchant's business with a little help from his brothers. In the early years, Jimmy's wages from football helped the family overcome the burdens of poverty. The younger children had benefited the most and, to help Jimmy set up his own business, Bill and some of the others dug into their pockets.

The middle brother was John, at 5ft 6 inches, he was the smallest of the Shanklys. While he was still a teenager, John was spotted playing at inside right for Nithsdale Wanderers and was immediately snapped up by Portsmouth, then in the English Third Division. But life at Fratton Park was not easy and, after just three appearances and one goal, all during the 1922/23 season, he dropped a division, joining Guildford United in the Southern League. The lower league seemed to rejuvenate him, to such an extent that Third Division South Luton Town stepped in and offered him another opportunity.

The following season, 1924/25, he hit 20 goals in 46 appearances, but although the next campaign started brightly enough a strained heart muscle began to cause problems and in mid-season he was transferred to Halifax Town where he scored twice in seven matches. Following a brief spell with Coventry City, he returned to Scotland and joined Alloa Athletic, but by then his heart condition was causing concern and he was forced to quit the game, returning to Glenbuck and the coalmines. John lived on until 1960 when he collapsed in the stand at Hampden Park with a heart attack during the Real Madrid/Eintracht European Cup Final. He died later that evening at the Victoria Hospital in Glasgow.

Then there was Bob, a few years older than Bill, and strikingly similar looking. Bob also ended up in football management, as boss of Dundee after spending seventeen seasons playing with Falkirk. In 1935/36, he was a member of the Falkirk side that won promotion to the First Division and, a year later, was selected for the Scottish League against the Irish League in Belfast, his only international recognition. But, as with so many players of that era, the onset of war effectively ended his career.

In 1950, he returned to Falkirk as manager, taking over the manager's job at Dundee nine years later. Within two years, Dundee were Scottish champions and the following year enjoyed an outstanding run in the European Cup that took them into the semi-finals. En route, they defeated Cologne 8-1, followed by victories over Sporting Lisbon and Anderlecht. But in the semi-final they lost 5-1 away to the eventual winners AC Milan, although there was some measure of revenge when they defeated the Italians 1-0 at home. Two years later, brother Bill would take Liverpool to a European Cup semi-final. Bob Shankly later became manager of the Edinburgh club Hibernian, and finally general manager and director at Stirling Albion.

When Bill finished school, there was only one place to go and that was down the mine. Schooling had never held much for him. His education was basic, uninspiring and regimented. It was little wonder he was keen to get out into the real world. There were some farming jobs in the community, but the Shanklys were not a farming family. They were miners and, as soon as he was old enough, it was down the mine for Bill where he joined his brother Bob.

At first, he worked at the pithead, earning a couple of shillings a day, unloading the coal from the wagons as they reached the surface. After six months, he went down the pit itself, shifting the wagons from their loading area near the coalface to the cage which brought them to the surface. It was hard work pushing the trucks full of coal along the dimly lit corridors of the mine and then racing the empty trucks back to the coalface. Sometimes, pit ponies were used for the job, at other times it was the miners themselves.

In some ways, Bill Shankly was lucky. He never worked at the face itself, hewing coal – he was too young. Eight hours a day, he would be down there, nostrils full of coaldust, lungs rasping when he returned to the surface, sucking in gulps of cool, clear Ayrshire air. At lunchtime, they ate down the mine, tucking into the sandwiches his mother had cut and drinking lukewarm tea from the flask that had been with him since early morning. If you wanted the toilet, you found a quiet corner. The conditions may have been undignified, but the men themselves were lordly and proud.

The mine provided a wage, but all Bill Shankly lived for was the hooter and daylight. Then he'd race home, grab his football boots and be off to the nearest pitch for a game. That was what really counted in his life. He didn't watch a lot of football in his early days, other than games in Glenbuck or other local villages.

If he wanted to see a professional match, he had to go to Glasgow, the nearest soccer city. Once he had started work, he could afford the 1s 6d return train fare. He'd go up there most weekends – one Saturday watching Rangers, the next supporting Celtic. And as he travelled back on the train on the Saturday evening, he'd be dreaming of playing for one of the big clubs. If he'd been to see Celtic, he'd be imagining he was Charlie Napier, an elusive runner. If it was Rangers, then he'd be dreaming of David Meiklejohn, that most noble of Scotland and Rangers' captains.

Given the sectarianism of the West coast of Scotland, it was remarkable that Shankly should divide his allegiance between Rangers and Celtic. Coming from a protestant family, a pillar of the Presbyterian church, he should have been a Rangers man alone. Yet it never even seems to have crossed his mind that Parkhead was forbidden territory. It says much for his upbringing that his family held none of the bigoted views that divided Glasgow in two. This cosmopolitan attitude was to remain with him throughout his life.

Thankfully, Bill Shankly's days down the mine were numbered although release arrived in unwanted fashion. It came in the form of unemployment, the latest in a long line of pit closures. The mine was worked-out and, when it closed, Glenbuck's long history of coalmining was over.

There were other pits in the area and some of the men, particularly those with families, had little alternative but to trek further afield. Two of his friends walked seven miles each morning to their new pit, getting up at five to start their 7 am shift. If the mines had left a sharp impression in his mind, then a couple of months of unemployment was to leave another lasting memory. There were no other jobs in Glenbuck. The thirties were beginning and unemployment was set to soar. The only money he could earn was by doing a paper round.

Shankly's games with the Cherrypickers were few. He was a member of the club and trained with them, but he was still considered to be on the young side – in later years it never stopped the club from boasting that Shankly had been a regular! But with the closure of the local pit, the Cherrypickers went into decline. Shankly played for another village side, Cronberry, about twelve miles from where he lived.

Word soon spread that he was a player of considerable potential. Kilmarnock were said to be keen, but instead interest came from south of the border, from Carlisle, where his uncle was a club director. Bill's father had passed the word on to his brother-in-law, who sent a Carlisle scout to watch him playing for Cronberry in a game at Sanquhar. Within a few days, he received a note asking him to go down to Carlisle for a month's trial. Young Shankly jumped at the opportunity.

3 Uncle Bill

S HANKLY ARRIVED at Brunton Park in August 1932, a bony eight-een-year-old but boasting enough natural strength and determination to survive the rigours of Third Division North football. Coalmining had at least done him one favour. That year Everton were the English league champions; Newcastle the cup-winners. But Shankly would not be seeing much of them. In store for him were trips to Southport, Darlington and Hartlepool.

Shankly pulled on the colours of Carlisle for the first time in a pre-season Possibles versus Probables trial match on 20 August, playing for the Possibles, or the stripes as they were known that day. It was the start of a month's trial. Seven days later, he made his debut for the reserves, playing at home to Middlesbrough reserves. The Boro won 6-0. It was not an auspicious start for the young half back although the local paper reported encouragingly that 'Shankly played strenuous-ly and might develop into a useful left back'.

After his month's trial with the club, Carlisle, no doubt encouraged by his uncle Bill Blyth, as much as manager Billy Hampson, decided to take him on for the rest of the season. For the remainder of 1932, Shankly played with the reserves in the North Eastern League, reckoned to be one of the strongest reserve leagues at that time, giving some promising performances. Then on the final day of 1932, he was called up to the first team, making his league debut at home to Roch-dale in a 2-2 draw. Two days later, he was selected again, this time for an away fixture at Barnsley. Carlisle lost 4-1. Five days later, they lost again, 4-0 at Southport.

But it wasn't all gloom; there were a few wins. The team slammed five goals past both Halifax and York, but then conceded six at Hull and on the final day of the season lost 5-2 at Darlington. It was not a good season for Carlisle. By the end of their campaign, they were in nineteenth spot having scored fewer goals than any other side in the Football League.

Shankly had played sixteen first team games, but had only been on the winning side on seven occasions. But one local newspaper had at least spotted his potential. 'Shankly is a most promising player,' it reported, adding, 'he is attracting attention'. They were right too. The word was out. The scouts were already reporting on the young Shankly and within a couple of months their flattering reports would be turned into at least one firm offer. Shankly's last game for Carlisle was with the reserves on 4 May, when they beat Wallsend 6-0 at Brunton Park.

At the end of the season, not surprisingly, most of the side were transfer-listed. But young Shankly at least escaped that humiliation. Carlisle's demise was hardly his fault and, while many of his colleagues found themselves looking for new employment, Shankly was instead offered a new one-year contract.

Shankly got on well with both manager Billy Hampson and trainer Tommy Curry. Hampson had played with Newcastle before the War, but then joined Leeds before returning to Newcastle after hostilities ended. He even won an FA Cup winners medal with the Geordies and at one time was the oldest man to have ever played in a Cup Final. When he hung up his boots in 1930, Hampson joined Carlisle as manager but in 1935 left to become boss at Leeds United.

A quiet gentlemanly character, Hampson was protective of his younger players. He would leave Shankly out of the side if he thought it was going to get a bit rough, preferring to let him develop at his own pace. There was no point in forcing him into games where he might be overawed or clattered too often. In those days, there was time to develop players at a more leisurely pace with few of the pressures of today's game.

It was Tom Curry who probably had more contact with Shankly than anyone. An unfussy kind of character, the pipe-smoking Mancunian stood for no nonsense. Shankly warmed to his discipline, something he would pass on in later life. A year after Shankly left, Curry would part company with Carlisle as well to join Manchester United. There, he helped Matt Busby train United's post-war championship and FA Cup-winning side as well as the famous Busby Babes. Curry would later die in the Munich air disaster.

The other big influence at Carlisle was his Uncle, Billy Blyth. He was one of Bill's mother's two brothers. Bill had played with Portsmouth and Preston before joining Carlisle United where he was now a club director. Shankly got on well with his uncle Billy who also owned a pub in town. He went to see him regularly and his uncle passed on invaluable advice as well as making sure that the youngster stayed on the straight and narrow.

Shankly shared digs, just a few minutes from the ground, with the former Celtic goalkeeper Johnny Kelly who at one time had been understudy to the great John Thompson. Also in the same digs was club captain and full back Bob Bradley. The height of their mischief appears to have been a singsong around a piano or the occasional card school. Shankly was not averse to a game of cards in his younger days and, on more than one occasion, came away more than a few pounds down.

The advantage of being at Carlisle was that it was not too far from Glenbuck and, every other weekend, for 12 shillings, Shankly could catch a train home to the family. He was earning £4 10 shillings a week, not a bad wage for an eighteen-year-old, especially considering that the maximum in English football at the time was £8, paid only to top-rank players. It was also more than he would have been earning back at the coalface.

These were difficult days. Unemployment was nearing its peak and Carlisle was suffering the effects as much as anywhere. It was a town dependent upon coal and agriculture and, during the Depression, these industries suffered more than most. Back home at Glenbuck, money was tight. Most of the mines had closed; jobs were scarce. Shankly was the first to dig into his pocket, ready to slip his mother some money to help keep mouths fed. Nothing was said. He regarded it as a natural duty and never looked for thanks.

That summer, as soon as the season ended, Shankly went home to Glenbuck. He was still only eighteen, single and eager to see his family and pals. But no sooner had he walked in through the door than he was told that a telegram had arrived for him. He tore it open. 'TRAVEL TO CARLISLE TOMORROW STOP CARLISLE UNITED.'

Shankly was puzzled. He couldn't make out why they wanted him back so urgently. He was worried that maybe he had done something wrong and went off in search of a telephone. He was surprised when he called Brunton Park. He had done nothing wrong. On the contrary, it was just that another football club was after him and the chairman wanted to talk it over. But they would not say who it was or whether anything had been agreed.

As he replaced the receiver, he was unsure of what to do. He had mixed feelings. For a start, he had no idea which club was trying to sign him. It could be Tranmere Rovers, or equally it could be Arsenal. He had played just 16 league games for Carlisle United and, although the team had struggled, he knew his performances had caught the eye of more than one scout. He would simply have to be patient. There was no point in getting excited until he discovered which club it was and precisely what was on offer. Maybe Carlisle would be glad to be rid of him.

The following day, accompanied by his brother Alec, he caught the train to Carlisle and went immediately to his Uncle Billy's.

'So who's after me?' asked Shankly, almost before he was through the front door. 'Preston North End,' answered his uncle smiling. 'They've offered £500 for you. That's a lot of money for a small club like us and for someone as young as you. We're happy with the deal. It's up to you now.'

Shankly was slightly surprised, but not overawed at the prospect. Preston were certainly a more famous and glamorous name than Carlisle. Founder members of the Football League, they had been its first champions in 1889 and in that same year also became the first club ever to win the double when they beat Wolverhampton Wanderers 3-0 in the Cup Final. They had won the championship again the following season, and then in the next three years had been runners-up. But since that glorious era, Preston's fortunes had been mixed. In 1925, they had been relegated and ever since had been languishing in the Second Division, at one point almost dropping into the Third Division North.

Shankly was quite happy at Carlisle. He seemed guaranteed first team football for the forthcoming season and had settled well in the borders town. He wasn't convinced that he really wanted to leave. What's more, Carlisle was close to home.

'How much are they going to pay me?' asked Bill. 'You'll get £50 plus a signing on fee of £10,' answered his uncle, 'and wages of £5 a week.' It was little more than Bill was already earning. 'Go and see Bill Scott the Preston trainer,' his uncle told him. 'Talk it over with him. It's a good opportunity, you know.'

Bill Scott was still in town and the following morning he met up with

Shankly outlining his plans to the youngster. He was convinced that they had the makings of a good side at Preston. They had signed a couple of experienced players and promotion to the First Division was undoubtedly on the agenda for the forthcoming season. Shankly was not entirely convinced by all that he heard and especially by the money, which amounted to little more than he was already earning.

'Ten bob a week more wages,' he said. 'I'm not getting anything out of it.' 'Well, that's all I can offer you,' replied Scott, a little surprised at the young man's response.

There was little more to be said. Scott shrugged his shoulders and said he was going off to Newcastle there and then to sign another player. He had to have an answer now. Shankly was still reluctant and couldn't figure out the advantage in moving to somewhere like Preston. With that, they parted and Scott made off for the station.

Bill and his brother Alec looked at each other. Alec was sure Bill was being a little headstrong. 'You should reconsider,' he told him, 'it's not what you're going to get now, it's what you'll earn later.' For half an hour, they mulled it over. 'Preston's a bigger club,' came the brotherly advice. 'They used to be a great team and they might be again.'

Alec's words began to sink in. It was an opportunity and he would be silly to throw it away, even if it meant reserve team football for a while. Preston had the history and Bill Scott had the ambition to make them great again. Nobody at Carlisle ever dreamt as ambitiously as this, let alone voiced his dreams in public. Carlisle were a Third Division North side and that was it. And given the mass exodus of players at the end of the season, there was little chance that next season would bring any major miracle. He wasn't wrong either. The following season Carlisle ended up in thirteenth spot, while a season later they were bottom with fewer points than any other club in the Football League. It would be another 30 years before they climbed out of the Third Division.

Of all the arguments against leaving, Bill especially did not want to let his uncle down after he had given him his first opportunity. 'But uncle Bill's already agreed a fee,' Alec pointed out. 'He's happy to see you progress.' Shankly was suddenly convinced. 'Right,' said Bill. 'Come on. Let's see if we can catch Scott at the station.'

The brothers grabbed their jackets and raced off down the road. The train for Newcastle had just pulled in as they ran into the station. Passengers were already begining to board. Bill and Alec sprinted down the platform looking in each carriage for Billy Scott. Then, Shankly spotted him further down the platform about to get on the train.

'There he is,' he yelled. 'What are we going to do?' asked Alec. 'I'll get on the train and talk to him,' replied Bill, opening the carriage door just as the train was set to pull out of the station.

Alec stood there shaking his head and laughing as the train moved off.

When Shankly poked his head into Billy Scott's carriage, the Preston manager was more than surprised to see him.

'Changed your mind have you?' he asked with a grin. 'Yes,' replied a slightly shame-faced Shankly. 'Come on then, let's talk a bit more.'

The pair of them sat down and thrashed out the final details. Scott then produced a contract and, as the train rattled through the borders, Scott's latest recruit had signed on the dotted line. At the next station, Haltwhistle, Shankly stood up. 'I'd better get off here,' he said. The two men shook hands, with Scott clutching his contract in the other hand. 'See you next season,' said Bill.

It had been a close shave, but Shankly would not regret it. He was about to embark on the most important years of his playing career. The *Carlisle Journal*, which had hinted the previous week that Shankly might be on his way to another club, confirmed the move in its 18 July issue. 'Some prophesy his promotion to Division One before long,' it suggested, 'adding cautiously that "as yet, he is in the raw state. He is only nineteen."' They were not wrong. By the end of the following season, Shankly would have made the leap from the Third Division North to the First Division.

4 For the Love of Deepdale

I
N 1933, PRESTON NORTH END were a club with a rich history but a gloomy-looking future. All that would soon change. Preston had been one of the founding fathers of English soccer, that was soon to be exported to every corner of the globe. Oddly enough, the club was founded by some local cricketers, keen to play another team sport in the winter. In 1881, the cricketers called a meeting and after some discussion set up a football club which was to become Preston North End. They were by no means the first football club in the area. Up the road, Blackburn Olympic, Blackburn Rovers and Darwen had set the pace but North End were soon to become one of the most glamorous names in soccer.

They first entered the FA Cup during the 1883/84 season, but almost immediately found themselves disqualified for fielding professional players. The situation caused a massive row that eventually led to Preston and eleven other clubs from Lancashire and the Midlands setting up the Football League in 1888. Preston were champions for the first two years. What's more, they were runners-up in each of the following three seasons. In 1888, they were Cup finalists and a year later they went a step further winning the FA Cup to add to their league championship. There was no other team in the country to compare with Preston North End. They were known as the Invincibles.

From then on, it was downhill all the way. True, they were league runners-up in 1906 behind Liverpool, but no further honours came their way, but they remained a club of undeniable quality. They even suffered periods in the Second Division and, when Bill Shankly landed on their doorstep, they were little more than a moderate Second Division side. They had been relegated in 1925 along with Nottingham Forest and had struggled ever since to escape the anonymity of Second

Division soccer. In the season before Shankly arrived, they had finished ninth in the table, fourteen points adrift of champions Stoke City.

Like so many other industrial cities, Preston suffered appallingly during the thirties. The Depression hit Lancashire hard. Across the country, the number of unemployed rose to 2.9 million, a staggering 20% of the working population and, if those who were unregistered were included, the total was nearer three-and-a-half million. Everywhere, the unemployed protested.

In Lancashire, they marched to Preston and in Scotland they descended on Glasgow, while those from Jarrow in the North-east marched bravely to London, pricking the conscience of the nation. The politicians called the unemployed regons Distressed Areas. It somehow sounded better. Unemployment benefit was basic if not downright miserable. The Means Test, with its crippling rules, ensured that money was only forthcoming if certain stringent criteria were met. And, when money was paid out, it was done so begrudgingly and in small amounts. Few claimants met the criteria; most survived thanks only to family and friends.

In some areas of Lancashire, unemployment topped the 25% mark. Preston was a cotton-spinning town and like all the cotton towns of Lancashire had been severely shaken by the Depression. Almost half a million cotton workers were on the dole. Exports to India had crashed. Looms lay idle; mills were closing. Unemployment in Preston, even though it hit an all-time high, may not have been as bad as some parts of Lancashire, like Mersyside and Blackburn, but there were still more than 15% on the dole.

You could spot the unemployed wherever you looked. Men congregated on street corners in small groups, idling their time away, maybe playing cards or passing round a newspaper. Women stuck to the house, busying themselves as much as they could. When a job was advertised at a factory, the queues stretched halfway down the road. There was no spare cash; everyone suffered.

Shop windows were bare, paint peeled off door frames, and children romped about the streets in rags. Picture houses played to half-empty auditoriums; even football attracted sparse crowds. Few could afford the coppers to go to a game when the family was half-starving.

Shankly was as aware as anyone of the problems of unemployment: he'd seen it all before. In Ayrshire, his family and friends had suffered as the mines closed and it was little better in Carlisle. He'd spent a couple of months on the dole himself and was well aware of the humiliations that unemployment brought. But in case he had forgotten, he was to be rudely awoken by what he saw in Preston.

Shankly was lucky. At the end of his first season, his wages had risen to £8 with £6 in summer, a small fortune in a place like Preston. It allowed for the luxury of going out occasionally though, as ever, much of his money was sent home to his family in Ayrshire. But it would get better. Shankly arrived at the peak of unemployment and, as the thirties unwound, jobs were beginning to return and with them wealth creation. Even the fortunes of Preston North End began to look up.

Preston's stadium, Deepdale, was a neat little ground with a fine grandstand dating from 1906. You felt at home here, unlike at many grander, stadia. Shortly after Shankly arrived, they built a pavilion, opposite the grandstand. It was another distinctive piece of architecture that set Deepdale apart from other grounds. Preston was a cosy, friendly club, and Shankly was soon lodged just a stone's throw from the ground.

It was some months before he made his league debut with his new club. He began in the reserves, playing in the Central League, pulling on a Preston shirt for the first time for a match against Blackpool reserves, which Preston won 2-1 at Deepdale. The reserves were the usual mixture of experienced old hands and younger, untested players like Shankly. The hope was that the older players would help develop the youngsters.

It was a learning process and Shankly was developing as rapidly as anyone. By December, he had made the first team. He made his debut against newly promoted Hull City on Saturday 9 December. Ironically, Shankly had played against Hull just a few months earlier when he was with Carlisle and had been on the wrong end of a 6-1 drubbing. This time, the boot was on the other foot. Preston won 5-0. Preston were three goals up within half an hour with Shankly having a hand in the second goal. His arrival did not go unnoticed in the press. 'Shankly passed the ball cleverly,' reported the *Sporting Chronicle* without going into further detail. It was probably the first time his name had appeared in a national paper.

By the end of the season, Preston had clinched promotion as runners-up to champions Grimsby. It was to be the start of a famous period in Preston's history. They had begun the season confidently and after a couple of games were topping the table. By October however, they had slipped and by early December they were down to seventh place. But then the inclusion of Shankly seemed to revive them. Their win over Hull hoisted them into sixth spot, some way behind Grimsby who were runaway leaders almost the entire season.

Preston were not always obvious promotion candidates. One week, they would shoot up the table and, overtake their promotion rivals, only to lose their next game and slither back the following one. Grimsby had clinched promotion by early April, but the second promotion place remained in doubt until the final day of the season.

It was neck and neck between Bolton Wanderers and Preston, two of Lancashire's most famous clubs. Both teams had 50 points from 41 games: Bolton looked to have the easier final fixture with a visit to Lincoln, while Preston were at Southampton. But much to everyone's surprise, Bolton could manage only a draw while Preston won 1-0 and were into the First Division. After making his debut in December, Shankly had gone on to play all season. Once he was in the side, he was there to stay and undoubtedly became an important influence on Preston's promotion challenge.

As the side travelled back the long distance from the South coast, Shankly, still only twenty-years-old, reflected that a year earlier he had been playing his football in the Third Division North and now he was on the verge of the First Division. Next season, he would be lining up against the likes of Arsenal, Huddersfield, Newcastle, Everton and Liverpool, and doing battle with players such as Alex James, Hughie Gallacher, Dixie Dean and Pongo Waring. The prospect might have put the fear of God into most twenty-year-olds but not Shankly. It didn't seem to bother him. On the contrary, he relished the prospect.

Shankly spent that summer back home with his family, but, as ever, he was out every day running in the fields, playing football in the evening, preparing for the new season. He was determined to be as fit as anyone at Deepdale. It was a self-discipline that was to remain with him for the rest of his life. The thirties were painful years and anyone who lived through them would never forget the hardship. Shankly's family suffered more than most. Things had barely improved since he left. There was still little work in Ayrshire. More mines had closed; business was bad everywhere. They were years that no one would forget.

Towards the end of July, Shankly returned to Deepdale for pre-season training. Preston's first game back in the First Division, and Shankly's first-ever game in the top flight, was against Grimsby, the side that had walked away with the Second Division title the previous season. The odds were on Grimsby who had won 2-1 at Deepdale six months earlier. But in front of a crowd of 28,000, Preston won 1-0. Although they were beaten 4-1 at Everton, Preston made a sparkling start to their season and, after beating Huddersfield 2-0 at Deepdale, they leapt into second spot behind Sunderland.

They were still there a fortnight later after beating Chelsea, but then they began to run out of steam, tumbling steadily down the table. A 3-1 win over Blackburn in front of a record crowd at Deepdale briefly halted the slide, but it wasn't long before they were losing heavily once more. The problem seemed to be upfront. The defence was holding steady, but the forwards were simply failing to produce the goods.

Christmas brought a dramatic turn of events with Preston travelling to Highbury to face the league's top club in a Christmas Day fixture. Arsenal won 5-3, but the following day, in the return at Deepdale, Preston had their revenge with a 2-1 win. It might even have been more had a Shankly shot been a few inches lower instead of skidding off the bar. That game produced another record Deepdale attendance of 40,000. By this time, Preston had slipped into the bottom half of the table.

There was never any serious threat of relegation but for the remainder of the season it was always a case of looking over their shoulders. In the end, they wound up in mid-table with Arsenal as champions. Considering all the years they had spent in the Second Division, it had not been a disastrous season. At least, they had survived, and fairly comfortably. They had also put up a fine show in the FA Cup, reaching the quarter finals where they lost to eventual finalists West Bromwich Albion.

The 1935/36 season kicked off with Shankly about to celebrate his 22nd birthday. Despite his youth, he was already a well-established professional at Deepdale. Peter Doherty, the Northern Ireland international, remembered making his debut in a Manchester City shirt against him that season. 'Preston gave a wonderful exhibition of football, beat us 3-1, and Bill Shankly, at right half, blotted me out completely. Bill has always been a wily tactician, but that day he excelled himself. He dogged my footsteps all afternoon, muttering "Great wee team North End, great wee team," and subduing me so effectively that I must have been a great disappointment to all the thousands of City fans who had come along to see the club's expensive capture.'

Bill Shankly

It was to prove another season of consolidation both for Shankly and Preston. They began the season in dismal form, losing their opening fixture 1-0 at Huddersfield, before being slaughtered 5-0 at Deepdale by Middlesbrough. Things seemed to go from bad to worse. After five games, they had only two points to show for their endeavours and were propping up twenty clubs. There hadn't been any improvement by November either as they struggled to escape the bottom two places.

The problem was that they couldn't score goals. Two Scottish brothers had been signed – Hugh and Frank O'Donnell – but neither had really settled into the pace and style of English football. But at the end of the year, helped by a 4-0 win over Huddersfield, the brothers finally began to find their feet. So much so that by the end of the season Preston had climbed out of the relegation zone and ended up seventh in the table, just a point behind Arsenal who had begun the season looking set for a fourth consecutive title. The championship was eventually won by Sunderland, 14 points ahead of North End.

On the field, Shankly had developed into as tough a half back as any in the Football League. With his short-cropped hair, his welterweight shoulders and his underlying strength, he was a frightening prospect for any forward. 'Just to look at him was enough to put the fear of God into you,' remembers Newcastle and Liverpool centre forward Albert Stubbins. Shankly never shirked a tackle; he was always prepared to go in where others might have pulled back. He was as much a leader on the field as he was off it. He played by example.

The following season, 1936/37 was almost a repeat of the previous year. Preston began in poor form, hitting rock bottom in mid-September after a 3-1 defeat at home by Wolves. But sometimes they played perversely well, visiting top of the table Derby, 'a certain home banker' according to the *Sporting Chronicle*, yet coming away with a surprise 2-1 win. The fans were not impressed. Gates slumped to around 10,000 although the appalling autumn weather, rather than the football, doubtless deterred many from their regular jaunt to Deepdale.

Shankly missed the visit to Derby through injury and was to miss a few more that autumn as injury interrupted his playing career for the first, and virtually only, time. Throughout his playing days, Shankly was rarely absent through injury. He kept himself fit, on and off the field, and when he did pick up an injury he seemed to shake it off quicker than most. He reckoned most injuries were in the mind: you had to grit your teeth and battle through. It was a simplistic view and, as a manager, it did not win him many friends as he cold-shouldered players who were repeatedly injured. In his books, you simply did not get injured.

But at least being injured allowed him to pursue his favourite pastime, watching boxing. He became a regular visitor to the Liverpool stadium and to Belle Vue in Manchester where Glaswegian Benny Lynch was a regular attraction. There were also fights at Anfield with 20,000 turning up to see Neil Tarleton lose his British featherweight title on points to Scotsman Johnny McGory that autumn.

There were even fights in Preston, though nowhere near as important as the ones in Manchester and Liverpool. This was boxing country and Shankly was indulging a love of the fight game that would stay with him to the end of his days. In particular, he loved the big men, Joe Louis, Jack Dempsey and Sugar Ray Robinson. It was the spirit of boxing, the passion, that appealed to him most. A big punch might have been useful, but more important was that never-say-die, battling attitude.

By Christmas, Preston's season had picked up. In early December, they had signed Scottish international Tom Smith from Kilmarnock for £3,000. Smith would go on to captain the club and pick up another cap for his country. But the most exciting signing that season was undoubtedly the capture of Willie Fagan in October 1936 from Celtic for £7,000. The auburn-haired Fagan was a goalmouth raider, a man who could score goals as well as set them up.

Deepdale was rapidly becoming something of a Scottish enclave in Lancashire. Besides Shankly, Fagan and Smith, there was also Andy Beattie from Kintore in Aberdeen, Shankly's fellow half back, now established in the side. Beattie and Shankly would remain close friends throughout their lives with Shankly taking over the managerial reins at Huddersfield from Beattie in later years.

On top of those two, there were also the O'Donnell brothers, Frank and Hugh. Shankly, Beattie, Smith and Frank O'Donnell would all play for their country, with Fagan winning wartime international honours as well. It was an astonishing line-up of Scottish internationals for a club as small as Preston, even if it wasn't a million miles from the border. The following season they would add another to their ranks.

The presence of so many Scots undoubtedly helped cement team spirit, making Preston one of the most attractive footballing sides in pre-war football. They liked to play the Scottish game – craft, accurate passing and hard tackling, aligned with passion. Manager Tom Muir-head and coach Billy Scott had drawn together a formidable combination. In later years, Shankly would point to that Preston side – they were his inspiration. 'That's how football should be played,' he would tell future generations. His aim was simple: to produce a similar, if not better, eleven than the one he had played with at Deepdale.

After their poor start, Preston's league form picked up though it temporarily slumped again as a run in the FA Cup took its toll on league results. In the end, they finished in 14th place. They had begun their cup run with a fine win over Newcastle United at Deepdale. It had been the plum draw of the round and it did not go unnoticed that, the last time the two sides had met in the cup, Preston had gone on to reach the final. It was a good omen though, yet again, Preston would not go on to win the Cup.

In the next round, Preston were drawn at home once more, this time entertaining Stoke City, now boasting the precocious Stan Matthews. But even his wizardry was of little use against Preston's Scots who romped home 5-1. In the fifth round, there were another five goals as Preston beat the season's giant-killers Exeter City of the Third Division South in a thrilling eight-goal battle at Deepdale. After three successive home draws, Preston were finally drawn away in the quarter finals, to Tottenham. It was a difficult tie even though Spurs were lying in mid-table in Division Two at the time. As it was, Preston cruised to a 3-1 win and were in the last four, their next opponents West Bromwich Albion. Like Preston, West Brom were similarly positioned in the middle of the First Division. Preston strolled it, winning 4-1 at High-bury in front of a disappointing crowd of only 42,000.

Their opponents in the Wembley final were Sunderland, champions the previous season, and still among the strongest sides in the league. In young Raich Carter, they had one of the brightest talents in English football, while in Bobby Gurney they had a proven goalscorer. Between them, they would prove to be the undoing of the Lancashire club. Preston's main concern was the loss of their goalkeeper Harry Hold-croft who had been injured. His place was taken by Mick Burns. In the end, it would spell the difference between the two sides.

Boasting seven Scots in their line-up, Preston began brightly enough, with Frank O'Donnell edging them ahead in the 38th minute. Preston had the ball in the net again just before the interval, but the referee had already blown for a foul and the goal was disallowed. In the second half, Sunderland slowly began to take charge with Carter getting the better of Beattie. Just after the turnaround, Gurney flicked an equaliser and then missed an open goal a minute later. But Carter made amends in the 73rd minute, firing the Wearsiders into the lead. Five minutes later, Burbanks hit their third and it was all over.

For Shankly, there was an awful feeling of disappointment. To have come so far and then to have lost. Nobody could be blamed, least of all Shankly, who had battled throughout the game. There had been periods when Preston looked the better side, but class told in the end. It was to be Raich Carter's day. After the game, a tearful Preston chairman James Taylor vowed that they'd be back the next year. Nobody believed him at the time, but it helped lift spirits. Taylor was a master of the off-the-cuff quip, always ready with some witty line or sardonic remark. Shankly may well have picked up more than a hint or two from him over the years.

Shankly had become a major influence at Deepdale, but in 1937 he was to be joined by a player who would, over the years, become an even stronger influence. His name was Tom Finney. Finney was only a teenager when he signed up with his local club, a small, delicate-looking lad but as brawny and skilful as anyone on Preston's books. Shankly spotted his ability instantly and took him under his wing.

'He was always keen on helping the juniors as much as he could,' remembers Finney. 'He would come and talk to us at the end of each game giving us advice and telling us how we could improve our game.' The two soon struck up a friendship that was to last through the years.

Admiration for Shankly did not stop with Finney. 'All the other players had a tremendous respect for Bill,' says Finney. 'He was always full of fun in the dressing room before the game and he gave everybody a totally relaxed feeling.' On occasions, Shankly would get up to the most extraordinary antics, at one time dressing up as the famous boxer John O'Sullivan, pulling on long pants and a cotton wool moustache, just to amuse his team-mates. But it was infectious, good for morale. 'It never affected him how big the game was,' says Finney, 'and everybody improved as a player as a result of being around him.' Even then, his ability to motivate was obvious. 'He lifted people to being ten feet tall. He used to talk them into being good players and as a result they would perform better than anyone would have expected.'

Paddy Waters remembers coming to Preston as a youngster, just after the war. 'I landed at Heysham with another Irish player. Peter Corr, who was at North End, told us that Bill Shankly wanted to see us. I never knew him from Adam, but we went to his house on Deepdale Road and he sat us down to a feed. "Eat up, boys," said Shanks. And I could eat in those days. "Don't ever go short of grub just because it's rationed. Just come and see me." '

Shankly and Waters were to become good friends and Waters even followed him to Carlisle during the fifties. On away trips, they would often room together. 'On a Friday night, he would have me in and out of hot and cold baths. I felt sure he was a nutter, but it was his sheer enthusiasm for the game and the people who played it.' It was also an indication that Shankly was a natural born leader.

During the 1937/38 season, Preston, by common consent, were the side of the season, coming within a whisker of lifting the league and cup double. It would have been an achievement to match the famous Preston Invincibles, the last side to claim the double, back in 1889.

They were in contention all season, nicely poised in fourth or fifth spot but never more than a couple of points adrift of the leading bunch. Much of their success was due to the recruitment in September 1937 of the enterprising George Mutch, who was signed for £5,000 from Manchester United. Mutch was yet another Scot, an Aberdonian, whose goal-striking instincts were to be crucial as Preston steadily climbed the table. Also scoring that season was Shankly himself, hitting his first-ever goal for the club in a 2-2 draw with Liverpool at Deepdale in February 1938.

As Easter approached, Arsenal looked clear favourites for the title, but then, to the surprise of everyone, they slipped up home and away to Brentford and dropped a further point to Birmingham. Preston meanwhile took both points at Chelsea before drawing with the other title contenders, Wolves, the next day. On Easter Monday, they dropped a further point at home to Chelsea though they could so easily have sneaked the game when, with four minutes remaining, Shankly had flung a free kick into the box that was scrambled into the net only for the referee to disallow it for a foul on the Chelsea keeper Woodley. That result left Preston, Arsenal and Wolves all on 46 points with only three games remaining.

The decisive game came the following Saturday when Arsenal visited Deepdale. A record crowd of 42,684 squeezed into the ground, where queues had been forming all morning. At lunchtime, as the hooters sounded across Preston, thousands poured out of the factories to make for the ground. It was the most important league game in decades. A win for Preston would almost certainly have handed them the title, but unfortunately, Jimmy Milne was injured just before half time and Preston, playing with just ten men throughout the second half, lost 3-1. It was 'Boy' Bastin who did the damage. Two more wins and the Gunners had sewn up the championship. Preston finished in third place, three points behind with Wolves sandwiched in-between.

But Preston's moment of glory was to come at Wembley that season as they erased memories of the previous year to finally lift the FA Cup. With the words of chairman James Taylor still ringing in their ears, they kicked off their assault on the cup with a home tie against Second Division West Ham United. Given the way Preston were playing in the league, it was hardly surprising when they won 3-0. Next in line were First Division Leicester City, comfortably shunted aside in a 2-0 win at Deepdale.

Then in the fifth round came the match of the season, Arsenal v Preston, with just over 72,000 shoe-horned into Highbury, a near record crowd. The inter-war years had been dominated by Arsenal. It was all down to one man – Herbert Chapman – who had arrived from Huddersfield in 1925 after taking the Yorkshire side to a couple of championships. After Chapman left, Huddersfield went on to collect a third successive title.

Over the next few years, Arsenal would win two more titles and the FA Cup under Chapman before he died in January 1934, though that was not to spell the end of Arsenal's success. They picked up a third league championship in 1935 and won the FA Cup a year later. It was a glorious era with a rich crop of players. Alex James and David Jack may have departed by 1938, but against Preston they could still muster men like Ted Drake, Eddie Hapgood, Cliff Bastin, Bernard Joy, Wilf Copping and George Swindon. The names tripped off the tongue, most of them internationals of the highest calibre.

With the match scheduled for Highbury, the odds had to be on the Gunners. But instead it was Preston. Arsenal played poorly and, by all accounts, Preston just about deserved their win. 'Preston teamwork tells in notable Highbury triumph,' read the *Sporting Chronicle*. The Preston goal came from Dougal midway through the second half.

After that result, confidence was sky-high at Deepdale. 'We just knew we were going to win the cup,' said Shankly. In the quarter final, they were drawn away yet again, this time to Brentford, then a useful

First Division side. But Preston walked it, winning 3-0 and they were into the semi-final. As luck would have it, they drew Aston Villa out of the hat, a Second Division side about to win promotion. In the other semi-final, Sunderland took on Huddersfield Town and the odds were on a repeat final. As it was, Sunderland lost to Huddersfield, while Preston beat Villa 2-1 at Bramall Lane, Sheffield with over 55,000 watching.

Preston may have been only a small town but, even though the remnants of the Depression still lingered, it didn't stifle the rush for tickets. Cup fever had hit Lancashire. In those days, only 10,000 tickets were allocated to each of the finalists. More than 50,000 applications poured into Deepdale.

Huddersfield were no longer the force of old. The loss of Chapman had been too great a burden. The 1938 final was to be their final show of glory, and even that would not be enough against a Preston side riding on the crest of a wave. Yet, there was little to choose between the sides. In the *Daily Express*, Henry Rose was predicting a drawn final after extra time. Another 60 seconds and he would have been right. The two sides had met in the 1922 final when a disputed penalty led to Huddersfield's winning goal. This time, the roles were reversed.

A week before the final, Jimmy Milne had fractured his cheekbone in the decisive league game against Arsenal and he was ruled out of the final. That defeat had hardly been ideal preparation for the final. As if that was not enough of a problem, days before the match centre forward Dougal broke down in training and also had to be counted out. In their places, the directors chose Robert Batey and Maxwell. Preston's injuries, argued the *Sporting Chronicle*, tipped the balance in favour of their Yorkshire rivals.

It wasn't the best of finals, even though the weather was as glorious as it could have been: sweltering heat and a shirt-sleeved crowd. After 90 minutes, neither side had scored and the game went into extra time. Opportunities had been few and far between. It was much the same in extra time.

Then, with just one minute remaining on the clock, George Mutch picked up a pass from Shankly and began a menacing run towards the Huddersfield penalty area. For a moment, the Huddersfield defence hesitated until Alf Young raced in to tackle Mutch on the edge of the area. Mutch tumbled, sprawling headlong on the lush turf. The referee pointed to the spot without a flicker of hesitation, although later photographic evidence suggested that Mutch was out of the area when he was actually fouled. There was no doubt that it was a foul but there would always be doubt as to whether it should have been a penalty. The dazed Mutch picked himself up and was promptly handed the ball.

Shankly had been a regular penalty taker, but on this occasion nobody was volunteering. In a career at Preston that brought him 13 goals, eight were to come from the spot. 'I was ready to take the kick had Mutch been injured,' claimed Shankly years later. Mutch in fact was injured and was in no condition to take such a vital kick.

After the game he told *Daily Express* reporter Henry Rose, 'when I came round I was only conscious that my body was one mass of aches. I did not understand that a penalty had been awarded. They handed me the ball. I placed it automatically, thinking it was funny they had given it to me, an injured man. As I took my run, I wondered what I was doing and why. I don't remember aiming at goal.'

Shankly stood poised on the edge of the box ready to seize on any rebound. Mutch ran up and hit the ball as hard as he could. It was a case of hit and hope. The ball scurried through the air, slammed against the underside of the crossbar – crossbars were square at that time – then dropped down over the line. Preston had won the cup. There was barely time to restart the game. Afterwards, the white mark from the crossbar still showed on the ball.

Shankly collected his medal from King George VI, and Preston returned to Lancashire for a tumultuous welcome though it was nothing in comparison with the next time he came home with the FA Cup. Huddersfield's Alf Young was left in tears. 'Of course it was a penalty,' grumbled Shankly, years later, 'it's a terrible thing when a man has nothing left to do but bring down another man.' Shankly had little sympathy for Young. As they lined up to receive their medals, tears streamed down Young's face. Shankly walked over to him, but instead of a friendly arm all he could say was, 'Ay, and that's nae the first one you've given away!'

Back in Preston the following Monday evening, a crowd of more than 80,000 lay in wait for the team. On the journey from London, they had enjoyed a special British Rail lunch of Mutch Mock Turtle Soup, Fillet de Sole Wembley, North End sauce, Roast Lamb, Sauce Smith and Pineapple Penalty. The streets of Preston were thronged with supporters. It was like a royal visit, reckoned the local paper, describing 'scenes unparalleled in Preston's footballing history'.

Bill Shankly

Tom Smith led the way, clutching the cup in the first of four coaches that wound their way out of the station. Shankly stood alongside him. In Market Square, a crowd of over 20,000 cheered as the band struck up 'See The Conquering Hero Comes' and the North End theme song 'Keep Right On To The End Of The Road', a song no doubt chosen because of Preston's strong Scottish connections. The coaches slowly edged their way through the crowds towards Deepdale where Preston reserves were entertaining Blackpool reserves. They arrived just in time for the interval and went straight out on to the pitch. It was a record crowd for a reserve match.

It had been a magnificent season for Preston and, for Shankly, the finest he would experience as a player. His international career had also begun that season when he was invited to turn out for Scotland against England at Wembley in April, just a few weeks before the Cup Final. It was what he had wanted most from football. His selection came as no surprise. The sporting papers had all been predicting it.

Alongside him that day were his Preston partners Andy Beattie, Tom Smith and George Mutch, another new cap, an undoubted reflection on Preston's success that season. Frank O'Donnell, by this time with Blackpool, was also in the line-up. The programme described Shankly as 'a hard worker who wants a lot of knocking off the ball and tackles cleanly', adding that 'Shankly is adept at feeding forwards and is a real team man.'

But even if the match itself was not to be memorable, at least the occasion turned out to be worth celebrating as Scotland won 1-0 with Tommy Walker hitting the winner from a Frank O'Donnel backheader in the sixth minute. It was Scotland's first shut-out at Wembley. Scots fans, who seemed to make up at least two-thirds of the 93,000 crowd, went wild.

But for Shankly the occasion always carried the memory of an unpleasant clash with England and Arsenal's Wilf Copping. Shankly had always been known as a hard player, a man who went in to win the ball and who never shirked a tackle. But it was always a fair and honest challenge, aimed at winning the ball and not crippling the man.

Copping however had been bred in the Barnsley school of football, where you were taught to win the ball no matter what. Copping was renowned for his toughness, some might even say roughness. And at Wembley he was intent on taking Shankly out of the game, lunging in on him within the opening ten minutes. It was one of those challenges designed to show who was boss. Shankly's stockings were left torn, with his shin pad flying through the air. Shankly picked himself up and got on with the game without complaining, though others glared threateningly at Copping. The pair kept out of each other's way for the rest of the afternoon, though it would not be the only afternoon when they clashed.

After their wonderful triumphs of the previous season, Preston's efforts in the 1938/39 season, the last before the war, were poor by comparison. They finished the season in mid-table, with Everton as champions and Portsmouth as cup-winners. In the Cup, it had seemed that Preston might be set for a third consecutive final. They began by beating non-league Runcorn 4-2 away from home and then, in the fourth round, took on Aston Villa beating them 2-0 at Deepdale. In the fifth round, they were drawn against Newcastle United again, this time at St James' Park. Would the omens prove true again? Briefly, it seemed they would as Preston won 2-1. But, in the quarter finals, they were pitted against Portsmouth, then of the First Division. Portsmouth won 1-0 at Fratton Park.

But for Shankly there were compensations. His international career continued as he won his second cap against Northern Ireland in Belfast. Scotland won again: 2-0 with Tommy Walker and Jimmy Delaney scoring.

The following month, Shankly was wearing the number four shirt again in a 3-2 win over Wales at Tynecastle. In December, he faced the Hungarians, then a weak side, as Scotland won 3-1 at Ibrox. Four games for Scotland and Shankly had yet to play at Hampden. His wish finally came true when Scotland faced the auld enemy in April 1939. England hadn't won at Hampden for twelve years, but in one of the most memorable of pre-war internationals they pulled off a remarkable 2-1 victory. In driving rain and wind and on a gluepot of a pitch, both sides slithered and battled to produce a classic: England's winner arrived with just a minute to spare as Matthews lobbed the ball over Shankly for Tommy Lawton to smash in at the near post. Shankly was distraught. 'If the ground had opened up and buried me, I'd have been happy,' he recalled.

Just under 150,000 had watched, the biggest audience Shankly would ever perform in front of. The defeat was hardly his fault: it was a formidable England side with the likes of Tommy Lawton, Eddie Hapgood, Joe Mercer, Stan Cullis and Stan Matthews. And the way

England celebrated at the final whistle was acknowledgement enough that they had beaten a formidable Scottish side. Sadly, it was to be Shankly's final game for Scotland under normal conditions.

The storm clouds of war were already gathering over Europe in 1938. England played Germany that May in Berlin, destroying them 6-3 though not before they had suffered the humiliation of taking part in the Nazi salute. Goebbels, Hess and Von Ribbentrop watched on gleefully. It was quite clear where German ambitions lay. But for the moment, nobody in authority wanted to believe it.

Austria had already been annexed by the Germans. And as the second World Cup began in Italy, the Austrians, perhaps the finest side on the continent, were forced to withdraw while Germany promptly annexed their best players as well. In the event, it made little difference: the Germans were humbled by little Switzerland. The winners were another Fascist nation, Mussolini's Italy, who had recently plundered Abyssinia. Elsewhere civil war still raged in Spain, a blueprint for what lay round the corner.

5 The War Years

O N SUNDAY 3 SEPTEMBER 1939, Prime Minister Neville Chamberlain made his historic broadcast to an apprehensive nation. Britain was at war with Germany. Shankly, like everyone else, listened silently by a radio set. The day before had been Shankly's 26th birthday. There wasn't much to celebrate: Preston had lost 2-0 at Grimsby in front of a meagre crowd of just under 7,000. Nobody was much interested in football, they had other concerns. The season was only three games old and Preston had lost two of those games. They stood fourth from bottom in the First Division.

Shankly had gone into Deepdale that morning for his usual Sunday massage, fully expecting a game to be played the following Saturday. Everyone had been hopeful up to the last moment of a German withdrawal from Poland, or some compromise. But there had been no news, no diplomacy. Chamberlain had been pushed to the brink and, having issued a threat, was now forced to carry it through. Life would never be the same again.

As Shankly turned off the radio, he must have known that the football season would soon be abandoned but he could never have guessed that it would be seven long years before he kicked a football in serious competition again.

Within hours, the armed forces were on the move. The large barracks in the town, billeted in Preston Castle, had been on hold awaiting the Chamberlain broadcast. As soon as the news was official, they began to put their plans into action. Along with the declaration of war came a ban on the assembly of crowds. It meant the end of football for the foreseeable future, although nobody really expected the war to last longer than a couple of months maybe, a year at the most. Like everybody else, Shankly faced the prospect of serving his country in some way. The obvious choice might have been for him to return home and go back down the mines. Coal-mining was a reserved occupation, registered as a vital service with jobs protected. But instead of going back to Glenbuck, one of the directors at Preston fixed up a job for him working in another reserved occupation, as a riveter at nearby English Electric. It didn't last long. Shankly couldn't stand the routine, or being indoors all the time. Before long, he decided to enlist. He was off to join the RAF.

He began his service at Padgate in Yorkshire. That was followed by a stint at St Athan in South Wales. But Shankly was never to be a frontline fighter. He never flew any sorties, or fired guns in anger. In general, he was doing menial work, the occasional repairs, cleaning floors, anything that needed doing. But he also kept fit. Although the Football League had been temporarily abandoned, the government soon relaxed their ban on crowds. It was of course impossible to reinstate the Football League as so many players were serving in the armed forces, but instead they agreed a system of regional leagues. Preston played in the North West league for the remainder of the 1939/40 season and finished in second spot, just two points behind Bury. Shankly played 23 games for Preston that season. Attendances at wartime league games were generally low. Nobody had much enthusiasm for the game. Money was short, people were preoccupied and many were away serving in the armed forces.

That spring, in May 1940, Shankly was awarded the first of his wartime international caps when he was selected to play for Scotland against England at Hampden. It was the first time the two sides had met at Hampden since the outbreak of war and an astonishing 75,000 turned up for the occasion which ended in a 1-1 draw.

The following season, 1940/41, Shankly was still turning out for Preston on a regular basis, this time in a North league which basically constituted about 36 clubs north of the Midlands. Preston topped the league and then played the champions of the South, Arsenal, in the final at Wembley. A limit of 60,000 was put on the gate, making it one of the biggest turnouts for a football match since the war had begun.

Preston were back at Wembley for a Cup Final, their third in the space of four years. All 40,000 terrace tickets were sold within 24 hours. The game ended in a 1-1 draw and, in a replay at Ewood Park in front of 45,000 three weeks later, Preston won 2-1. But there were no medals. Instead, Shankly and his victorious Preston team-mates were given savings certificates. Shankly had played 25 games that season, scoring four goals. He again played for Scotland against England in May 1941 as Scotland went down 3-1 at Hampden.

The following season 1941/42, Shankly played an identical number of games for North End but this time Preston could only reach third spot, just two points behind Blackpool. And that in effect was the end of Preston for the war period. Organising fixtures and players had been a constant struggle throughout the period. Then in May 1941, the army moved in, taking over Deepdale for their own purposes, paying £250 a year compensation to the club. Two years later, they even commandeered the club's car park. Doubtless, Preston could have found alternative accommodation, but it was all too complicated. So, Preston decided to wind themselves up for the duration of the war, or until the army found alternative accommodation.

It left Shankly at a loose end, but at least he was free to play for more or less whoever he wanted. But he missed the quaint old grandstand, pavilion and the friendly terraces of Deepdale. The league had relaxed their rules, so that players could play with clubs close to where they were billeted. Some clubs like Aldershot with its huge army base benefited enormously and were able to choose the top players of the time simply because they were based in the town. Other, better known clubs, with fewer local bases, had problems. There were also travel restrictions, and many players were unable to get time off from their duties to play soccer.

For much of 1942, Shankly was stationed in Manchester and played a number of games in the Manchester and District League. He even had a game with Norwich but mainly he played for Arsenal during the 1942/43 season, making eleven appearances with the London club. Arsenal topped their regional league that season and played Charlton Athletic in the League South Cup Final at Wembley.

Unfortunately, most of Arsenal's missing stars suddenly became available for the Wembley final and Shankly found himself missing from the line-up with their registered players taking precedence. Shankly was furious. He stormed out of Highbury, vowing never to play for them again although he did go and stand on the terraces to watch Arsenal win 7-1. Joe Mercer remembered him losing his temper. 'He was most indignant and his language was dreadful.' That season, he also managed a game with Cardiff City.

Shankly played five more games for Scotland during that period. In

Bill Shankly

October 1941, he lined up at Wembley as Scotland lost 2-0 to England. Then in January 1942, he was at Wembley again as Scotland lost even more heavily, 3-0. But in April 1942 came one of the great wartime internationals as Scotland beat England 5-4 with Shankly scoring one of his country's goals. It was an outstanding Scottish side with players such as his old friend Andy Beattie from Preston, Matt Busby and Billy Liddell of Liverpool, David Herd from Manchester City, Jock Dodds of Blackpool and Willie Waddell of Glasgow Rangers. Liddell made his debut for Scotland that day, while Dodds scored a hat-trick. It wasn't a bad English side either with Hapgood, Mercer, Lawton and Matthews.

In October 1942, Shankly returned to Wembley with the Scottish side when they drew 0-0 and then, in April 1943, he played his final game for Scotland. Sadly, it was a 4-0 defeat at Hampden by the auld enemy in front of 105,000, many of them soldiers dressed in the khaki uniforms, turning Hampden into a sea of brown that day.

After that, Shankly was left out of the Scotland line-up with Adam Little taking his place. But he wasn't too bothered. He'd seen how England were beginning to shape up and was more than impressed by it. 'When I heard the team for the next game against Scotland I said two prayers,' remembered Shankly, 'one of thanks to the Scots for leaving me out, and one on behalf of Adam Little who had taken my place.' He was right to be concerned. Scotland lost 8-0 at Maine Road, their worst-ever defeat. Shankly was lucky not to be part of it. And nor would he be a part of any other Scotland squad. In all, he had played five full internationals for his country and seven wartime internationals.

The following season, 1943/44, he turned out for Bolton Wanderers on three occasions and with Luton Town five times. But that season was interrupted by yet another new posting. He was going back to Scotland, this time to Glasgow. His father had been taken ill and Shankly had been granted a posting to Bishopbriggs camp in Glasgow. It was a compassionate camp, designed to accommodate such problems. He had left Manchester a few years earlier and had then been posted to Arbroath for a junior NCO's course. After that he had been billeted at Great Yarmouth, followed by Henlow in Bedfordshire. It was a case of join the forces and see the country. But now he was off to Glasgow where he would remain until the end of the war.

Glasgow of course presented a new problem: who to play for. English soccer was now out of the question. It was too far to travel. He telephoned the secretary of the Scottish Football Association and told him that he was coming to Scotland and would be looking for a team.

He was hopeful that the word might be passed on to someone at Ibrox. Shankly had always wanted to play for Rangers, now was his chance. Or so he thought. He arrived in Glasgow a few days later and as he was walking down the platform at Central Station someone called his name. But instead of an official from Glasgow Rangers, it turned out to be someone from Partick Thistle who had come to collect him. He was told that the secretary/manager of Partick, Donald Turner, wanted to see him. It transpired that the Secretary of the Scottish FA had passed the word on to Partick.

Turner and Shankly were soon enjoying steak and chips in a local restaurant with Turner asking Shankly to play for his team. Shankly still held out hopes for Rangers and was reluctant to take up Partick's offer. But Turner was quick to point out that Partick was the closest ground to his camp at Bishopbriggs and, under service rules, you were obliged to play for the team nearest your camp – though it was a rule that was generally ignored. Shankly smiled and duly signed.

It turned out to be a fortuitous partnership. Shankly enjoyed his time with Partick, and even helped them to the Scottish Cup Final where they beat Hibernian 2-0. Shankly could now boast wartime cup-winning medals north and south of the border, a rare distinction. He continued to play with Partick until he was demobbed in January 1946. They were a fine young side and, after the war, continued to challenge for honours, finishing fifth and then third in the Scottish First Division.

It was in Glasgow at this time that Shankly met a young ginger-haired woman by the name of Agnes Fisher. She was in the WRAF serving at the same camp as a teleprinter operator. She watched Shankly many a morning as he went jogging around the camp with Jock Porter, the Scottish heavyweight boxer. 'Who's he?' she asked someone. 'Oh, that's Bill Shankly, the international footballer,' she was told. But it meant little to her. Agnes, or Nessie, as she was to become known, had little interest in football at the time. She shrugged her shoulders and wondered why he went out jogging so much.

In fact, Shankly was recovering from a cartilage operation. He had been injured playing with Preston at Halifax during the early years of the war. At first, they had thought it was a broken leg and had put his leg in plaster, but before long the plaster was off. The leg wasn't broken, but the cartilage was seriously damaged. With a war on, it was hardly the most vital surgery and Shankly was forced to play on. But at Partick, they realised the extent of the damage and the club paid for Shankly to go into hospital and have the cartilage removed. He was forever grateful.

Eventually Shankly and Agnes got talking and the inevitable happened. Shankly had never really been one for the women. He was shy and usually too busy with his football to have much time for them. But at the Bishopbriggs camp, there was a little more time for reflection. Nessie Shankly was born in Dennistoun in Glasgow in 1920. Her father had been a motor mechanic and she had worked as a bookkeeper typist in a plumber and gas fitters' office before the war. She had wanted to join the Wrens, when war broke out, but her eyesight failed her and instead she enlisted with the WRAF. Like Bill, she found herself at Bishopbriggs for compassionate reasons – in her case it was an illness to her mother. Bill and Nessie were married in Glasgow in the summer of 1944. A year later, a daughter, Barbara, was born at Nessie's house in Glasgow.

In January 1946, Shankly was finally demobbed. The war had ended six months earlier, but it was a slow process releasing everyone from the forces. As soon as he was released, he was on his way back to Preston and the following day played for North End in the cup against Everton. League football would not restart until the following August. In the meantime, Shankly played with Preston in the regional leagues, but it was not a good season for them as they ended up just a few places off the bottom. In the Cup, they beat Everton in a two-leg third round and then beat Manchester United in the fourth, before losing heavily to Charlton next time out.

The war undoubtedly robbed Shankly of his best playing days. Six years is a long time out of anyone's life. When war was declared, Shankly had just celebrated his 26th birthday. As it ended, he was coming up to his 32nd birthday. The war years came as a cruel intervention. The peak years of his footballing career had been lost to the war effort. But there was still some football left in him.

Before the war, Shankly had played in an outstanding Preston side that might well have gone on to win more honours, especially with young Tom Finney emerging. Shankly might also have boasted a dozen or more international caps. But there was no turning back the clock. At 32, he had to make the best of the next few years. Fortunately, he had kept fit, unlike many others of his age. Some had been frontline fighters and found it impossible to maintain any fitness regime; others, based at camps in remote parts of the country, had simply not played regular football. There were also those who, without the discipline of a club trainer, had grown complacent.

But Shankly had always had self-discipline. He didn't need a trainer to put him through the motions. He'd get changed and go running, by himself if necessary. Throughout the war he had kept himself fit, even winning a boxing medal, and at the end of hostilities it showed. Many of those around the age of 30 returned to their clubs after demob and simply could not keep up with the pace of league football. They had lost that edge. Within a season, most had drifted out of the game. But Shankly had a few more seasons left in him, thanks to his self-imposed fitness regime.

Within a few weeks of returning to Preston, Shankly had found accommodation for Nessie and their young child Barbara who had been born in Glasgow. It was a very different Britain after the war. Thanks mainly to the forces' vote, a Labour government had been elected with a substantial majority. They faced a thankless task. Europe had been devastated. Re-equipping industry for the future and repairing the infrastructure would be time-consuming and difficult. There was rationing and austerity. It would take years before the nation was back on its feet again.

But at least there was peace. The street lights were switched on again, queues formed outside cinemas once more and football was back in the diary. After seven years, it was hardly surprising that just about every ground in the country was packed for the return of the nation's most popular game. Over the next few years, attendances reached an all-time high. Deepdale was no exception. The queues snaked around the ground, and the town buzzed with people on a Saturday lunchtime all making their way towards the stadium. It was also said that women never ventured downtown on a Saturday because there were so many men.

That first season back, 1946/47, Preston were a side to be reckoned with. Andy Beattie was still there although he was beginning to show his years, but the Preston team had been regenerated by a young winger called Tom Finney. He may have been slight of build, but Finney was as strong and nimble a flankman as any the game had seen in 30 years. His only rival was Stan Matthews. With his powerful running, inch-perfect crosses and ability to score goals, Finney was one of the biggest attractions of post-war football. With sudden acceleration, he could whip the ball past defenders, taking the ball with either foot, and cause panic wherever he strode.

He was Shankly's hero. The two first met in 1937, when young Finney came along to sign up with his local club. Shankly spotted his ability from the outset. The youngster always had a tennis ball at his feet and Shankly was ready to give him any advice he might want. 'He was always keen on helping the juniors as much as he could,' recalls Finney. He might have been a seasoned professional, but he always used to come and talk to us at the end of each game giving us advice and telling us how we could improve our game.'

Finney had started playing for Preston during the war years, but did not make his full league debut until after the war. Yet, within weeks of the start of the season, Finney was winning his first international cap. His England career would last for twelve years.

Over the next 30 years, Shankly never tired of talking about Finney. 'He was grizzly strong,' he once said, adding, 'he could run for a week. I'd have played him in his overcoat.' As far as Shankly was concerned, Finney was the finest player of all time. Nobody was fit to tie his bootlaces.

During the 1970s, Elton Welsby produced Shankly's chat show for Radio City. 'Beforehand, we used to warn all his guests on the show not to mention Tom Finney. As soon as you mentioned Finney, it was the signal for an onslaught. You wouldn't be able to get him off the subject. He'd go on and on about Finney.'

The Preston side of the post-war years was undoubtedly dominated by Finney. He was the man the fans paid to see. And they flocked in their thousands to watch him, not just to Deepdale but wherever he played. Army uniforms gave way to demob suits and brown trilby hats that summer of 1946. Football was back in business, and the new Labour chancellor had decreed that admission prices would be restricted to 1s 3d, acknowledging that this was the working man's game and should remain as such. Wages for players were also up, with Shankly, as an established professional, now taking home the princely sum of £10 a week. It was a welcome rise.

The new season kicked off on Saturday 31 August 1946 amidst thunder, lightning, floods and sunshine. It was extraordinary weather for the time of year. Football was even back on the nation's radio network on the old Light Programme. Elsewhere the Nuremburg trials were hitting the headlines, while riots were raging across India.

Preston's opening fixture was at home to Leeds United. Finney scored the winner in a 3-2 win in front of 25,000 spectators. Attendances that day were a record high, just under the million mark, a huge increase on the 600,000 who had watched the last proper opening day in 1939. Preston had decided on a change in their line-up that day with Shankly playing at centre half. It didn't last long; he soon reverted to his old right half spot. But the performance of the day came from Wolves, who hit six second half goals to beat Arsenal 6-0. A couple of days later Preston entertained Sheffield United at Deepdale and lost 2-1. By mid-October, they were in the middle of the table, with Blackpool and Manchester United making the early running.

In that first season of league football after the war, Preston eventually finished in seventh spot ten points behind champions Liverpool. In the FA Cup, they reached the quarter finals before going down to Charlton Athletic again. The Londoners eventually went on to win the cup. All three goals came from defensive slips as the two sides struggled to play football on an ice-bound pitch.

The winter of 1946/47 was the worst in living memory. Temperatures plummeted, snow fell endlessly and the nation ground to a standstill. In the bitterly cold weather, mountains of coal were frozen solid at the pitheads. They couldn't be moved and, with so much coal trapped at the pitheads, train services soon ground to a halt. This also meant no domestic supplies of coal were available for the home; people were forced to huddle around half-empty fireplaces.

With a young baby, it was a difficult time for Bill and Nessie. The child had to be kept warm and bathed, and many was the time Shankly would return home with a few splinters of wood. Football matches galore were called off that winter with the season extended into the middle of June. Anyone who lived through it remembered it. 'It was terrible,' recalls Nessie. 'There was rationing, no coal, and we had young Barbara. They were difficult years for all of us.'

Shankly always maintained that those post-war years had a profound effect upon him. 'Everyone was out for themselves,' he claimed. It taught him that you had to stand on your own two feet and that nobody was going to give you anything for nothing. In many ways, such thoughts contrasted with his sharing view of socialism, but it was one of the tough lessons of life and not entirely incompatible with his politics.

The 1947/48 season brought little respite. There were still massive economic problems. On the opening day of the season, there was a dollar crisis with new motoring cuts just announced. The government was trying to get the miners to work longer hours and there was speculation that Prime Minister Clem Atlee was about to resign through ill health and hand over to Foreign Secretary Ernest Bevin. But as the season wore on, there would be more goods in the shops. Growing self-confidence and optimism were appearing on the horizon.

Shankly hadn't lost any of his enthusiasm either. He was still chasing every ball, still putting in his famous challenges. 'How Shankly keeps it up game after game, year after year, I don't know' commented one reporter in the *Sporting Chronicle*. On the opening day of the season, with temperatures in the 80s, Preston visited champions Liverpool and lost 3-1 in front of 50,000. But for much of the game they had held their own, leading 1-0 at half-time. Shankly and Liverpool's Albert Stubbins were the stars of the game. One paper described Shankly as 'the attacking power in the half back line,' adding that 'Shankly was grand throughout'. Finney was also in awe. 'He was always a 90-minutes man. The last thing he ever wanted to do in a match was lose. He didn't understand what defeat meant, and more importantly he didn't want to know.'

As captain of the club, Shankly had also become something of a minder to Finney, whose skills made him a target for the hatchetmen. When Finney was buttonholed by a half back who threatened to break his leg, Shankly intervened warning the half back that if he so much as touched Finney, he'd be the one with a broken leg. It was little wonder that in the years ahead Shankly would favour players like Tommy Smith or Ron Yeats in his side.

Finney remembers Shankly towards the end of his last season with Preston. 'We were away to Sunderland and he was twelfth man. On the way up to the game, he was telling me what a great side Sunderland were and how big a graveyard Roker Park was for Preston as we hadn't won a game there for ten years. Anyway we went and beat them 2-0 which was a great result. On the way back, I was sitting next to Bill and I said, "By god, Bill, that was some result." "Aye. It was a great win but that's the worst bloody Sunderland side I've ever seen," he snapped.' For Tom Finney, that summed up Bill Shankly.

At the end of that season, Preston ended up in seventh place again, with Arsenal champions. Preston had mounted an impressive challenge for much of the season. Going into the New Year, they had been in third spot behind Arsenal, but as the season wore on results trailed off. In the Cup, they had another noteworthy run, beating Millwall and then Portsmouth before travelling to Maine Road and beating Manchester City in the fifth round. Unfortunately, they then drew Manchester United in the quarter finals, and lost 4-1.

It was a game that brought Shankly up against his old friend Matt Busby, now managing United. When he saw what Busby was doing at United, it set off more than a few thoughts about his own future. All season, there had been rumours that Shankly was set to retire. He denied them strenuously, telling one reporter that he intended to go on playing as long as possible and to lead Preston out at Wembley. But United scotched that ambition.

The truth however was that Preston's league position flattered to deceive. Many of the club's players were now too old while the post-war replacements did not match the stars of pre-war years. Men like George Mutch and Andy Beattie were almost impossible to replace, while Shankly himself would be 35 when the next season kicked off. He was still full of enthusiasm and energy but he was losing the necessary edge for top-flight football, and it was noticeable. Joe Mercer remembered one player turning to him and jokingly pointing out, 'Shanks is getting past it. He's letting the left half take his own throw-ins.' It's difficult to imagine Shankly allowing anyone to do that!

Manager Billy Scott noticed the change as well. For much of the season, Shankly had been left out of the line-up while Finney had also missed large chunks of the season through injury. There was no one to carry the side. At the end of the season, when the retained list went up on the player's board, Shankly's name was not among them. He stormed in to see the manager only to be told that he was being given a free transfer. Shankly was fuming, still convinced that he had some football left in him. But Scott was adamant. It was a sad way to end his career.

Preston may well have kicked off the 1948/49 season flush with optimism after their previous campaign, but it was soon to evaporate as they discovered the truth. At the end of the season, Preston were relegated though one point would have saved them. Shankly again missed most of the season, this time through injury and, although he did return as the side struggled on, there was little he could do to avoid the inevitable.

Bill Shankly

By then, Shankly had come to terms with his own predicament. He could foresee Preston dropping into the Second Division and he did not want to carry on his career in the lower leagues. Nobody had come in with an attractive enough offer from elsewhere. Now was the time to quit. Ever since he had been playing, he had harboured ambitions to become a manager. That season, he kept his eyes pinned to the small ads that would appear on the sportspages inviting applications for any football jobs that were going. He thought that at first he might have to begin as a trainer. He'd even taken a course in physiotherapy and massage to equip himself.

Then in February came word that Carlisle United were looking for a new manager. It spelt the end of Bill Shankly's Deepdale days. He played his final game in Preston's famous white shirts on 19 March 1949 against Sunderland at Deepdale. It was his 297th league game for Preston. In his time, he had scored thirteen goals, including eight penalties, and picked up a Second Division championship medal and an FA Cup winners medal as well as a loser's medal. As he left the club, he handed his number four shirt to the manager. 'It'll run around by itself,' he told him. And with that, he walked out.

6 First Foot on the Ladder

N JANUARY 1949, IVOR BROADIS, then player/manager of Shankly's first club Carlisle United, took the unusual step of transferring himself to Sunderland for a fee of £18,000, an astonishing amount of money for a Third Division North man. It meant there was a vacancy for a manager at Brunton Park. Shankly's uncle, Bill Blyth, who had set the young Shankly on the early road to a footballing career back in 1932, was still a director at the club. Shankly decided to give him a call.

'Put yourself up for it,' suggested his uncle, 'you've nothing to lose. It's as good a place as any to begin a managerial career.' When the advert appeared, Shankly applied for the position along with some 30 or 40 others. Two were shortlisted, and invited for interview at the ground on 28 February. Shankly was one; the other was Bobby Gurney, the ex-Sunderland centre forward who was then managing Horden Colliery in the North-east League.

The two men turned up and were duly interviewed with both reportedly performing well. At the end of the day however, the board decided to offer the post to Shankly. But the position was not straightforward. Shankly was being offered less than the £14 a week he was earning at Preston, and he was not prepared to take on a managerial role that did not reflect his seniority and experience. The two sides haggled but could not agree: Shankly left Carlisle half-hoping that they might increase their offer, but fully expecting Bobby Gurney to be given the job. Shankly also knew that, with £18,000 pocketed from the sale of Ivor Broadis, Carlisle could well afford his meagre demands.

As it was, Gurney was not offered the post and all went quiet. A week later there was talk in the local papers of the Rotherham manager being offered the post, but in the event nothing was forthcoming. For the next few weeks, Shankly sat at home, keeping a watchful eye on the latest managerial sackings.

Back at Carlisle, overtures to various managers had proved futile. They had even considered giving the job to the club secretary, but in the end had rejected that notion. After all, Carlisle was hardly the most attractive of clubs. They had ended the previous season in the middle of the Third Division North and were doing little better in the current season. Appointing a new manager was becoming crucial to save the ship from drifting on to even more dangerous rocks. The board met and decided to up its offer to Shankly. He was immediately telephoned and, on the 22 March 1949, he accepted Carlisle's offer and was formally appointed the club's new manager.

Nessie was thrilled. She had worried about what would happen when Bill retired. He didn't have a trade or a skill to offer an employer. Nor was he a drinker. So running a pub, the role many ex-players took on, wasn't a possibility. She was also aware that finding a job in football would not be easy since there were plenty of other distinguished ex-players in the hunt as well. But what also delighted her about the Carlisle job was that she would be nearer her family in Scotland. That meant a lot to her.

Shankly had few doubts about leaving Preston. He may have been captain of the club, but at 35 years of age he had to be realistic. He could not go on forever. Tom Finney begged him to stay, arguing that they'd organise a benefit game for him and that he'd make money that way. Finney knew that Shankly would be earning no more in his new job than he was already getting at Deepdale. Shankly thought about it, but there were never really any doubts. He had made his mind up and he was going. He always believed that, when an opportunity occurred, you had to grasp it.

Finney was sad to be losing someone who had become a close friend; but the club was furious. Preston suddenly needed him as they struggled to avoid relegation. 'You've got a benefit due you,' they said. 'Yes,' replied Shankly. 'That's right, but you could still give me the benefit game without my being at Preston.' They looked in disbelief at him. Needless to say, Shankly never got his benefit. It disappointed him that after the years he had been at Preston, and all the heights they had climbed together, they should deny him a benefit match and look so grudgingly on his departure. After all, they knew as well as he did that his days as a player were numbered and had told him so when they transfer-listed him at the end of the previous season.

'It wasn't a pleasant business,' remembers his wife. 'Bill was so up-set. He loved Preston and then they treated him like that. It wasn't nice. We had to leave the club house and go back to Glasgow until Bill had settled everything.'

The club even held him to his contract, refusing to release him for Carlisle games until mid-April when they hoped he might have saved them dropping into the lower flight. Carlisle played on without him.

Shankly finally took up his duties at Brunton Park on 4 April 1949. His first game in charge was the Cumberland Cup Final, Carlisle against Workington at Brunton Park. Carlisle won 2-1 and Shankly had picked up his first trophy. It was a useful start. But his first league game in charge came a few days later as Carlisle drew 2-2 at home with Tranmere Rovers.

There was little Shankly could do that season other than to sit back, watch and make plans for the following season. Carlisle were stuck in the middle of the table, free of relegation and some way off promotion.

'One of the first things he did,' remembers Geoff Twentyman, then a nineteen-year-old at the club, 'was to arrange a friendly with Queen of the South. It was near the end of the season and he wanted to check on the players. Twentyman had been in and out of the team all the season, but has cause to remember that game. 'I played in that friend-ly,' he recalls, 'and after that got a regular place in the side.'

In all, Shankly took charge of just seven games in that first season but could win only one of them. Two were lost, with the other four drawn. He must have known then that he had taken on a hopeless cause. But at least it was the first step in the managerial ladder.

In fact, Shankly had spotted some potential. There were a few useful players, including Geoff Twentyman himself a half back whom Shank-ly converted into a centre half. Twentyman was born in Carlisle and had been on the club's books since 1945. He was then apprenticed as a body builder in a local garage. Two years later, he turned profes-sional and in 1947 made his debut as a seventeen-year-old. After six useful years with the Cumbrian club, he was transferred to Liverpool where he enjoyed a highly successful spell before eventually returning to Brunton Park. Twentyman however would be best remembered for his period as chief scout at Liverpool, when he teamed up with Shankly to discover some of the finest talents in British football.

It didn't take Shankly long to realise that Carlisle needed to strengthen their squad. While there were youngsters like Twentyman

who could be encouraged and developed, the side needed a few seasoned professionals. One of his first signings was Billy Hogan, an
outside right from Manchester City who joined the club in late August
1949. Hogan had only made a handful of appearances with City but
at Carlisle he was a revelation.

Geoff Twentyman could never understand why City let him go. 'Hogan was a clever player, always keen to carry the ball down the flanks,'
though as Twentyman adds, 'totally incapable of heading the ball if he
ever got into the box.' Hogan was a well-respected figure at Brunton
Park, the only player on Carlisle's books who Shankly allowed to live
outside the area. Hogan came from Salford, but Shankly trusted him
and agreed to his remaining there. It was a firm rule of Shankly's that
all players had to live within easy striking distance of the club.

In those days, it was not unusual for a player to live at the other end
of the country. Ivor Broadis, for example continued to live and train
with Carlisle, even though he had joined Sunderland. But Shankly
never encouraged that attitude, making an exception only for Billy
Hogan who he knew to be a level-headed, law-abiding character. 'Play
the game always, and be a gentleman off the pitch,' was the motto on
the club's registration card.

'Shankly was a strict disciplinarian,' remembers Twentyman. 'He
was always up-to-date on any player's misbehaviour. If he heard that
players were womanising or drinking, he'd be down on them like a ton
of bricks. He'd be very angry. He was a good masseur and, while he
was giving a player a massage, he'd also be giving him a bit of advice
about his private life and how he should be looking after himself.'

Over the years, Shankly was to remain a strict disciplinarian although there was always room for a laugh and a joke. Even then,
Shankly was beginning to develop his famed antipathy towards injured
players. Goalkeeper Jim MacLaren recalls having a leg injury and telling Shankly that he couldn't walk very well. Shankly glared at him.
'Just walk slowly then,' he told him, 'and the opposition won't see
you've got a limp.'

Carlisle hadn't changed much since before the war when Shankly
had begun his career there. The small Cumbrian outpost seemed almost
untouched by the years of hostilities. Had it not been for rationing, the
usual queues and the general lack of choice on shop shelves, you might
just as well have been in pre-war Carlisle. The Shanklys moved into a
small terraced house in Tullie Street, opposite the rugby ground and a

stone's throw from Brunton Park. Shankly always liked to be close to his work. Like any other community, the people of Carlisle made do as best they could, improvising here, being provident there. It was still largely an agricultural town, as it had always been.

Every Friday, a local farmer would call in with a few dozen eggs and some butter for the players. It was a welcome gift in those days of continuing austerity. Shankly and his trainer Fred Ford would divide the eggs and butter up for the first team players. If you didn't get your ration, then you could take it that you would not be in the first team the following day. It was certainly a novel way of breaking the news to a player.

But when players were dropped, it would always be accompanied by some logical reasoning, remembers Alex McIntosh. 'If you were dropped, he would tell you why. You didn't feel that you were being dropped. It was simply that the pitch wasn't suitable for you!'

When Shankly arrived at Carlisle, the players were visibly bored with their training routines. Training never added up to much more than running a few laps around the pitch. It was all physical. Little work was done with the ball and five-a-side games were unknown. Shankly changed things immediately. 'He sharpened up the training,' remembers Twentyman, 'and made it a whole lot more enjoyable.' Over the years, his training methods would be refined, but the basics were apparent in those early days. Five-a-side games became a regular feature. 'Sometimes we would play for an hour,' remembers Twentyman. Ivor Broadis, who was training with Carlisle, remembers going back to the ground one afternoon for extra training. At first, Broadis had trained on his own, away from his former team-mates, carrying out the kind of exercises he reckoned Sunderland would be doing.

Shankly watched him and told him he was doing it all wrong. 'Come and join in with us,' he said, 'our training is far better.' Shankly finally suggested they have a kick-around. 'The two of us played one-a-side in the car park with chimney pots as goal posts,' he says. 'If I was in front, we didn't stop until he was in front, even if it meant playing until it was dark.' Shankly's managerial style was beginning to take shape.

Shankly also encouraged the younger players, taking them and the part-timers for training every Tuesday and Thursday evenings. After that, they'd go to the pictures, normally to the Lonsdale cinema, and usually paid for by Shankly himself.

On match day, the team would meet up at noon in a local hotel.

They would have a bit of fish and toast for lunch, or maybe chicken and toast. Rationing was still enforced and fresh vegetables were at a premium. Then, after their light meal, they would settle down in the lounge for Shankly's team talk. He would start building them up – never suggesting anything too complicated – and would make a few points about the opposition, telling his backs to watch the winger because he was nippy and liked to cut inside. And then he would tell his forwards that the defenders were suspect.

'Push him over to his left,' he'd say, 'he's only got one foot. And that centre half, he doesn't like physical contact. Rough him up a bit.' It was never any more detailed than that, though Jackie Lindsay remembers that while you were eating at the table your plate would suddenly disappear and be taken down the other end of the table, so Shankly could explain some tactical move or other. It was all a process of building up confidence for the game. After the team talk, brimming over with confidence, they would either walk to the ground or catch the local bus. If someone had a car, then as many as possible would pile in for the short journey, with usually a couple of them sitting on knees in the back.

Once at the ground, the players would make for the dressing room and, at 2.45 pm prompt, Shankly would climb up into the announcer's box where he would address the crowd over the tannoy. Instead of writing a column in the programme as some managers did, he decided to speak to the fans personally, explaining why he'd changed the team, and talking about the way they had played in previous games. It proved popular and, of all the innovations that are remembered from his days at Carlisle, it is this one in particular that is recalled most often.

Shankly also took a pride in how the players turned out: he liked them to look smart, convinced that it impressed the opposition. He wanted them to take a pride in their kit, even encouraging them to take their shirts home to repair themselves. On a trip to play Lincoln one Saturday afternoon, Shankly spotted a well-equipped sports shop as the team coach drove through Doncaster. He promptly ordered the coach to stop, got out and went into the shop, reappearing proudly ten minutes later with a whole new set of playing strips. That afternoon, the team wore them for the first time as they lined up against Lincoln. Shankly probably paid for them out of his own pocket.

Shankly's assistants at the club were Jimmy Wallbanks, a Geordie who had played with Carlisle, and Fred Ford who had come to the club from Millwall. Ford was still young and was particularly popular with the players. Among the playing staff was Phil Turner, an inside forward who had previously played with Chester. Turner had joined Carlisle in September 1948. There was also Lloyd Iceton, a forward who had joined Carlisle from Shankly's old club Preston, back in 1946.

Then there was Jackie Lindsay, a fellow Scot from the West coast who would soon strike up a rapport with Shankly. Shankly called him 'Hector'; he called Shankly 'Tam'. Lindsay was a centre forward whose promising career had been interrupted by war. His goalscoring exploits had attracted the attention of clubs on both sides of the border and in the early 1940s he was snapped up by Sheffield Wednesday. He scored at a prodigious rate in the latter years of English war football but, immediately league football was resumed, he was transferred to Bury. In August 1947, he had joined Carlisle where he struck up an effective partnership alongside Ivor Broadis and Billy Hogan. Shankly would often go to Lindsay's house for lunch. 'The wife would give us some soup,' he says, 'but before long Bill would be moving the salt and pepper cellars around the table, explaining some tactics.'

One of Shankly's first signings was full back Alex McIntosh recruited from Barrow in October 1949. McIntosh was another Scot, from Aberdeen, and was soon made club captain. Shankly's first full season in charge showed only hints of promise. There was no doubt that team morale had surged, but, when it came to collecting points, Carlisle ended the season in ninth spot, though they were only eight points adrift of champions Doncaster. At that time, only one team from each of the regional divisions was promoted.

But at least Shankly could look back with some satisfaction. The previous season, Carlisle had finished 15th, well short of the top place. No matter how you looked at it, things had improved at Brunton Park. But to win promotion, new blood was needed.

One of his first recruits for the new season, 1950/51, was Alex McCue, an outside left from Falkirk who joined in October. Towards the end of the year, Paddy Waters was also recruited. Waters was to be one of Shankly's most notable signings that season.

A Dublin man, Waters had also been a team-mate of Shankly at Preston after the war, playing alongside him in the half back line. But after a bad injury, Waters had lost his place and was unable to fight his way back into the Preston side. Shankly knew he was too good to be sitting on the sidelines and reckoned he could do a useful job in the Third Division.

In December 1950, Waters teamed up with Shankly again at Brunton Park where he went on to make more than 250 appearances. When he arrived at Brunton Park to talk over the move with Shankly, Waters took one look around him and asked, 'What time is the next train back to Lancashire?'

'It was just like a big wooden rabbit hutch,' Waters remembers. 'The facilities were shocking, especially for someone like me who'd been used to Preston's ground.' Shankly knew Waters well and realised that his experience and commitment might just be the vital ingredients in Carlisle's championship chase. But persuading him to sign was another matter. 'When I left Deepdale in the morning, I told the Preston manager I had no intention of signing for Carlisle and, when I arrived and saw the ground, I knew I was right,' remembers Waters. 'By the evening and after a day of listening to Shankly, I had signed.'

Shankly's side was still a patchwork of players, though, as usual, he was oozing optimism prior to the opening of the 1950/51 season. Indeed, his mood turned out not to be totally unfounded as the side ended up in third place, some nine points off promotion. 'Shankly got the town buzzing that season,' remembers Waters, 'with gates of 18,000 and 20,000.' But Rotherham, without any doubt the best side in the division, still romped to the title.

At one stage, Shankly even tried to enlist the army's help in the push for promotion. Geoff Twentyman, who was doing his national service that season, was forced to miss a number of games due to his military commitments. He was stationed at Oswestry and remembers shortly before Easter being called into the adjutant's office.

'Gunner Twentyman,' asked the adjutant. 'Does the name Bill Shankly mean anything to you?'

'Yes sir,' replied the young soldier.

'Well, he's been on to the War Office and says that if he can get you off to play football for Carlisle, then you'll win the Third Division North championship.' Twentyman could barely believe it. The army did let him go but it was of little use. He played three games that Easter, but they didn't bring sufficient reward and Carlisle ended the season in third spot.

The highlight of the season unquestionably came in the FA Cup when Carlisle came within a whisker of pulling off one of the biggest giant-killing acts of post-war football. Carlisle had reached the third round of the Cup after wins over Barrow and Southport. Then out of the hat for the third round came the juiciest draw of all – Arsenal v Carlisle. As players and staff huddled around the radio at Brunton Park to listen to the draw, they didn't know whether to laugh or cry.

It was January 1951 when the northern no-hopers travelled to Highbury with the football world expecting a massacre. It was little wonder Carlisle were being written off: the Arsenal side was littered with talent. They had two international full backs, Wally Barnes of Wales and Len Smith of England; an all-international half back line of Alex Forbes, Ray Daniel and the evergreen Joe Mercer; while upfront they boasted Jimmy Logie, Reg Lewis, Don Roper, Freddie Cox and Peter Goring.

Nobody gave Carlisle a chance, except for one man – Bill Shankly. As far as he was concerned, when you went out on to the pitch, especially in the Cup, you started off at evens. But Carlisle were not without their worries. Just before the tie, Jack Lindsay suffered a broken jaw in a league game and had to be ruled out. Geoff Twentyman was also carrying a hamstring injury, but was determined to play even though he was not fully fit.

Ever since the day of the draw, Carlisle had been suffering from cup-tie fever. Everywhere you turned, talk was of the FA Cup and Arsenal. Shankly was besieged by well-wishers and ticket demands. Yet that was to be nothing to what would occur a week or so later.

Fans travelled in their thousands to Highbury, all determined to enjoy their day in London. Shankly took his side to the Mount Royal Hotel at Marble Arch, a far more salubrious hotel than they would normally have stayed at. This was a special occasion and the directors were determined to make the most of it. On the morning of the game, Shankly took the team to Highbury early to give them a conducted tour of the famous ground and to get them used to the atmosphere.

Apart from the injury to Lindsay, the side almost picked itself. In goal was Jimmy McLaren who had come to Carlisle from Chester on a free transfer in 1948. In front of McLaren were Norman Coupe and Alex McIntosh with a half back line of Tommy Kinloch, Geoff Twentyman and Paddy Waters. In attack were Billy Hogan, Phil Turner, Jimmy Jackson and Alec McCue, with Jack Billingham drafted in at centre forward to replace the injured Lindsay.

In the dressing room prior to kick-off, Shankly was doing his best to rally his troops, telling them to get the ball to Hogan whom he reckoned could spring a surprise or two on the Gunners' defence. He also told Jack Billingham to play as deep as he could. It was a novel role, and one that would some years later be perfected by Don Revie in the 1956 FA Cup Final.

Then as the whistle sounded in the corridor outside the dressing rooms, warning the two teams that it was time to come out, Shankly lined his eleven men up against the wall. And like a sergeant major he began to inspect them. The team were wearing a new strip for the occasion with a special badge carrying the coat of arms of Carlisle. As he walked along the line, he made minor adjustments here and there. 'Pull those socks up! Tuck that shirt in!' he ordered. Then he turned to them. 'Whatever happens on the field today,' he barked, 'you are going to go out of this dressing room a credit to the city of Carlisle!'

'That day we had a confidence instilled into us by Shankly, that I don't think has ever been equalled,' confesses Jimmy Jackson. 'The Shankly brand of enthusiasm made you feel there was no team in the country that you were not able to match!'

Arsenal supporters had also done Shankly's side proud, turning out in force for the game, with just under 58,000 of them packed into Highbury. It was the biggest gate of the day, and for almost every one of the Carlisle players, the biggest crowd they would ever play in front of.

It was a fearsome prospect, and Carlisle nerves were soon jangling. Arsenal won the toss and decided to play down the Highbury slope. Within a minute, they were swarming all over Carlisle, setting up chances galore.

'I remember there was a big clock in the ground and, after seven minutes, I turned to Geoff Twentyman and said, "We're going to lose here 20-0 at this rate," ' remembers skipper Alex McIntosh. 'Then suddenly Billy Hogan got the ball and made a great run. He dribbled past a few defenders. Immediately, confidence surged through everyone and we were away.' Shankly's plan to get the ball to Hogan as early as possible was paying dividends.

Hogan was the one player who could hold the ball and slow the game down, allowing less experienced players to acclimatise themselves to the atmosphere. Hogan had soon forced three corners and Arsenal's England full back Smith was scurrying in circles. Carlisle went on to give as fine a performance as they had ever given and, in the end, it was a case of Arsenal hanging on for the goalless draw rather than the other way around. It might even have gone Carlisle's

way but for a miraculous save by Platt in the Arsenal goal after Turner
had stolen a yard on the Gunners' defence. Shankly was overjoyed, and
walked slowly on to the pitch at the end, arms raised above his head
to greet his eleven heroes.

After the game, Shankly was besieged by reporters, all wanting to
know the Carlisle secret. It was his first experience of such fervent press
attention. He was only used to having to deal with Bob Wood, the
sports editor at his local paper. 'If only Twentyman had been fully fit
and Lindsay had been playing, we'd have won,' he claimed. Indeed,
Twentyman had played very much within himself, rarely venturing
over the halfway line for fear that he might get caught out and be
unable to sprint back.

That evening, the team returned to their Marble Arch hotel. Some of
the players went to the cinema but not Shankly. Rather than go out
celebrating, he invited Tommy Kinloch, Geoff Twentyman and Paddy
Waters up to his room where he was soon demonstrating slide tackles
across the floor, showing them how best to deal with the Arsenal attack
in the replay. It was typical Shankly.

The following day they returned home where a huge crowd lay in
wait. In all its 47-year history, Carlisle United had never experienced
anything like this. Thousands thronged the railway station, the court
square and surrounding areas. It seemed as if the entire population of
this small Cumbrian town had turned out. Nessie remembers the excitement in the town. 'Everyone was talking about the game and the
famous draw with Arsenal. It was the talk of the town.'

A couple of days later, the scenes were even wilder as 22,000 tickets
for the return went on sale. It became known as 'Black Tuesday' with
scenes of chaotic disorder. Tickets went on sale at 6 pm and the first
supporters began queuing at dawn that morning. By the evening, some
25,000 were packed six-deep in a queue that stretched two miles. Then
as the tickets went on sale, the queues broke up and the crowd surged
on the Market Hall where Corporation staff were distributing the
tickets. It was chaos.

Time and again, there would be a surge in the crowd with police
unable to cope with the swelling numbers. People fainted; others were
injured. Many left disappointed even though they had queued for
hours. Shankly watched in horror at the disorder, but could do nothing. At least he knew, there would be a full house and plenty of
support.

Sadly, the replay, despite all expectations, turned out to be something of a one-sided affair. Carlisle had had their hour and Arsenal were not a side to allow a minnow to escape a second time. The Gunners won 4-1, though Carlisle were denied a justifiable penalty as Wally Barnes fisted the ball off the line. Unfortunately, the referee did not spot it and Barnes wasn't admitting it until he was safely back in the dressing room at full time. Paddy Waters reckoned it was the pitch that cost them the tie. 'Although it was our ground,' he says, 'I felt the pitch beat us. It was very heavy.'

The Cup run probably cost Carlisle promotion. It had taken its toll on the players. After the excitement of the Highbury draw, defeat at Brunton Park came as a let down. After that they struggled, losing a string of games, many against poor sides. Rotherham meanwhile broke free of the pack and were never caught again all season.

The Liverpool centre forward Albert Stubbins remembers bumping into Shankly in those days. Stubbins was on a train returning to Liverpool with his wife, sitting in a carriage, when he heard a rapping on the window. 'I looked, and I said to Anne, "It's Bill Shankly." Bill was pointing urgently down the corridor – he wanted me to come out – so I said "Excuse me," to Anne and went out.

'Bill never wasted any time on any preamble, not "How's the family?" or "How are you?" or whatever. "Albert," he said, "When you move to the wing, do you like the opposing centre half to go with you?" I said, "Oh yes, it can leave a gap for somebody else, like Jack Balmer to go through the middle." He said, "Fine, that's what I wanted to hear. I've been trying for weeks to get them to play like this, but I'll certainly tell them next week." He shook hands and I never saw him again for four years.'

Shankly got on reasonably well with the Carlisle directors, probably better than any set of directors he ever worked with. They had no pretensions, and most of them didn't have much money either. Johnny Corrieri, the chairman, owned a fish and chip shop in the town as well as an ice cream business. Corrieri was an Italian, a generous man who would often dig into his own pocket to give a player a few quid. And of course there was Billy Blyth, Shankly's uncle, who had been at the club for many years. But of all the directors, Shankly was probably closest to Johnny Miller, a scrap iron dealer with a fine sense of humour.

Shankly was deeply disappointed that the club's form slumped after the Arsenal games. Before the transfer deadline, he approached the board seeking money to buy new players. He was ambitious for them. But Carlisle was not an ambitious club. The huge fee they had received for Ivor Broadis seemed to have been frittered away on trivia, or used to pay off debts. Shankly pointed out that Carlisle had made a considerable amount of money from the cup run. Eighty thousand had watched the two games against Arsenal, and Shankly felt, with justification, that some of it should be ploughed back into the side. But the directors were reluctant. It was probably pointless expecting much else. The club had no history, no pedigree and was hardly in a catchment area of rich footballing talent. It was just an isolated town in the borders that had briefly been seduced by a famous cup run.

Earlier that year, Shankly had applied for the vacant manager's job at Liverpool, then a First Division side. George Kay who had been managing the club since 1936 had been taken ill and was unable to carry on. The job was advertised, and Shankly applied.

It was an ambitious, seemingly wild bid, yet much to his surprise he was invited to Anfield for an interview. As he stepped off the train at Lime Street station, he spotted his old Scotland and Preston friend Andy Beattie. There was no doubt where Beattie was heading. They looked at each other and laughed. 'Well, you won't be getting the job either,' joked Shankly.

Neither of them rated their chances of securing what was even then one of the most prestigious management jobs in football. After all, they were both novices at the management game. Also joining them for an interview that day was the far more experienced Scott Symon who had to be clear favourite.

The stumbling block for Shankly turned out to be who would choose the team. The directors were quite clear about that responsibility. They were in charge of team selection. Of course, the manager would have his say, but there would be a small committee of directors and manager and it would be their job to meet on a Friday night and choose the side.

Shankly did not like that notion and told them so. If he was going to be manager, then he had to choose the side. It didn't go down well with the Liverpool directors. Needless to say, Shankly didn't get the job and nor did Andy Beattie or even Scott Symon. A few weeks later, the Liverpool board appointed the former Charlton player Don Welsh to the post. But Shankly had not gone unnoticed. One of the Liverpool directors T. V. Williams was quite taken with his enthusiasm and bold approach. He would remember Shankly and keep a close eye on his future career. There was one other compensation. On the evening of his interview, a second daughter, Jeanette, was born back in Carlisle.

Liverpool might not have wanted him, but in the spring of 1951 Second Division Grimsby Town approached Shankly and asked him if he was interested in a coaching job. The club's long-serving manager Charlie Spencer had been taken seriously ill early that season and assistant manager and former goalkeeper George Tweedy had initially stepped into his shoes as caretaker manager. Later that season, another former manager Frank Womack had taken temporary charge as the club battled hopelessly against relegation.

At the time, Grimsby were a Second Division club, only a few seasons out of the top flight. Shankly however was sceptical about taking on a coaching role when he had spent a year in management. He promised to think about it and was clearly tempted by the money on offer.

Shankly was now married with a family but his salary at Brunton Park was derisory. He could have been making just as much as a tradesman had he a skill to offer. Shankly let it be known that he had been offered another job. He also told the board that he had been offered a higher salary at Grimsby, even though the job was that of coach and not manager. Carlisle, to their credit, decided to make amends and immediately upped his pay. But the writing was on the wall. The fact that Shankly had been tempted was enough to unsettle him.

By the end of the season, Shankly knew he was banging his head against a brick wall at Brunton Park. Without money, he could be there for the rest of his life trying to get them out of the Third Division North. If they would not dig into their pockets after the cup run, what hope was there for the future. He made a further appeal for funds, but it fell on deaf ears. Geoff Twentyman is convinced that Shankly felt let down. 'He'd been very successful, but there just wasn't the backing from the club,' he says.

Then came news that Charlie Spencer would definitely not be returning to Grimsby. He was too ill to continue in such a demanding role and had decided to call it a day. Rudderless and reeling under so many managers Grimsby had crashed into the Third Division North. They now needed to make a permanent appointment.

Grimsby had been impressed when they talked to Shankly and admired his loyalty to Carlisle. But they had also realised that what

Shankly really wanted was to be in charge. Although he was a natural coach, he had spent two years managing and it was not in his nature to take what he might consider a backward step. The solution was simple: offer him the manager's job.

7 Fish and Rugby League

RIMSBY'S DEPARTURE FROM ANY DIVISION was always mourned by the clubs in that league. Visiting players to Blundell Park had become accustomed to finding a bag of fish hanging on their peg in the dressing room at the end of a game. It was a typical gesture of the time, though, God forbid, the smell must have been pretty appalling on the journey home. But now Grimsby were back in the Third Division North after an interval of 26 years. They had finished bottom of the Second Division, a welcome relief in many ways after a season of struggle against relegation and worry. With Charlie Spencer officially retired and a new manager in place, they could forget the traumas of the previous season and begin to look to the future with some optimism, and certainly a little more stability.

When Shankly took up residence at Blundell Park in July 1951, he discovered a depleted and demoralised squad of players. He was particularly shocked to find that the club had released a number of players who he had anticipated would be at the club ready for the forthcoming season. The directors had simply gone ahead and transfer-listed them without considering the new manager's wishes. But that was the way of football in 1951, when directors ruled the day even over team affairs.

Shankly's first task was to recruit a new bunch of hopefuls. They included Jimmy Hernon from Bolton Wanderers, Bill Brown from Elgin City and Walter Galbraith from New Brighton. But perhaps his brightest recruit was Alec McCue, whom he persuaded to leave Carlisle for a fee of £3,000.

The season began disastrously. As if losing their opening game at Chesterfield was not enough, Grimsby then lost their second game at home to Lincoln along with goalkeeper Stan Hayhurst who broke a finger and Alec McCue, who suffered a broken leg. With a crisis on his hands, Shankly turned to former England and Grimsby goalkeeper George Tweedy, who was then assistant manager at the club, and persuaded him, at the age of 39, to pull on the goalkeeper's jersey once more. Tweedy had kept goal for Grimsby since 1932, but agreed to give it a go and went on to make 32 more league appearances before finally retiring.

Given their appalling bad luck in the opening fixtures, Grimsby went on to do remarkably well that season. The experienced players that Shankly had brought in blended successfully with the less-experienced youngsters. They even put eight goals past Halifax and, between January and March, strung together eleven straight wins to take them into the promotion challenge.

Shankly called them 'pound for pound and class for class, the best football team I have seen in England since the war.' It was another slight exaggeration, but he meant well and that kind of talk could only boost morale at the club.

By the end of the season, the mood in the dressing room had lifted. Veteran Billy Cairns was the star of the season, knocking in 35 goals in 45 outings. Shankly rated him the finest header of a ball in English football, 'equal to Dixie Dean', an opinion that held substance. In April, promotion hopefuls Stockport visited Blundell Park and, with the gates closed and a record 26,605 inside, the Mariners triumphed 4-0. But in the end, it was all to no avail. With only one club promoted, it was Lincoln City and not Grimsby who were the champions.

That fateful early season start had robbed Grimsby of promotion. The players were all bitterly disappointed. Yet again Shankly had nearly led a team to promotion, and yet again they had failed by a whisker. Grimsby finished up in second place, a mere three points adrift of Lincoln.

The disappointment melted away with the summer warmth and, by the start of the new season, there were high hopes once again. For once, Shankly did not feel the necessity for too many changes and seemed happy with his squad of players. His only signing was Fred Smith from Manchester City for £6,000 who went on to net four goals in seven minutes as Grimsby thrashed Hartlepool 7-0.

Shankly's early confidence looked to be fully justified when the side began the 1952/53 season with five straight wins. It was not until their tenth game, away to Carlisle, that they suffered their first defeat. By then, they had stormed to the top of the table. They were to remain in the top three for much of the season and looked odds-on favourites for promotion until a run of four successive defeats at Easter put the championship beyond them. They slipped into sixth spot and, although they recovered, all hope of promotion had gone. Grimsby ended the season in fifth place, trailing champions Oldham by seven points.

Shankly had now enjoyed four full seasons in the Third Division North. In the last three seasons, his sides had challenged for promotion but on each occasion they had missed out. It was frustrating and tiring. All the time, Shankly was having to lift his players, to keep them at their sharpest.

Grimsby's team of veterans had served him well but the truth was that many of them were past their peak and in the twilight years of their careers. He had seen many of his players tire as the season wore on. New blood was needed if Grimsby were to sustain a challenge that would take them back into the upper division.

This fact was obvious to everyone it seemed, except the club's directors. Not that they were averse to new blood; it was, as always, a question of cost. And so, Shankly was forced to begin the 1953/54 campaign with pretty much the same line-up as the previous season. There was however a new goalkeeper in place – Clarrie Williams – who had made his debut towards the end of the previous season, while Archie Wright had stepped in to partner Fred Smith.

But the changes did not augur well. Shankly had a feeling in his bones, and it was not long before the rot had set in. By mid-September, the team had already lost five games, winning only three and drawing the other. Shankly knew it was pointless approaching the board for money to buy new players. During the 1952/53 season, the club had enjoyed good gates, usually in the region of 10–15,000 with more than a few around the 20,000 mark, especially early in the season when they looked championship hopefuls. But as their season slumped, so did attendances. Yet money ought to have been made available. Grimsby were without question one of the best supported Third Division clubs and had not long been out of the top divisions.

Shankly was depressed. He knew he had reached an impasse. What's more Nessie was homesick. She missed the North. Neither of them had ever lived on the East coast. All their lives had been spent on the West. They had gone home to Scotland during the summer, but if anything it had only made matters worse. Shankly missed his regular jaunts to

Ayrshire as well. Grimsby was bleak and cold, a stiff wind whipping in off the coast. They also missed the friends they had made at Carlisle and Preston. Even when he was managing at Carlisle, it wasn't far to travel down to Preston to see old friends such as Tom Finney. But from Grimsby it seemed such an effort. 'We had a lovely house in Cleethorpes,' says Nessie, 'but I didn't like Grimsby. It was so cold.' All that Jean remembers is the smell of fish.

Then, out of the blue, came the chance of a job at Workington, back on the West coast, and not a million miles from Carlisle, Preston or Scotland. The only problem was that Workington had finished the 1952/53 season next to bottom in the Third Division North.

Shankly knew he would be taking a risk, going to a club that had never known success, and one which clearly had no money to invest in players. What's more, gates were meagre and, as he was soon to discover, Workington was more of a rugby league town than a football town. But he met with the directors of Workington in a Blackpool hotel on the 19 December. He listened carefully to what they had to say, then told them that he was interested, but wanted a little time to think about it. 'Think about it over Christmas,' they told him. 'Get in touch with us in the New Year.'

It was a dilemma. Shankly knew that in Grimsby he would be leaving a club with some pedigree and tradition where gates were high and success was not a complete stranger. He knew that he would be taking a gamble if he went to Workington. They had only been in the Football League since 1951 when they had been elected to take the place of New Brighton.

Over the Christmas period, he and Nessie talked about little else but there was no doubt that their minds were made-up. Immediately after Christmas, and a couple of wins over Tranmere Rovers, he rang Dan Richardson, chairman of Workington, and told him his decision. Richardson was a delighted man.

On 2 January, Shankly met with the directors of Grimsby and formally gave them the news. It came as something of a shock to them, especially when they discovered that he was bound for Workington. But try as they might to change his mind, he was adamant. Once Shankly had decided something, that was it. Four days later, he was formally appointed manager of Workington although he was only given a temporary contract. But contracts never meant much to Shankly; far more important was a shake of the hand.

Within a few days, he must have been wondering what he had let himself in for. Previous manager Ted Smith had left the game to take up a job with the prison service. Shankly soon realised that, if Smith reckoned the prison service was more attractive than Workington, there was not much to be said for Workington. His first shock came when he discovered there was no electricity at the club. When he walked in on his first day, his hand automatically moved to the wall to switch on the light. But there was no light switch. The reason; the club still had gas.

His second surprise was to learn that the rugby league club trained and played many of their games at Borough Park. Nobody had bothered to inform him; perhaps the club's directors just assumed that he knew. Every Thursday night, the rugby league players would be out training under their coach Gus Risman. The rugby league club had won the championship back in 1951 and, under the guidance of Risman, was among the best clubs in the country.

Shankly was horrified by the state of the pitch after their sessions. The ground was cut-up and, in the winter months, it would finish up either as a mud bath or frozen like a ploughed field full of bone-hard ridges. It was impossible to play decent football on it. The situation led to numerous arguments.

Shankly had not been told of the arrangement until he saw it with his own eyes, but his protests fell on deaf ears. The board was stacked with rugby league men whose interest in football took second place to rugby. At least, the arrangement provided much-needed finance to keep the ground and league football in Workington alive.

The driving force behind the club was Ernest Smith, a director more popularly known as ED. Smith was a local headmaster, who had also been a league referee and officiated at the 1946 FA Cup Final. He was forever resigning as chairman, after battling long and hard to get the club into the Football League, and he was never prepared to put the club's existence at risk. The season before, he had even addressed a meeting of local traders to persuade them to dig deep into their pockets, so that the club could buy a new centre forward. Smith knew full well that, if Workington finished in the bottom two of the division, then the odds were that they would not be re-elected. Shankly would just have to make do with the situation.

Borough Park was as antiquated a ground as any in the Football League. Compared to Grimsby, it was appalling. The dressing rooms were bare and cold; the manager's office, little more than a wooden hut, was depressingly small. There was a smell of damp everywhere.

Even when the sun shone, and that wasn't often, you still felt a chill to the bone. You could hear Shankly's steel-capped shoes echoing down the concrete-walled corridors as he made his way about the place.

Workington Football Club was run on a shoestring. The club employed a part-time secretary and, when he wasn't there, Shankly would be the only person around to answer the telephone. The manager's first job every Thursday morning was to stroll down to the bank and draw out the players' wages. He would then return to the office, and he and the club secretary would make out the pay packets. There wasn't even a safe to keep the money in, and the wages would be handed out as quickly as possible. It was the kind of club where you had to account for the most meagre of items. 'Elastic to repair pants, 10 shillings; postage stamps, three shillings,' read one typical invoice, dated 29 September 1955, neatly typed and signed by Shankly.

When Shankly wasn't out training with the players, he liked to spend his time in the boiler room with Billy Watson, the groundsman. It was warm in there, even on those stark Cumbrian mornings. The two of them would huddle around the boiler, surrounded by paint pots, and Billy's gardening tools. Billy would get a pot of tea brewing, and the two of them would gossip for hours about football. Ironically, Watson had been appointed to the job on 12 January 1952, the day Workington played Liverpool in the third round of the FA Cup. Watson did his best to keep a good pitch at Borough Road, despite the hammering it took from rugby league, and Shankly was always there to encourage him. It was perhaps those chats in the boiler room at Workington that inspired the idea of the famous bootroom at Anfield years later.

'I can still hear his steel-tipped heels as he walked down the tunnel,' remembered Watson years later. 'He would pull up a lemonade crate to sit on and I would say to myself in anticipation, "What will he reminisce about today?" Would it be Tom Finney, or maybe West Brom's Ronnie Simpson with his emerald green overcoat?' Shankly was fond of telling the groundsman about the old lady at Cleaton Moor who tried to hit him with her walking stick, shouting 'Get back to Workington,' just because his A team had beaten her beloved Cleaton Moor Celtic. Watson would sit enraptured, listening to Shankly's tales.

Workington was not a wealthy town. It's just about as isolated a spot as you could imagine. Perched on the West coast on the edge of the Lake District, it had none of the beauty of the Lakes, nor the trading possibilities of a coastal town. It still boasted a harbour, but the days when it was an important trading port with Ireland had long gone. There were still a few coalmines in and around the area, mainly near Whitehaven, but they were closing rapidly during the 1950s as richer seams were unearthed elsewhere.

Workington was a town of little history, other than for appalling mining disasters, and even less future, out on a limb miles from anywhere. Unemployment was high among a population of little more than 25,000. Barrow and Carlisle were the nearest football clubs, both a couple of hours journey in those days. There must have been many times when Shankly wondered just why he had taken on the job, although he was to always maintain that he was happy there. 'We made the best of it,' he once said, adding, 'Deep down I enjoyed it.'

Bill might have liked it but Nessie wasn't so sure. 'It was bleak,' she says. 'We moved into a big old club house which was nice, but Workington just seemed to be miles from anywhere. We didn't have a car there either. And that made things difficult.'

But the abiding memory for Nessie was the haze. 'There was always this film of dirt everywhere. I think it must have come from a chemical plant or something. Every time I put the washing out it was always dirty when I brought it back in.'

Shankly's first, and possibly most challenging job in football, was to get Workington into a safe position. Weeks before his arrival, they were bottom of the Third Division North with just 12 points from 21 games. Had Shankly realised that his new club's very existence was at stake, it is hard to imagine he would ever have left Grimsby. But now he did, and he had to make the best of it.

The transformation was almost instantaneous. His first game in charge was, ironically, against his former employers Carlisle. Workington managed a 2-2 draw in front of 13,000 at Borough Park. During January and February, they lost just two games, winning four and drawing three.

The crowds started coming back with 14,000 flocking to see them beat league leaders Port Vale. On *Sports Report*, Raymond Glendenning was forced to eat his words after predicting a comfortable win for Port Vale the previous week. When they beat Barnsley a fortnight later, Workington had clawed their way out of the bottom four for the first time that season. They were on their way, although not without a few more scares.

It would be a struggle, but Shankly was always confident. 'I can't see us being beaten at home and we can grab some points away,' he told the local paper towards the end of the season. But luck arrived in the shape of Ernie Whittle, a North-east lad and ex-miner, who had started his playing career with Newcastle and then gone on to become a prolific goalscorer with Lincoln. Whittle was to be the answer to Borough Park's prayers, hitting some vital goals as they battled against re-election. He opened his account with a goal against Grimsby as Workington won 2-1.

From the start, Shankly instilled discipline into the side. Things had got lax without a manager and discipline had been allowed to drift. But Shankly's reputation went before him. When the team were playing away, he would bid his players goodnight at 10.30 pm, glance very deliberately at his watch and expect them to get up and retire to bed. Once they had all gone, he would take guard in the hotel foyer, waiting to catch anyone with ideas about a night out.

With two games to go, Workington needed just one point. It came against Halifax in a 3-1 win, with Whittle hitting a couple. Workington were saved although they went on to lose the final game of the season. They eventually finished in 20th spot with 40 points, four places off the bottom and just four points above Halifax who were forced to apply for re-election. They had taken 22 points from 20 games since Shankly had taken over. It had been a narrow squeak, but it was an achievement that should rank alongside any of the more famous honours he was to win.

Workington's directors were delighted, none more so than ED. A cartoon in the local paper depicted them looking gloomy and dejected early in the season, but dancing a jig after humbling leaders Port Vale. Indeed, four of the directors were so ecstatic that they decided to sever their life-long association with the rugby league club and to concentrate solely on the football club.

What's more, they agreed to invest money in new players and to redecorate the changing rooms. Things were looking up. Goalkeeper Malcolm Newlands was voted *West Cumberland Times* Sportsman of the Year. 'He thoroughly deserves it,' said Shankly, 'after saving us so many times.'

At the end of the season, Shankly had a clear-out. Eight players were transfer-listed, and six given free transfers. There were only nine full-time players left on the staff, along with seven part-timers and another five part-timers currently on national service.

It turned out to be a glorious summer of hot balmy weather: time to relax and reflect. Shankly was even becoming involved in community activities. He judged a beauty competition, appeared at local fund-raising dances and organised Sunday morning training for the A team, so that he could assess young local talent. A Workington and Whitehaven Ladies section of the club was also formed, bringing in additional funds of £230. It may not have been much, but it all helped.

Shankly and Nessie had moved into a club house in Harrington Road not long after arriving in Workington. It was a typical 1950s, semi-detached house about a mile from the ground: smart, efficient with a trimmed hedge and neat garden where children could play safely. Shankly walked to work each morning and then strolled back at lunchtime to eat with Nessie.

After spending much of the summer decorating and sorting things out, Shankly set off in search of new players. His first signing was Stewart McCallum from Wrexham who had formerly been with Hearts. A week later, he snapped up Ken Rose from Exeter. Goalkeeper Wilf Billington was signed from Blackburn as cover for Newlands, and Jimmy Fleming, a half back from Stirling Albion, was also recruited along with Des Jones, a tricky reserve winger with Bristol Rovers. In the main, players were bought for reserve team football. It had been a busy summer, but Shankly felt well-pleased with his business.

In the season's pre-trial, the Probables thrashed the Possibles 8-4 with Ernie Whittle and Jim Dailey hitting hat-tricks. It seemed that Shankly had discovered the right blend. But after winning their opening game against Darlington, the team stumbled at home to Chesterfield. Shankly decided to ring the changes although it did not bring immediate success. More defeats followed, more switches were made. Eventually, Des Jones was given his chance and slowly the side began to settle.

But if things were improving on the field, the same could not be said for the boardroom. That autumn, there was an almighty behind-the-scenes row. It was an unusually large board and consequently their deliberations could be tortuous. Meetings were said to be chaotic. Shankly attended the monthly meeting to give his report, but frequently found himself watching dumbfounded as the directors bickered. On occasion, their arguments almost came to blows. The bitter rivalry between the football club and the rugby league club was usually the source of disputes, along with the board's inclination to be involved in team selection. But sometimes, like most families, it was just about money.

Prior to Shankly's arrival, the team had been managerless for some months with trainer Tommy Jones running affairs. But his authority stopped firmly at the training ground. It was the board who chose the team and the board who signed new players.

Shankly, of course, did not like that, but on occasion was forced to at least go along with some of their 'advice' over team selection. Certainly, he would never have allowed them to usurp his position when it came to operating in the transfer market but the occasional 'word of wisdom' from above could just about be tolerated. In truth, he didn't have much option. It was the case with most clubs.

'Board meetings were as good as going to the music hall,' joked Shankly. But that autumn, after yet another stinging internal row, Ernest Smith took over as chairman again from Dan Richardson. The local papers were full of it although nobody could ever fathom precisely what was going on. Workington was that kind of a club. But no matter how you analysed it, the return of ED had to be good news. He was, after all, a football man.

There was an all-round improvement in morale. Even though results that autumn remained inconsistent, there was a new buzz about the dressing room. 'There was more laughter, more pulling together,' remembered one player. 'You could hear the players singing together in the bath.' The team soon climbed to ninth in the table, the highest Workington had ever been. Shankly had also instituted his five-a-side games, although, in place of the usual England/Scotland tussles, it was now bachelors against the married men.

After knocking Cheshire County side Hyde United out of the FA Cup in the first round, Workington were drawn away to Leyton Orient of the Third Division South. It was the biggest game Shankly had faced since taking charge at Borough Park. There was a long-held belief in football circles that the southern section was much stronger than the northern – and it was a view that had some validity to it – but on this occasion Workington surprised everyone by winning 1-0. The explanation, according to Shankly was simple: it was the influence of the great Ferenc Puskas and his Hungarian side.

After training on Friday, the team had taken the team coach to Carlisle station where they caught the midday Flying Scotsman to London. On the train, Shankly heard that the great Hungarian team were in another carriage, travelling back to London after having beaten Scotland 4-2 at Hampden Park. The year before, Hungary had destroyed England 6-3 at Wembley.

That was enough for Shankly. He was up out of his seat and off in search of Puskas, Hidegkuti and Kocsis. He eventually found them up in the first-class carriages, introduced himself, got Puskas to give him his autograph, and then brought the rest of the Workington side down to meet them. The players exchanged pleasantries and stories for the rest of the journey. 'Some of their magic rubbed off on us,' Shankly told the papers after beating Leyton Orient. A few days later a postcard arrived at Borough Park, addressed to Mr Shankly. 'Congratulations on your historic win,' it read, 'from the Hungarian FA.' Unfortunately, the magic did not last long. In the next round, they were thrashed 5-0 by Luton.

Meanwhile in the league, the goals were rattling in. After hitting five against Hyde United in the Cup, they struck four against Stockport and six against Darlington. Jim Dailey and Ernie Whittle were proving to be an effective partnership upfront helping Workington climb to fifth spot, within four points of leaders Scunthorpe. With Christmas on the horizon, the talk around Borough Park was not so much about turkeys and plum pudding as about promotion. The board was even considering a plan, codenamed 'Prepare for Promotion', that involved raising £10,000 to bring the ground into line with those of the Second Division. But it was all wishful thinking. By February, the team had slipped out of contention, picking up only four points out of a possible eighteen during the first months of the year. And with it gates slumped. Eventually, Workington wound up in eighth place having been out of contention since the back end of the year.

Since his arrival, Shankly had been keenly developing a youth policy at the club. The reserves had done particularly well and had become known locally as Shankly's Babes. Every game, at least eight or nine of those fielded would be local lads under the age of twenty. That summer, Shankly decided to take out an advert in the local press asking youngsters in the area, who were interested in a football career, to get in touch with him and come along for a trial. Cumberland might not have been ideal hunting ground for the stars of the future, but you had to encourage as many as possible, screw every last drop of blood out of the stone. If youngsters knew they had a realistic chance at Workington, then they might just be tempted away from rugby league. And with no money to buy players, Shankly was left with little option but to concentrate on a youth policy.

During the 1953/54 season, the club spent a total of £18,480 on transfers and was now financially embarrassed. The slump in form had been accompanied by a drastic fall in attendances. Just 2,660 turned up for the final match of the season. Shankly was told, quite firmly, that the club could not afford to sign any new players for a short while. Indeed, matters were so grave at one point that the board accepted a proposal to cut the players' wages by £1 a week to bring them in line with other Third Division North clubs. The total wages bill for the year had been little over £13,000, yet it needed to be trimmed even further if the club was to survive.

Shankly didn't like it. He always believed that a working man should be paid his due but now found himself having to set an example and take a cut in salary himself. It was no use expecting the players to accept a reduction, if he didn't as well, and the way the players were complaining, it was the only way out of the problem. In the end, everyone accepted the pay cut and most of the players spent the summer working elsewhere to earn a bit more cash. Jim Dailey drove a van for the Co-op, while Jack Bertolini worked for the Coal Board.

Things improved slightly over the summer. Andy Mullen was sold to Scunthorpe for £1,000 and it was announced that gate prices for the new season would be increased, though this came with a warning that if attendances didn't rise, the club would be 'facing impossible problems'. It gave Shankly just enough space to be able to sign Tony Spink from Doncaster for a nominal fee.

And yet despite all the problems – a dilapidated stadium, wage cuts, no money for transfers – morale remained high. Everyone was bullish, as the new season kicked off, especially wing half Rex Dunlop who was predicting, 'We'll win the championship.'

There was a new sense of purpose about Borough Park and it showed on the field. They beat Hartlepool 5-1, and won 5-4 away at Stockport. By early October 1955, they had climbed into fourth place. Aston Villa had been making inquiries about Wilf Billington, and there was talk of a hefty fee although the club was still awaiting an offer. Billy Robson was also attracting the scouts to Borough Park and, although Shankly would have been reluctant to release either of them, he was realistic enough to know that in the end he would have little say in the matter. The club was still in dire straits with yet more talk of a price increase at the turnstiles.

That autumn, Shankly made an audacious bid to sign Stan Mortensen, the Blackpool and England striker who had scored three goals in the famous 1953 Cup Final. Mortensen was nearing the end of his career and, after being dropped by Blackpool, was looking for a fresh challenge in the lower divisions. Even though Workington was not too many miles from his home in Blackpool, Shankly could not persuade him to try the Cumberland outpost. Instead, Mortensen chose Hull.

On Saturday 12 November, Workington travelled to Accrington for a top-of-the-table clash. It was to prove Shankly's last game in charge, but one he would rather forget. Workington were thrashed 5-1.

A couple of weeks earlier, Shankly had taken a phone call from his old Preston North End friend Andy Beattie. Beattie was then manager at Huddersfield Town. He wanted to know if Shankly would turn out for him in a testimonial game. Shankly was delighted to be asked and particularly relished the prospect of playing under floodlights, something he had rarely done.

The game was to be played on Monday 14 November. Shankly had a hectic schedule that day with a practice match at Workington in the morning and a meeting with the Football League in the afternoon in Manchester. But that was not going to stop him. Shankly duly turned up and played. After the match, Beattie took him aside. 'How's things at Workington?' he asked. 'Well, it's going pretty well,' replied Shankly, 'but it's not easy.' He explained the various problems. Beattie sat, listening carefully.

'Look,' he said. I don't know whether you'd be interested in this, but I'm looking for an assistant at Huddersfield. I need someone to bring on the youngsters. You've done a good job at Workington, developing young players. Fancy joining a First Division club?'

The offer was highly tempting. Workington's problems were too numerous to list. It wasn't just the lack of funds either. One of Shankly's toughest jobs had been to try to persuade players simply to come to Workington. It was so out of the way. The club had only been in the Football League a handful of years, and most people still thought of it as a non-league club. In the end, Shankly was having to rely on home-grown talent and, in an area like Workington, that was always going to have its limitations. Shankly told Beattie he would be interested. Beattie promised to talk to Huddersfield the next day and to phone him as soon as possible.

Within a few days, it had all been sorted. The Workington directors were upset but not bitter when Shankly informed them of his decision. It was an amicable parting. Shankly had enjoyed his time with the club, even if it had been an exasperating experience at times. He had made many friends, but in his heart he knew that Workington was going nowhere and probably never would. He wasn't far wrong.

8 Back Across the Pennines

HUDDERSFIELD IS ONE OF THOSE TOWNS that seems to have avoided the worst vicissitudes of history. The Depression of the thirties passed it by with barely a ripple. There were always jobs here in the rich woollen industry. The war also came and went. The only excitement Huddersfield experienced was a single bomb landing without causing too much damage, and a plane, which turned out to be British, crashing on nearby Castle Hill. Huddersfield just got on with life, the world passing by with a slight nod in its direction. It's a friendly town though with a slight reserve and suspicion of outsiders. Proud, industrious and provident are the words that spring to mind when it comes to Huddersfield.

During the fifties, it was also a comfortable place. Comfortable with its position in life; comfortable with its own community. There were even elegant trolley buses that hummed along its busy streets.

During the sixties, it was to change dramatically, but in the fifties there was no doubting the prosperity and status of the town. Wool was what made Huddersfield; the town produced the finest cloths you could find anywhere. They sold them to America, to kings, princes, maharajas and to the best Savile Row tailors. In the days when suits were made to measure, the finest cloths and cuts came from Huddersfield.

It's also claimed to be the largest town in Britain. In the mid-fifties, it boasted mills galore, the grandest of town halls, the finest of parks. Think also of Handel's *Messiah* and you think of the Huddersfield Choral Society. Then there was the most elegant of railway stations, where you could still catch a train direct to London and, finally, of course, there was Huddersfield Town Football Club, rich in history and still something of a force in the soccer world.

The northern code might well have been founded in Huddersfield's

George Hotel, but the town has always been unashamedly soccer rather than rugby league. Huddersfield Town Football Club, founded in 1908, was once the finest football club in the land. They had 30 years in the First Division between 1920 and 1952, and between 1924 and 1926 were the first club ever to lift the league championship in three consecutive seasons. The following two seasons they were runners-up. They also won the FA Cup in 1922, having been losing finalists in 1920, 1928, 1930 and 1938.

The interwar years may have left painful memories on the rest of Britain, but for Huddersfield it was a glorious era. Much of the club's success was due to its legendary manager Herbert Chapman, who between 1921 and 1925 guided them to phenomenal success. When he left, it was for Arsenal and even greater glory. The football club epitomised the town. It enjoyed universal respect.

But after the war, times were hard for the club. Much of the postwar period was spent perched in the lower reaches of the First Division, staving off relegation season after season. It was somehow unimaginable that a club with a history like Town could ever be relegated. But history is no respecter of pedigree. And eventually, at the conclusion of the 1951/52 season, the inevitable happened: Town were relegated.

Andy Beattie, the former Preston and Scotland full back was installed as manager in April 1952, once relegation had been settled. Under Beattie, success was instant with the club promoted the following season and finishing up in third place a season later. But slowly they fell apart again and, in the spring of 1956, slid half-expectedly out of the First Division.

The pressures on the manager were considerable, not least in the dressing room where Beattie had an uncomfortable relationship with one or two of his players. A tough disciplinarian, he took a schoolmasterly approach to football management. He was aloof, always keeping distance between himself and his players. 'When we went on away trips, he would be up the other end of the carriage with the directors,' remembers, former *Huddersfield Examiner* reporter Alan Driscoll, 'When you wanted to see him, you had to book an appointment.' Town full back Brian Gibson remembers him as 'a worrier. All the time he was worry, worry, worry, even when you were winning.'

In November 1955, Town had suffered perhaps the worst run in their history, beaten 5-2 at Everton, then 6-2 at home to Newcastle, followed by a 5-0 defeat at Birmingham. The Birmingham game marked sixteen goals conceded in three consecutive games and their seventh successive defeat. It was depressing, enough to make anyone quit. Earlier that month, Beattie decided it was time to go. He had had enough of the penniless struggle, the uphill battle to win promotion. Beattie asked for a meeting with chairman Bernard Newman and told him he was unhappy.

The day-to-day running of the club and its players was a 'mental slog', he told the chairman, especially without any money. He couldn't go on. But Newman was having none of it and quietly persuaded Beattie to continue.

'I know we have no money,' the chairman agreed, 'but there is potential in the youngsters.' It was Beattie who had put a youth policy into place, he insisted, and it would soon pay dividends. In the end, Beattie agreed to remain at the helm. But on one condition, that he could bring someone in to act as his assistant to look after the reserves – with the intention of taking over at some point in the future. That would take pressure off him and would give the club the chance to groom the new assistant for the top job when Beattie eventually quit. Newman agreed without hesitation.

Beattie already had a coach at the club in Eddie Boot, a veteran Town player, but he wanted someone with managerial experience who could take on the role of developing the pool of young players. Beattie had visions of a Busby/Murphy partnership and wanted someone who could give the team a boost. He knew precisely the man he wanted.

Shankly and Beattie had been colleagues at Deepdale before the war: and had even played in the Preston North End side that defeated Huddersfield at Wembley to win the 1938 FA Cup Final. A few weeks earlier, they had both linked up at the same venue, this time in Scotland shirts, in a memorable Scottish win over England.

Shankly was surprised to hear the voice of his old Preston pal when he picked up the phone that afternoon in early November. He thought over the offer. The important thing was that Huddersfield was a club with a rich history; ambition and success were not foreign to them. And in Andy Beattie, there was a manager he knew he could work with. What was more, there was also the likelihood that within the year he could be manager. Nessie was consulted, but as always, she agreed to go where her husband wanted. And so, in November 1955, Bill and Nessie Shankly packed their belongings and left the dampness of the Lake District behind them for the chill of the Pennines.

Shankly was publicly welcomed at Leeds Road as Town took on Tottenham Hotspur in a First Division relegation battle. The date was Saturday 10 December 1955. Town were in bottom spot with just ten points from eighteen games, while Tottenham sat two places above them. Shankly's arrival had an immediate impact as Town won 1-0, thanks to a Jimmy Glazzard goal, although the game was played in front of 11,000, the lowest crowd so far that season.

'Mr Shankly is a man with a reputation for living football,' was the welcoming note in the programme, adding that he had recently played a 90-minute practice match with Workington, before rushing to Manchester for a meeting and then making a further journey to play in a floodlit match that evening. His duties, they noted, would be to supervise the Central League side 'and correct their faults in training sessions'.

Shankly's job was to look after the reserves with the specific task of grooming the younger players. Helping him was Eddie Boot, something of a Huddersfield Town legend. Boot had been one of Town's leading players in the post-war years, a left half and expert penalty taker who had arrived at Leeds Road from Sheffield United, twenty years previously. He had even played for Town against Shankly and Beattie in the infamous 1938 FA Cup final. When he retired from playing, Boot was taken on as a coach, and in due course he would become manager.

But those first few days were not without incident. On his first day, Shankly and Eddie Boot went down to the training ground. As they prepared to go out, Shankly called Boot over. 'Just ignore the first team,' he told him. 'Let them run around on their own. We'll just concentrate on the second team.' Boot was astonished. 'We left them,' he says, 'and they just messed about.'

Word filtered back to Leeds Road. The next day, Andy Beattie called Eddie Boot into his office and closed the door behind them. He'd heard what had happened the previous day at the training ground. 'Eddie,' he said, 'I've just made the biggest mistake of my life bringing Bill Shankly here. I should never have hired him. We never agreed at Preston. I can see it's going to be the same here. I thought things might have improved, but I can sense that they've not.'

From that moment on, there was a rift between Beattie and Shankly. 'They were at it all the time,' says Boot. 'They never got on. They were always scoring points off each other.' Boot was friendly with both men but could understand the friction. 'Bill could get on with people. He was rough and ready. Andy Beattie was a totally different kettle of fish.'

Shankly liked what he saw in the reserves, but in particular there were two youngsters who stood out above all others. They were Denis Law and Ramon Wilson. Law was a mere fifteen-year-old playing with the juniors. He had come to the club from his home town of Aberdeen, but as yet had not signed professional forms. Law had been spotted by the manager's brother, Lawrence Beattie, playing up in Aberdeen. A skinny, eight-stone, squint-eyed youth, he hardly looked the part of a footballer. When he arrived at Leeds Road, there were some mystified looks. Yet on the pitch, he was already showing signs of developing into a major player.

Shankly was not the only one who realised that here was a player with a great future. In an FA Youth Cup tie against Manchester United, shortly before Shankly became manager, Law gave United's Busby Babes a roasting. Town led 2-0 at half time, but finished up 4-2 adrift at the end.

As the final whistle blew, Matt Busby caught Shankly by the arm. 'That's a promising young lad you've got,' he said. From the glint in his eye, Shankly knew Busby had marked him out. Half an hour later, Busby approached Andy Beattie offering him £10,000, a not inconsiderable sum in those days, especially for a sixteen-year-old. Beattie politely but firmly turned him down. It would take Busby another six years before he finally got his man though this time it would cost him a record £115,000.

United weren't the only club interested. Over the next few years, the offers flooded in – from Chelsea, West Brom, Wolves and a £40,000 offer from Johnny Carey's Everton. Much of Shankly's time at Leeds Road would be spent fending off attempts to sign the young Scot. Eventually he would be sold, three months after Shankly had left, with Manchester City paying a record British fee of £55,000 for him. When Arsenal had approached the club earlier offering a similar fee, Shankly had told the board not to sell. 'Mark my words,' he prophesied, 'one day, this lad will fetch £100,000.'

Shankly's initial problem with Law was that the sixteen-year-old was still an amateur, not yet old enough to sign professional forms. In effect, he was a free agent and could go to whichever club he wished. Shankly's first task, as soon as Law was sixteen, was to persuade him that his best interests lay in remaining with Huddersfield. Law's father was brought down to Yorkshire, billeted in the George Hotel for the weekend, supplied with a fine cut of cloth from the chairman's mill, and subjected to the silver tongue of Shankly. Not surprisingly, by the end of the weekend, Law's father had advised young Denis to sign with Huddersfield.

Shankly enjoyed looking after the reserves. They were a solid bunch of players, at one point going sixteen matches without defeat. Alongside Law, at outside right, there was another youngster, Kevin McHale who would go on to play more than 300 games for the club. Together, the two sixteen-year-olds would form the youngest, right-sided attack in the history of the club and one of the youngest ever in the Football League.

But it was another youngster, Ray Wilson, who really caught the eye. Wilson had already played for the first team, making his debut against Manchester United at Old Trafford, a few weeks before Shankly arrived at Leeds Road. He made six league appearances that autumn, as a half back, before returning to the reserves where Shankly converted him into a left back. Strong, deceptively capable and committed, Wilson would go on to win glory elsewhere, a lion at the heart of England's defence as they lifted the World Cup, and a battler at Goodison in Harry Catterick's attractive side. And there were others: Gordon Low and Les Massie among them. All in all, Shankly's reserves were a useful side; young, spirited and confident, each one testifying to the encouragement of Shankly.

Shankly used to annoy Andy Beattie with his quips. Every Friday morning, the teams for the weekend would be pinned up on the noticeboard. Shankly would wander over to join the lads as they read the list. 'Oh I see you've been promoted, son,' he would say to some tearful first team player who had just been dropped. 'You're coming to play with my side instead of Andy's.' There may have been a little bit of psychology there, but it was more to do with an attitude that his reserves were much better than Beattie's first team. 'He was trying to undermine Beattie all the time,' remembers Boot.

'He was good for us young lads,' remembers Kevin McHale. 'You didn't need motivating, it just rubbed off on you. When he was around you felt that you could do something.' Manchester United's Busby Babes were clearly the inspiration. The youngsters of Manchester who were taking on the world with their spirited enthusiasm and uncomplicated style had caught Shankly's imagination. United were the talk of the Football League, champions in 1956 and 1957 with a bunch of kids not much older than the likes of Law, O'Grady and Wilson.

Shankly watched in admiration, enthusing over their dedication and ability. The night he saw his Huddersfield take on the mighty United in the FA Youth Cup was a proud moment. Town might have lost but, in the first half, Law and his friends had taught United a few lessons. There were signs here of a new Town developing that in future years might match United for passion and endeavour. Busby was an old friend and, even by 1956, it was clear that Shankly was basing his own thoughts upon those of Busby.

At the end of the season, relegation came hard to the club. Morale was low; shoulders dropped and the spring had all but disappeared from players' legs. Beattie found it increasingly difficult to lift his players. He was a strange mixture: quiet and thoughtful generally, he was also prone to exaggerated gestures. In 1954, he had been appointed manager of the Scotland team for the World Cup finals in Switzerland, but had resigned after just one game when selection restrictions became obvious. His actions may have had some justification but his timing was disastrous. Scotland were beaten 7-0 by Uruguay in their next game and were on the plane back home.

Beattie is remembered as a studious, thoughtful man, the very opposite of Shankly. 'He was extremely articulate,' recalls Alan Driscoll. 'He looked after the office side of the business, the off-the-field activities. There was never a thing out of place in that area. It was Shankly who looked after things on the field.'

It's a view confirmed by Eddie Brennan, Town's assistant secretary at the time. 'Beattie was a manager,' he says. 'He was the boss. Nobody called him Andy, not even the directors. But Shankly was a coach; everyone called him Bill. Beattie was a disciplinarian, strict but fair. When he walked into the dressing room, there was total silence and nobody ever swore in front of him.'

Eddie Boot was also a quiet customer; deep, keeping his own thoughts to himself, rarely showing much emotion or anger. 'He never really spoke his mind,' says Brian Gibson. 'He got others to do that.' Shanks was the very opposite: always the extrovert, outspoken, forever encouraging his players. His enthusiasm was infectious.

Shankly was so devoted to the game that he would have them playing three-a-side matches in the afternoon after they had trained in the morning, and that was often on the full-size pitch at Leeds Road. Denis Law called him 'football mad'.

Nor were his teams ever chosen at random. There was always a competitive edge. Most mornings, Brennan would cut the names of the players out of the programme and put them in a hat. He and Shankly would then draw the pieces of paper from the hat, writing down the half-a-dozen or so five-a-side teams. 'We'd put one player down for each of the sides, continuing in that manner,' remembers Brennan. 'Then, when each side had four players, Shanks would carefully scrutinise the line-ups. 'Aye, that looks a good side, he'd say. Put my name in as the fifth player. He just wanted to be on the best side. He couldn't bear losing.'

On occasions, as Ray Wilson recalls, their five-a-side games took on a new perspective. 'It was England v Scotland on the asphalt car park at Leeds Road under the mill and the gasometer. We would keep playing until Scotland got in front and that was it.' Dave Hickson always did his best to get into Shankly's side. 'That way I knew I would be on the winning team because Shanks just kept us playing until we were a goal ahead.'

'All he ever talked about was football,' says Law, 'and I mean all the time. Shanks taught us all a lot. He would say "Don't work on your strengths, work on your weaknesses. Get your left foot going and get your heading going." His greatest strength was his enthusiasm. He loved playing football. He gave you confidence and made you feel a bit cocky. He made his players think they were the best in the world.'

But Shankly could never escape the game. He could never relax. Even on a Sunday afternoon, he would sneak out of the house, pretending he was off for a walk, instead going up to Heights Farm at Lindley near his home where he regularly met with a bunch of kids and their dads for a knock-about, a soft leather casey bobbing around on the uneven hillside.

'It's just a social gathering with the men in the locality,' he called it, 'a chance to get to know each other, good exercise and fresh air.' He'd been playing there ever since the family moved into their house at 113 Crosland Road, the Oakes. At first, the players were mostly schoolboys but the game snowballed until before long there were a couple of dozen of them, mainly adults playing every Sunday. It was usually about fifteen or sixteen-a-side, a mixture of ages from seven upwards to 40. As the housing scheme grew, they were forced to move pitch every few months. By the time Shankly left Huddersfield, they were reckoned to be on their sixth pitch.

'He'd come knocking on my door at about 2 pm every Sunday,' remembers Peter Gronow. 'He'd be bouncing his ball, like a ten-year-old. "Come on," he'd say, "let's go." It didn't matter what the weather was like – snow, pouring rain, whatever it was we played. When we got to the field, everyone would line up and Bill and I would pick the sides, just like kids. We'd play all afternoon, packing in about 5 pm.'

Even after he had gone to Liverpool, Shankly would come back on the occasional Sunday bringing some pals over. 'Joe Fagan came once,' remembers Gronow, 'and some of the other bootroom staff. Bill loved playing with us. The thing was that he had never really grown up – when it came to soccer, he was still a kid at heart.'

Eddie Brennan was round at Shankly's house early one Sunday. 'Every Sunday, Nessie made him clean the gas cooker. He was up to his arms in grease chatting to me when there was a knock at the door. A ten-year-old waif was standing on the doorstep. "Are you coming out to play Bill?" asks the ten-year-old. "Oh hello son," says Shankly. "How's your injury, is it better now? Aye, I'll be out in a wee while. Go, get the goalposts set up." ' Closing the door, Shankly turned to Brennan. "He's a dirty wee bugger that lad." Such was the man's passion for the game that he even took this ten-year-old seriously.'

A coolness remained between Beattie and Shankly. It had all come to a head when Beattie brought a reserve team player into the first team. It didn't work. Beattie's tactics were about man-to-man marking, whereas Shankly encouraged a sense of adventure in his reserves. The player had been all over the field and Town were beaten. Beattie was furious. He felt that Shankly was being disloyal, that it was his job to tutor the reserves in the same style as the first team.

'Beattie was very upset,' says Brennan. 'He felt that Shankly was not showing enough loyalty.' The rift was damaging. It was inevitable that Andy Beattie and Huddersfield would soon part company. Town had started their season back in the Second Division with a string of poor results.

It was the beginning of a new philosophy: blame the manager. And Beattie's record was not too impressive. Not that there was much public criticism. The local paper remained loyal and chairman Bernard Newman was putting no pressure on him. But, by the time Town met Yorkshire rivals Sheffield United at Leeds Road on Saturday 3 November, the pressure was intense. They had already lost six games and had only 16 points to show from their 15 fixtures, leaving them in the middle of the table. Promotion was already beginning to look out of the question.

That Saturday, in front of a crowd of 18,000, Huddersfeld went down 4-1, their seventh defeat of the season. The *Huddersfield Examiner* was scathing. 'Not since Newcastle United won 6-2 at Leeds Road almost exactly a year ago have Town been so outplayed before their supporters as they were in the closing stages of the first half,' thundered the *Examiner*, adding, 'United were superior in practically every department and no-one could grumble about the result.' The result left Town lingering in the middle of the table.

In November 1956, the world was in turmoil. Soviet troops had just stormed into Hungary to stamp out a popular uprising with Soviet Party boss Nikita Khrushchev making threatening noises to the West. But the West had problems of its own. President Nasser of Egypt had nationalised the Suez Canal and British Prime Minister Anthony Eden had sent an attack force into Egypt along with French and Israeli troops. For a day or two, the world tottered on the brink of uncertainty and a possible Third World War. It was all very unsettling.

The mood was catching. Beattie knew his time was up as well. There was no more he could do – too many groans on the terraces, too many long faces in the directors' box. People didn't criticise the manager to his face in those days, but you didn't have to be a mind-reader to know what they were thinking. Beattie told nobody. Shankly was at Barnsley with the reserves. After the game, Beattie went in to see Newman and told him that this time his mind was made-up. It would be best for everyone if he went. Newman did not really want to lose him: Beattie had been there since April 1952 and was a highly respected manager, but at the same time he recognised that Beattie was a tired man. The death of Tom Whittaker, the Arsenal manager, from a heart attack a few weeks earlier had deeply affected him. The pressure had finally killed Whittaker, and Beattie did not want the same thing happening to him. Until then he had intended to see out his contract, due to expire in 1958. He had even bought a small post office in Nottingham, all ready for retirement.

Now was the time to go, he told Newman – there was no more that he could do. If he remained any longer, it would make the task of his successor all the more difficult. There was still time for the new man to turn things round. Newman agreed reluctantly and quickly convened a board meeting. But before the two parted company, Beattie advised him strongly that Shankly ought to be appointed as his successor. 'Just look at his results,' he said. 'The reserves have gone fourteen games without defeat. He's my assistant, he knows the ropes.' Ironically, that afternoon, the reserves had lost at Barnsley, for the first time that season.

The chairman agreed with Beattie's recommendation. He liked Shankly and could see that the players liked him as well. 'I'll discuss it with the board tonight,' he promised.

Later that evening, after returning from Barnsley, Shankly and a few others retired to their favourite post-match haunt, the White Horse restaurant in Market Place. The club guessed that was where Shankly would be and phoned him. Shankly came back to the table. 'The chairman wants to see me,' he told the others. He had no inkling of Beattie's decision, but figured something must have happened. Another Saturday evening was about to be ruined for Nessie. Shankly jumped into his car and quickly drove the short distance to Leeds Road.

'I don't know whether you've heard,' said Newman as Shankly sat down in his office, 'but Andy's decided to call it a day. He's retiring, he's tired. He's handed in his notice and can't be persuaded to stay.' Shankly acted surprised although he was hardly shocked. He knew Beattie had bought the post office business. He had also seen Beattie each day suffering from stress; he knew many of the players did not like him. He and Beattie had been close as players, and he always respected him. But he still had his differences with him when it came to managing a club.

'Andy's recommended that we give you a try at the job,' he continued. 'How do you fancy it?' Shankly nodded his approval. 'Yes, of course. I certainly want the job,' he said. Newman outlined the offer. 'You can think about it overnight if you like,' he added. 'No, I don't think there'll be any need of that,' replied Shankly. 'You can take it from me that I'm your man.'

And so began a three-year stint as manager of Huddersfield Town. At the Curzon cinema that night, they were showing the film *Reach For The Sky*. Shankly had hoped to take his wife to see it. Instead, he was reaching for the sky himself.

As he left the ground, he decided to call in at Andy Beattie's house. Yet even though Beattie had recommended Shankly for the job and, even though he himself had recognised it was time to quit, the business still left a bad taste in the mouth. Shankly drove up to Beattie's house, but could not bring himself to go in. Instead, he drove the car half-a-dozen times around the block before he finally plucked up the courage. Unbeknown to Bill, Beattie was watching from the window with some amusement.

'We sat in the house together and talked about this and that,' wrote Shankly in his autobiography some years later, 'but the manager's job was never mentioned. I was waiting for Andy to say, "Oh, you've done it. You've got the job. Good luck," or something like that . . . Nothing was said. I knew I was the new manager: he knew I was the new manager, but we never mentioned it. It was a kind of mutual embarrassment.'

In truth, Shankly was really incapable of articulating his feelings and Beattie was not in the mood to help him. It was all too awkward for Shankly. In time, the rift would heal and Shankly would even give Beattie a job as a scout for Liverpool with Beattie repaying the favour by discovering and persuading Shankly to buy Kevin Keegan.

The following morning, Shankly's appointment was confirmed and officially announced. 'I expect to get 100% effort from the players,' he told the few pressmen who had gathered at Leeds Road. 'I gave that when I was playing and that is all I want of them – 100% effort. I want them all to fight.' But he was making no promises. 'I will work hard for the club, but I won't make predictions.'

Chairman Bernard Newman was at pains to point out that the departure of Andy Beattie had been entirely friendly. 'The board had known that Mr Beattie had wanted to be released at an opportune time,' he revealed adding, 'We are sorry to lose him but the parting has been very amicable, and we wish him every success.'

The man from the *Examiner* took a photograph, Shankly shook the chairman's hand and there were smiles all round. Bill Shankly was officially the new manager of Huddersfield Town Football Club. Eddie Boot was subsequently given a small promotion, taking on the responsibility of the reserves.

Shankly's first game in charge was a couple of days later, for a friendly against Stockport County, arranged to switch on the new floodlights at Edgeley Park. It was not a good result: Huddersfield lost 1-0 but there were compensations. Town did most of the attacking, hitting the woodwork three times, and showed plenty of effort. A few days later, Shankly handled his first league game as Town visited Barnsley where a week earlier the reserves' unbeaten run of fourteen games had come to an end.

This time there was a different outcome, as Town thrashed Barnsley 5-0, four goals coming in a breathtaking 20-minute spell in the first half. It was Town's best post-war score on an away ground. There were only two changes to the side, with Fearnley returning in goal and Massie coming into the side for only the third time that season. Simpson was also pushed upfront to play alongside Massie. It seemed to do the trick as Town played with more commitment than they had shown all season.

From the way they played, it was clear that the new appointment was popular with the players. 'The change was almost instantaneous,' remembers centre forward Dave Hickson. 'From the moment he took over, the atmosphere in the dressing room, changed. It was the same when he came to Liverpool as well.' Everyone recognised the new mood. 'The manager's door was suddenly open. With Beattie, you had to book an appointment, but with Bill you just strolled in without even knocking.'

The press noticed it as well. Beattie had never enjoyed the PR side of the job and could be blunt and unforthcoming. But Shankly revelled in talking to the press. If they wanted to talk about football, he was happy to oblige.

But the improving fortunes of Town did not last long: in December, they lost four consecutive games and began to slip down the table. On Christmas Eve, Shankly decided to play Santa Claus by giving youth its fling with a debut for sixteen-year-old Denis Law. The eight-stone Law had been put on a special diet of steak and milk to build up his strength. Shankly had arranged with the woman, who ran the cafe opposite the ground where the players had their lunch, to feed him up every day. 'I didn't argue,' recalls Law. 'I'd hardly eaten meat in my life before. Later on, he had me drinking Chinese tea without sugar or milk. It was diabolical.'

The diet did the trick. Law performed well at Notts County, with Huddersfield winning 2-1, and two days later having retained his spot for the return against County, scored his first league goal as Town ran out 3-0 winners. Shankly was so impressed by what the herbal tea had done for Law that he soon had the entire team drinking it. It might have worked for a while, but there were still some embarrassing moments, such as a 5-1 defeat at Stoke and a 7-2 thrashing at Middlesbrough.

Huddersfield ended their first season back in the Second Division in mid-table, in all honesty faring little better than they would have done under Andy Beattie. An exciting run in the FA Cup however took Town into the fifth round. Their three third-round games against Sheffield United were watched by a total of 61,000, while their fourth round match at Leeds Road against non-league Peterborough attracted 48,000. Then, in the fifth round with First Division Burnley the visitors, just over 55,000 poured into Leeds Road, the club's biggest gate in years. It all helped bring much-needed revenue to the club, though most of it was earmarked for ground improvements.

There were other compensations as well. By the end of the season, Law had signed professional forms and become a fixture in the side, bringing the media spotlight to Leeds Road with his electric performances, while Ray Wilson had been switched from wing half to full back, looking particularly impressive until injury disrupted his season. Now the battle was on to keep the pair of them at Huddersfield.

Sixteen-year-old amateur winger Kevin McHale had also been given his chance, linking up with Law to form a notable right-sided partnership, reckoned to be the youngest ever in the history of the Football League. McHale went on to make more than 30 appearances that season and, although he would never quite fulfil his early promise, he turned out 375 times for Town before joining Crewe. There was much to be satisfied about; prospects for the future looked promising.

At the end of the season, Dave Hickson, Town's centre forward, moved on, rejoining First Division Everton. Hickson was always a problem. He had been transferred from Everton to Aston Villa but had only stayed at Villa for a few weeks, managing just a dozen appearances, before Beattie signed him for a record Town fee of £16,000. He was a tough, effective striker, tall, powerful, bustling, not the most naturally talented of strikers but always difficult to defend against.

Hickson might have been a problem for defenders, but he was also a problem for his manager. On the field, he caused waves. 'We couldn't cope with him,' admits Eddie Boot. 'You were not safe standing next to him. If he got kicked early in the game, he would spend the rest of the 90 minutes hunting the man who had kicked him.' Even before the game in the corridor, he would be badmouthing the referee. His disciplinary record left little to be admired. His problems didn't stop there either. Off the field, he was shunned by many of his playing colleagues.

Shankly, even then a tough disciplinarian, was growing weary of dealing with Hickson. As far as he was concerned, Hickson was a disruptive influence and the club would be better off without him. In July 1957, he heard that Eveton might be interested in taking him back to Goodison. A deal was quickly set up, a fee of £7,500 agreed, and Hickson was off home. Shankly was glad to see the back of him, although Hickson maintains that he always got on well with the man. Little did either suspect that within three years their paths would cross again.

The Huddersfield dressing room might have been calmer without Hickson, but the team would never quite recover from the loss. Even Eddie Boot agrees that losing Hickson possibly caused more problems than it solved. In his two years at Leeds Road, the rumbustious Hickson had netted nineteen goals in 56 appearances, a goal every three games. In his first period at Everton, he had scored in virtually every other game. Over the next couple of years, Shankly would search desperately for a replacement but never found an adequate substitute. 'We struggled for goals after Hickson went,' admits McHale.

With Hickson gone, Shankly also decided to begin a shakeout of the older players with Watson, Kelly, Davie and Quested, all hanging up their boots, or moving on after long service at Leeds Road. Beattie had remained loyal to the older players, too loyal in fact, playing them when it would have been best to let them go. In all, thirteen players were listed as Shankly swung the axe. Shankly had decided that it was time for his youngsters.

The 1957/58 season brought only a marginal improvement in Town's fortune's as they wound up in ninth spot, nowhere near promotion. There was no luck in the cup either and the local paper could only describe their season as 'undistinguished.' Continuing his policy of hiving off the elderly, Shankly let veteran Vic Metcalfe go to Hull City for £5,000. On the positive side, Ray Wilson was maturing with every game and already beginning to look an England international in the making, while Law continued to catch the eye, even though his appearances were limited by injury. 'Shankly would also rest us youngsters,' remembers McHale. 'We'd have a few games, and then we'd be told to put our feet up for a week or so.'

That season, Shankly and Huddersfield were to be involved in one of the most extraordinary games in the entire history of the Football League. Town were playing Charlton Athletic at the Valley a few days before Christmas. Early in the first half, Charlton lost their centre half with a dislocated shoulder and Town soon swept into a lead. With 25 minutes to go, they were leading 5-1. Everybody on the Huddersfield bench was relaxed and enjoying it when suddenly Charlton struck. They struck again, and again, and again, and again. Suddenly they were leading 6-5.

Shankly could barely believe it. Then, with a minute to go, Huddersfield scraped an equaliser. It looked to be all over. But no. Charlton kicked off and immediately banged the ball into the back of the Huddersfield goal. Town had lost 7-6. The Huddersfield players trooped off, heads buried in their chests. Shankly stood by the bench and glared at them as they went down the tunnel. Within twenty minutes, they were all dressed and on their way home. There was silence. Shankly never said a word until they reached Peterborough. Then he finally broke his silence, lashing into them. It was beyond belief that playing against ten men, and 5-1 up, you could concede six goals in less than 25 minutes.

Midway through the season came the appalling news of the Manchester United air crash at Munich. It was a cold February day in Huddersfield with the sleet and wind ripping in off the black Pennine hills. Shankly was in his office. It was 4.15 pm when he took a call from a local journalist. 'Good God,' he said turning to Eddie Brennan. 'Manchester United. They've all been killed. I think we'd better get home. Look at the television.' Shankly and Brennan ran to their car and made towards town. There was total silence as they drove through the wet, snowy streets. Not one word was said. Then as he dropped Brennan off at the George Hotel, Shankly turned to him. 'You're a Catholic, aren't you, Eddie?' he asked.

'You know I am, Bill,' replied Brennan.

'You say a prayer for them,' asked Shankly, 'say a prayer for them.'

News of the disaster came hard for Shankly. He knew Busby well, idolised the man and his team. Fortunately, Busby lived but Tom Curry, Shankly's first-ever trainer when he had joined Carlisle United as an eighteen-year-old in 1932, was dead. Curry had left Carlisle to join United where he had trained the club's post-war championship- and FA Cup-winning side as well as the hugely successful Busby Babes. But now he was gone.

A few months earlier, Shankly and Brennan had gone to see Everton playing at Burnley. Busby was there that day. After the game, Shankly was having a chat outside the boardroom with Busby when the Burnley chairman Bob Lord wandered over.

'Hello, Matt,' said Lord. 'Would you care to come into the board-room for a drink?' The invitation clearly did not include Shankly.

'No thanks,' replied Busby. 'I'm having a chat here with my old friend Bill.' On the way home that night, Shankly turned to Brennan. 'Did you see that, McGuigan?' he said (he always called Brennan McGuigan). 'Matt, what a wonderful man. He wouldn't go off with Bob Lord because I had not been invited. What a man he is.'

The following season, Town were off to an appalling start. By the end of September, they had already lost five matches. Then in October came the highlight of the season as Town faced Liverpool at Leeds Road. When Kenny Taylor limped off with damaged ligaments after just five minutes, it looked as if Town would be in for yet another defeat. But the loss of Taylor seemed to make little difference as ten-man Town gave Liverpool a thrashing, eventually winning 5-0. It was Liverpool's biggest defeat of the season. Years later when he was at Anfield Shankly was fond of reminding everyone of the day 'his' Huddersfield whipped the mighty Liverpool. 'I remember the Liverpool directors leaving the ground in single file, with their shoulders slumped, like a funeral procession,' he recalled.

The Liverpool result promised an about-turn in Huddersfield's fortunes but it was not to be. By Christmas, they had lost another five games and any dreams of promotion were long-gone. At one point, relegation even looked a possibility. In the end, they finished the season in fourteenth spot, 22 points behind champions, Sheffield Wednesday.

Midway through the season, Shankly dipped into the transfer market. The club was seriously short of a quality goalkeeper. Goals were leaking through Town's fragile defence and South African Sandy Kennon was showing a distinct lack of confidence. Shankly turned to his old pal Matt Busby at Manchester United. Ray Wood, the former England international keeper who had won league championship honours with United, had only played once for United since being injured in the Munich air disaster and had been replaced by Harry Gregg. Busby suggested Wood might be the man to shore up the Town defence. What's more he was available for a mere £1,500, a bargain if ever there was one. Shankly snapped him up and Wood immediately stepped into the Huddersfield line-up, conceding five on his debut at Stoke and three more the following week. But eventually Wood settled, restored his self-confidence and over the next half dozen seasons would be a permanent fixture between the posts. Two months later, Kennon was sold to Norwich.

Alec Bain was also signed during the 1957 close season. Bain arrived with a sky-high reputation and Shankly was convinced that he would do the trick for Town. Eddie Boot had never seen him play and had not been consulted on the deal. 'He was no more than a second team player,' reckons Boot. Bain never lasted and was gone within three years, managing only 29 league games.

A useful side was beginning to take shape though, a blend of experience in England internationals Wood and McGarry combined with the youthful exuberance of Law, Wilson, Massie and McHale. But it was still a case of promise rather than fulfilment, and with just 63 goals scored it was clear where the problem lay.

Shankly was a players' man. 'I always thought of him as a coach rather than a manager,' says Alan Driscoll. 'He was very much a rookie, learning the ropes at Huddersfield. He didn't want to be in the office, signing letters, making telephone calls, like Beattie had. He wanted to be out there on the pitch, passing on his knowledge. In fact, he never struck me as being that ambitious.' Eddie Boot remembers how painfully slow he was at signing his name. 'It was laboured almost like a child,' he says. 'Sometimes it was embarrassing to watch.'

Driscoll also recalls his team talks. 'When the team went away in the coach, I was always invited along. The last twenty minutes of the journey to the away ground were always the same. Shankly would walk up and down the bus giving his team talk. He used to tell them they had nothing to worry about, 'You're playing a bunch of cab horses.'

Driscoll met Shankly on a daily basis. Every day, he'd go down to the club, to see if there was any news. 'He always called me "son" but he was totally trusting. We built up a close relationship,' he recalls. 'He knew I would report things accurately and not let him down. In return, he gave me snippets of information. I was always the first to know.'

'He always had the players' interests at heart,' says McHale. 'He was always loyal. He would never criticise any of us in public. Sometimes he would not even do it in front of others. He'd take you aside and have a word.'

'We always had a laugh in the dressing room with him,' says Brian Gibson. Shankly turned up for a match one day sporting a trilby with a feather in it. Nobody was quite sure where it had come from. It had probably been given to him by Nessie, but it was to be the source of some ribald humour. Shankly took it with good grace and was still wearing it for the next game.

Shankly also used to give his father-in-law a hard time though always with the best of humour. 'The old man would come down to the ground with Shankly to watch the training, and Shanks would be taking the mickey out of him all the time. He'd get mad with him. It was just good fun between the pair of them, remembers Eddie Boot.'

Every morning at 8.45 am, Shankly would pick Eddie Brennan up from outside the George Hotel, close to the railway station, and the pair of them would then drive down to Leeds Road in Shankly's baby Austin car. 'We'd have a good laugh,' he recalls. 'He'd yabber on about what he'd seen on television the previous night, some cowboy film or other. He liked cowboy films, but more than anything he loved American gangster movies. He was always going on about James Cagney, George Raft, Humphrey Bogart and the rest. He loved them. Little tough guys, just like himself.'

Shankly also continued to play in various charity and testimonial games, usually under floodlights. He turned out for an All Stars XI againt Tranmere, playing alongside Eddie Boot, Wally Barnes, Billy Liddell, Jimmy Hagan and Charlie Mitten.

There was always plenty of humour when Shankly was around, and yet he could be antagonistic to anyone suffering from an injury. He would cold-shoulder them, walk past them in the corridor. Denis Law was often on the receiving end of this hostility. 'If you were injured, you were no good to him, and he didn't want to know you. If I came out of the treatment room at the same time that Shanks was coming along the corridor, he would just walk right past me. It was incredible. Before the match I'd been the greatest player in the game, but now I'd try to catch his eye and he'd just whistle and walk past staring at the ceiling.'

Shankly worried about Law. He didn't share his doubts however with too many other people. He always reckoned Law was injury-prone, and indeed in those early years at Huddersfield he was, his young legs taking a battering from 'over-zealous' defenders. But it worried Shankly, and he often wondered if Law would survive the batterings to make a truly great player.

Shankly would go to some lengths to dismiss an injury. When Brian Gibson hurt his wrist in training one morning, Shankly diagnosed it as a small broken bone. They had a game at Swansea coming up. 'Go along to the infirmary, son,' he told the player, 'and get them to put a light plaster or bandage on it.' Gibson returned from the hospital a few hours later, his arm in a heavy plaster and sling. 'What the hell's that?' screamed Shankly. 'I told you to get a light plaster put on. How can you play with that?' Gibson clearly could not play but Shankly was not to be outdone. 'We'll take you with us to Swansea,' he said, 'and let someone down there have a look.' As soon as they arrived in Swansea, they made for the local hospital where Shankly tried to have the plastercast removed. Unfortunately, the hospital refused point blank, arguing that the cast was clearly new and that it was not their job to remove something that had been put on by another hospital. Shankly was furious, but even then was not to be outmanoeuvred. The arm was tied up in a bandage and Gibson was taken to the referee who was told it was only a light plaster. But the referee was not fooled and Shankly was reluctantly forced to concede defeat.

The 1959/60 season was to be Shankly's last with Huddersfield; it was also to be Denis Law's. Shankly was optimistic at the start, telling fans that he was looking forward to 'the fulfilment of everybody's hopes'. By the autumn, his optimism was looking justified. Town were in fourth spot, five points behind the leaders Aston Villa but with a couple of games in hand.

Principally however, it was to be a season when Town's search for an effective centre forward reached desperate heights as Shankly tried out half-a-dozen men in the position. None lasted more than a couple of games. Les Massie kicked off the season in the number nine shirt, but, after five games, moved to inside forward and handed the goalscoring role to Peter Dinsdale. After just one game, it was passed on to Sinclair who hung on to it for four matches before passing it on to Jack Connor. In November, he passed it on to Tony France and, before Shankly left, Ledger, Hawksworth and Kevin McHale had all had a go in the striker's role. And still goals were a rare commodity. Some of the changes had been forced on Shankly by injury but usually it was a case of give someone the striker's shirt and see how he copes.

Not surprisingly, Shankly was scouring the land in search of a genuine striker. The club was even linked with Brian Clough, then an emerging young goalsnapper with Middlesbrough, but the money was never forthcoming, and Shankly was denied the opportunity to play Clough alongside Law. His search for a centre forward also took him to Falkirk to watch Ian St John in a Scotland against the Scottish Second Division friendly.

Another man took his eye that night, the towering Dundee United defender Ron Yeats. Shankly fancied the pair of them. On the way home, he talked it over with Eddie Boot who had accompanied him on his scouting mission. They both agreed that St John and Yeats would complete the jigsaw and that it was worth trying to persuade the board to put up the money. The following morning, Shankly plucked up the courage to go and see his chairman. 'How much?' asked Stephen Lister. Shankly hesitated, 'Maybe £25,000 for St John, probably the same for Yeats.' 'We couldn't even afford one of them,' snapped Lister. 'You know we don't have that kind of money.' 'With those two in my side, I could guarantee you promotion,' insisted Shankly. 'It would be an investment.' But his promises fell on deaf ears. There had been too many years of struggle, either at the foot of the First Division, or in the anonymous midriff of the Second Division. Gates were low, averaging just 17,000. They hadn't even had a decent money-spinning cup run for a couple of years. The priority had been to spend money on ground improvements. A roof had just been erected on the popular side, and that had taken up most of the club's finances. Town were so poor they were one of the few clubs in the country that still did not have flood-lights.

Shankly kept it fairly friendly, biting his tongue as the chairman shook his head. It seemed pointless arguing or storming out. He'd known all along what the answer would be. At the end of the day, the money was simply not available. £15,000 was probably their limit, unless of course they sold Law. But that would have made a nonsense of everything. Above all, Shankly was not going to sell his young star and he was also unwilling to consider any of the offers for Ray Wilson that were beginning to pour in. If Town were going to win promotion, Law and Wilson had to be a part of the plan.

'Money was tight even then,' says Eddie Boot. 'The board's attitude was that the club must never go into debt. That was Huddersfield Town. They had no ambition. I had to sell a player every year in order to pay the summer wages. Shankly had the same problems.' Providence was the name of the game. It was part of the Huddersfield spirit.

Shankly had known from the outset of his managerial career at Leeds Road that money was short. That Saturday night when he was ap-pointed, the former chairman Bernard Newman had spelled it out to him. Town's policy was to build a side from its youth policy, finding youngsters and developing them. That's why he had been appointed in the first place because that was the policy he believed in. But it wasn't easy. You had to have the men in place to spot the youngsters, and even then you were always competing with the big clubs who had better scouting arrangements and more pulling power than Huddersfield Town. There were also under-the-table payments to youngsters and their families, something which Shankly would never have considered. At least Huddersfield was still a reasonably big name in football, even though they hovered in the middle of the Second Division.

Shankly was now realising what Andy Beattie had always known, that you could not build a side on youth alone. It was to prove a valuable lesson. It was all very well to point to Manchester United's youth policy, but even they had spent heavily in the transfer market bringing in the likes of Tommy Taylor for just under £30,000, Harry Gregg for £25,000, and Johnny Berry for £15,000.

Shankly had barely spent in the transfer market. He'd brought in Alex Bain and Willie Sinclair from Scotland as well as Ray Wood from Manchester United but in doing so had spent only a few thousand pounds. Had the likes of Clough, St John or Yeats joined Huddersfield, the Bill Shankly story might have had a very different outcome. Town would undoubtedly have been challenging for promotion with Shankly perhaps less likely to have been tempted away to Anfield. But football is packed with ifs and buts.

By the late autumn of 1959, Huddersfield were, for the first time in years, beginning to look like serious promotion candidates. They had won their first three fixtures of the season and topped the table. By early September, they had accumulated 11 points from a possible 14, but then they lost two games in succession and dropped another point at Sunderland.

The side was as settled as it had ever been under Shankly. He knew his line-up although injuries often interfered with selection. They were an attractive side with their mix of youth and experience. Besides the youngsters, Law, Wilson, McHale and Massie, there were the ex-England internationals Ray Wood and Town captain Bill McGarry. And yet they were still a couple of players short of being a genuine promotion-chasing side. The youngsters still had much to learn. Law was always capable of scoring goals, but not on the regular basis that was necessary, and even at that time injury was beginning to restrict his appearances.

Nor can you build a side entirely on enthusiasm. Shankly had tried that at Workington and Grimsby but in the end reality had found him out. Now at Huddersfield, the enthusiasm which he had generated in the dressing room earlier that season was beginning to wane as the results failed to match his confidence.

The board's refusal to give Shankly the money to sign St John and Yeats hurt. If only they could have agreed to let him have one of those men, it could have made all the difference. Shankly did not find it easy to deal with the board. He was not as articulate as they were, and always had difficulties selling ideas to them. He had none of their education, none of their standing in society. The directors were an odd mixture: chairman Stephen Lister was a solicitor and coroner; then there was the local Chief Constable James Chadwick OBE, a coal merchant Haydn Battye, mill owner Bernard Newman, and a few others, mostly retired. Shankly was always respectful, but sitting around a board table was not his idea of football. His forte was in talking to footballers, not directors.

Shankly had no plans to leave Leeds Road; he was perfectly content living in Huddersfield. His family were settled, his two girls both at school, yet he recognised the limitations of managing a club without much money. He'd done it before at Carlisle, Workington and Grimsby where he did not even have a Law or a Wilson to nurture. He knew he could be a lot worse-off than at Huddersfield, but he simply could not see where to turn to next.

On Saturday 17 October 1959, Huddersfield Town faced Cardiff City at Leeds Road. Huddersfield were fourth in the table that morning, Cardiff second. But by five o'clock, Town had slipped to their fourth defeat of the season, losing 1-0, a loss that only underlined the problems Shankly and Huddersfield still faced. But the match statistics were irrelevant. Of far more consequence were the post-match events. As a dispirited Shankly left the ground that evening, two figures emerged out of the gloom, walking down the Leeds Road slope. They called over to him. Shankly stopped and crossed towards them. One of them introduced himself.

'Good evening Mr Shankly, my name is Tom Williams,' he said politely. 'I don't know whether you remember me but I am the chairman of Liverpool Football Club and this is Harry Latham one of my directors. I wonder if we could have a word with you.' 'Of course,' said Shankly, expecting another bid for Denis Law or Ray Wilson. 'How would you like to manage the best club in the country?' asked Williams. Shankly looked at him quizzically. 'Why, is Matt Busby packing it in?' he asked. Williams smiled. 'No,' he answered. 'I'm talking about Liverpool. How would you like to manage them?' For once Shankly was lost for words. No mention of Denis Law or Ray Wilson. This time, it was him they wanted. 'What about your present manager Phil Taylor?' he asked. 'He hasn't left the job.' 'Mr Taylor is not very well and has asked to be relieved of his duties,' replied Williams. 'It's not been announced yet, but I suspect it will become public in a week or so. We'd like to sort something out before then.'

The three of them wandered over to Tom Williams' car and sat inside discussing the offer. Shankly knew immediately. He had no doubts at all about accepting the job, but he was not going to be rushed into it. 'I'll consider it,' he said. 'It's an interesting offer but obviously I've got to talk to the wife. And we're not doing too badly here, you know.' 'Yes, we can see that,' replied Williams, 'That's why we want you.' They shook hands. By now, it was dark and just a few lights were left twinkling inside the offices at Leeds Road. Williams and Latham edged their car out of the car park, its headlights catching in the pools of water on the potholed surface. Shankly waved farewell to them and turned to walk towards his own car. He had a feeling that his days at Leeds Road were numbered.

Nessie was not happy at the idea of leaving Huddersfield. 'We had words,' she confesses. 'I liked Huddersfield. It had taken us time to settle, to get to know Yorkshire folk, but once they had accepted us they were very warm and loyal.' Even today, she still keeps in touch with them. But her husband was adamant and she was not even going to try and change his mind. Once his mind was made up, that was it. He told his eight-year-old daughter Jean that Liverpool was 'by the seaside'. That was enough to persuade her.

It was a few weeks before anything formal was announced. Shankly held his silence at Leeds Road, not even telling Eddie Boot or his secretary Eddie Brennan. Talks between Shankly and Tom Williams at Liverpool continued but it was only ever a matter of settling the fine print of the contract. Phil Taylor formally resigned as manager on 14 November admitting that he was tired. 'The strain of trying to win promotion has proved too much,' he admitted. The way was now open for Shankly.

Word eventually leaked out that Shankly was the man Liverpool wanted and, when Liverpool came to play Huddersfield at Leeds Road on 28 November, the back pages were hinting that the Liverpool board would be arriving in force to steal Shankly away to Anfield. Rumours were rife. In the event, only one Liverpool director turned up and much to the relief of the Huddersfield directors announced that he had only come 'to scotch the rumours'.

Town beat Liverpool 1-0 and for a few days it looked as if the rumours were just idle gossip but then at the weekly board meeting held the following Tuesday, 1 December, Shankly was, as usual invited in to give his report. Before he began his report, he told the board there was something he had to say to them. 'This is my last report,' he began. They knew at once what he was about to say.

'I have received an offer from Liverpool Football Club to become their manager,' he began, 'and I have decided to accept the offer.' Members of the board stared coldly in his direction.

'I realise that this may come as something of a shock to you, but I have decided to go simply because I would like to take up the challenge of managing a big club in a big city. In many ways, I have taken my decision reluctantly. I have enjoyed my time here: the club, and its directors, have always been good to me.'

There was a silence broken only by Haydn Battye who leaned back in his chair. 'I wonder if Harry Catterick at Sheffield Wednesday would be interested in coming here?' he pondered aloud. Shankly looked at him. 'Harry Catterick. But he's managing a bigger club than this,' stuttered Shankly. The board members glared at him. Nothing more was said.

The directors were not pleased – they were especially angry that Liverpool had duped them. There was no attempt to persuade Shankly from resigning. 'I think at the very least,' insisted Lister, 'that you should give one month's notice.' The rest of the board agreed. Shankly had little option but to accept their condition. He would leave on 31 December, and that would be that.

Shankly returned to his office and taking Brennan aside told him. 'He was very excited,' says Brennan, 'talking about what a great club Liverpool was, how much potential they had and how money was going to be available. But then he started rubbishing Huddersfield, saying they had no ambition, no money, would never get anywhere, and that he was leaving Town for a better club. He was saying things that he would never have said to me 24 hours earlier. That upset me. I felt he was being disloyal.'

After the meeting, it was announced to the press that Bill Shankly was leaving. 'Liverpool are getting a good man,' said Lister.

'My wife and family have made more friends in Huddersfield than in any other town we have lived during my career in soccer,' said Shankly. 'It's going to be a terrible wrench saying goodbye.' He meant it as well.

The *Huddersfield Examiner* reckoned there was more to it. 'He had had a bellyful of this one; indeed of the entire heart-breaking business of having to balance promotion aspirations to a financial tightrope,' wrote Longfellow in his column adding, 'Bill Shankly can take every credit for his patient and untiring labours to transform an ageing team into a young, virile and successful combination.'

But it turned out to be an uneasy week. All week, he was down at the training ground but he was restless. His heart had already crossed the Pennines, there was little he could do at Leeds Road, except pick the team. He could lay down no plans and anyhow the next man might want to unpick them. He was in limbo and the board's decision to tie him to Leeds Road until the end of the month had been a knee-jerk reaction. They soon realised that it was an impossible situation.

At the board meeting the following Tuesday, Shankly's weekly report carried no weight and was received almost in silence. The board quickly realised that an immediate parting would be best for everyone. After the meeting, the chairman called Shankly into his office and told him that if he still wished he could go immediately. Shankly thanked him and agreed that it would be better if he went straight away. 'By the way, we've decided to make Eddie Boot caretaker manager while we find a permanent replacement,' said Lister as Shankly was about to leave the room. 'That's good,' said Shankly, half-smiling and closing the door behind him.

It was a cold night; winter had come early to that part of Yorkshire. There had already been a brief layering of snow the previous week. It might even be a white Christmas, Shankly thought as he wandered back to his room under the Main Stand. On the way, he bumped into Eddie Brennan. 'Well, I'm off,' he announced. 'The board aren't holding me to the month's notice. I'm going straight away. I'm just on my way to clear the office.' 'Will you be around for Christmas?' asked Brennan, following him down the corridor. 'Yes, I suppose I'll be in Huddersfield. We went to see a house in Formby last week,' he added, 'but it wasn't suitable, so I expect we'll be here until after the New Year. Eddie Boot's taking over by the way.'

Bill Shankly

Brennan left him in the half light of his office, a lonely figure picking his way through his desk, looking for a bag to put his few belongings into. He carefully folded his tracksuit and pushed his boots into another bag before putting his light out for the last time. There was a small Christmas tree in the foyer. As he walked outside into the car park, a few flakes of snow were falling. So that was it. Goodbye Huddersfield.

9 This is Anfield

'I AM VERY PLEASED AND PROUD to have been chosen as manager of Liverpool Football Club, a club of such great potential,' enthused Shankly to the press. 'I have known Mr Tom Williams a long time and have always considered him to be one of football's gentlemen. I am confident we will be able to work well together. It is my opinion that Liverpool have a crowd of followers which rank with the greatest in the game. They deserve success and I hope in my small way to be able to do something towards helping them to achieve it. I make no promises, except that from the moment I take over I shall put everything I have into the job I so willingly undertake.'

The *Liverpool Echo* was equally enthusiastic. 'Yes, Liverpool are getting the man they want,' wrote sports editor Leslie Edwards, calling him 'a 100% club man, an expert and an enthusiast rolled into one. In fact a one-man combination that will not rest until Liverpool are in the First Division.'

Standing on the brink of a new decade, the city of Liverpool could never have guessed that the sixties would rocket it to the centre of world attention. It was still an economically important city; the docks were still a thriving community. Ships would lie moored in the Mersey awaiting the next tide or a vacant berth, while the ferryboat that steamed from Liverpool to Birkenhead would meander its way through a maze of shipping. They were mainly cargo ships, but there was still also the occasional passenger liner, the *Empress of Canada*, the *Corinthia* and the *Empress of England* providing a gangplank to almost any port in the world. The whole dockfront was a whirl of ships, cranes, stevedores and chandlers.

Over in Birkenhead, they were beginning work on the first nuclear-powered Polaris submarines, while at the other end of the engineering pendulum, the overhead railway – better known in its time as the 'dockers' umbrella – had not long been pulled down, a sign at least that business was not quite what it was. The railway which had run the entire six-and-a-half miles of the docks, from Dingle in the south to Seaforth in the north, had carried the dockers to their workplaces since 1893, with seventeen stations one for each dock. And the docks themselves carried the names of Victorian England – Albert, Stanley, Huskisson, Gladstone. That was the era when Liverpool had burst on to the map, a world map largely painted in the red of Imperialist Britain.

Liverpool had first been given its city charter by King John in 1207 but had remained a minor port, trading principally with Ireland, until the late eighteenth century. The first dock had been opened in 1715. Forty years later came the first graving dock for the repair of ships, and in 1739 the first ship was constructed on the Mersey. Liverpool was always a port and with its western position offered potential for trade across the Atlantic. As such, it was to become one of the most important ports involved in the trade of slaves. Between 1700 and 1730, it became increasingly influential and by the mid-eighteenth century was the principal centre in Europe for the slavery trade. But as well as slaves, goods such as coffee, tea, sugar and chocolate were also being imported.

Liverpool soon became the focal point of a flourishing Empire. Not only was it an industrial port, it was also a passenger port, one of the busiest in Europe, carrying traders and settlers to Australia, America and India as well as Ireland. Emigrants arrived from as far afield as Russia, Scandinavia and Germany seeking passage to the Americas. Liverpool-based liners were the pride of the fleet with Cunard, Canadian Pacific and Elder Dempster heading the list of shipping companies that vied for the passenger trade across the Atlantic.

Victorian Liverpool was a busy city with its expanse of docklands and shipyards. Its population had grown from just 1,000 persons in 1670 to 7,000 by 1710. A century later, it had jumped to 78,000. By 1831, the population had almost doubled. Over the next twenty years, the population of the city was to increase rapidly before tapering off.

Much of the increase in population was due to Irish immigration, encouraged by the Irish famine of the 1840s. Some 500,000 Irish immigrants entered Liverpool before July 1848. At one point in the mid-century they were rolling in at the rate of 3,000 per day. Not all remained in the city. Many returned to Ireland, others ventured further afield to America, Canada and Australia, while many simply made for other major industrial centres such as Manchester and Glasgow. In the spring of 1847 it was estimated that 105,000 had remained. Immigrants came from elsewhere, particularly North Wales and Scotland, all attracted by the possibility of employment. This clash of cultures was to later give rise to religious friction that would also have its influence on football in the city. Between 1830 and 1930 it has been estimated that 9 million emigrants passed through the city of Liverpool.

The attraction of Liverpool lay not only as a port with passage to some foreign land but also as a city offering employment opportunities. Much of that employment was connected with the docks and trade. In 1800, 4,746 ships used the port. By 1857 this had increased five-fold. In the first half of the nineteenth century, 24 new docks were built, and by 1900 the number of docks had grown to 40, mainly due to an expansion on the other side of the river at Birkenhead and Wallasey. In 1840 Birkenhead had barely existed, its population no more than a few thousand.

Victorian Liverpool was as fine a city as any in Britain. Even today, the legacy of those years still survives. Just stroll around the financial district close to its elegant Town Hall and you can see the gothic architecture of the period. Heavy on the outside but ornate and proud inside, buildings that have withstood bombs, the vibration of traffic and the passage of time.

During both World Wars, it was one of the most important ports for the allies. Equipment, food and other materials vital to the war effort rolled in from America, Asia and Africa. Even after the war, trade flourished, mainly with America. But in the fifties came the first signs of a change in trading patterns. The growing importance of Europe, containerisaton and airfreight combined to swing trade away from Liverpool and to the eastern ports. Liverpool was hopelessly positioned for trade with Europe. Its docks soon gained a reputation for being slow and anarchic, with a lazy, strikebound workforce. Much of its reputation was ill-deserved, but that was the way the world perceived the city.

When Bill Shankly arrived, ships were still an important commodity. But to the discerning eye, the writing was already on the wall. Some docks had closed, others were half empty and the giant liners were spotted less frequently on the river. But even though unemployment had always been higher in the city than the national average, there were still only 4% or so unemployed, considerably less than the 15% that would dog the depressing years of the eighties. In Shankly's first week, the chairman of the city's Juvenile Delinquency committee was warning of problems to come. Juvenile unemployment stood at 800 but could grow to as many as 8,000 by the year 1963, he warned. He would not be far wrong.

Far more depressing than the economics of the city were the fortunes of the two local football clubs. Liverpool had been trapped in the Second Division since 1954 and hadn't won anything since they clinched the league title in 1947, the first season after the war. Since then, they had gone into steady decline, appearing in a Cup final against Arsenal in 1950, only to be soundly beaten and then relegated four years later.

Life in the Second Division had proved frustrating. In their first season, they had finished in eleventh spot. A year later, they climbed into third spot but just failed to make the leap. It was the same over the next three seasons. First, they finished in third spot again and then fourth the next two seasons.

Every year, they made the early running and looked set for the First Division only to stumble at Easter and miss out on promotion. Fate seemed against them. The FA Cup proved just as elusive. They had a few decent runs but that had to be balanced against defeat by Southend United in the third round in 1957, and then by non-league Worcester City in January 1959, a defeat that marked an all-time low in the fortunes of Liverpool Football Club.

Their neighbours Everton had not fared much better. Since the war, the trophy room at Goodison had been bare. They hadn't won anything since 1938, the last full season before hostilities broke out. Since then, it had been all gloom with not even a Cup Final appearance to boast. In 1951, they too had been relegated but had returned to the top flight in 1954, swapping places with Liverpool. Since then, they had lingered in the lower half of the top division, staving off relegation most of the time. For both clubs, it was as depressing a period as any in their history.

Yet Liverpool and Everton were clubs of undoubted pedigree. Liverpool had previously won the league title on five occasions, putting them among soccer's elite. If anything, Everton's history was even more impressive. They had also captured the league trophy on five occasions but had added the FA Cup to their collection twice, in 1906 and 1933. In 1958, they had installed Johnny Carey the former Manchester United captain, in the manager's chair, but so far there had been few signs of any improvement. At Goodison, there was more happening off the field as John Moores of Littlewoods began taking more of an interest in the club. Soon he would be chairman, pumping thousands into the club and appointing a new manager.

Elsewhere in Liverpool, five young lads had formed a pop group. They called themselves the Silver Beatles. But the days of Beatlemania were still some way off. Instead, it was Cliff Richard who was more likely to turn the heads of Liverpool's youth. In the first week of December 1959, Cliff and the Shadows were topping the bill at the Liverpool Empire, tickets 3/6d to 7/6d. And in the record charts, all ears were tuned to Duane Eddy whose latest record 'Some Kinda Earthquake' had just been released. The Liverpool scene was still at an embryonic stage, more a jazz scene than a new pop fashion.

The Liverpool music scene had its roots in the mid-fifties with groups such as the Bobby Bell Rockers, the James Boys and the Raving Texans. The influence was American music, much of it brought to Liverpool from the USA by sailors. At that time, imported American records were a rarity in the city's record shops and it needed a trip to the States to get hold of some of the more obscure American rock music. High on the list of wanted records were Chuck Berry, Little Richard, the Coasters and Bo Diddley. Liverpool lads returning home aboard Cunard liners would arrive with bundles of records as a present for families and friends.

But it was R&B artists, rather than old-style rock 'n' rollers, who captured the soul of Liverpool. There was a rawness about them that suited the mood of the city. Liverpool was somehow closer spiritually to the deep south of the USA. Memphis, New Orleans, Nashville, these were the places the merchant seamen visited on their travels, bringing home souvenirs, exciting tales and memories. Schoolboys wanted to go to sea, to become part of this roving community.

When Bill Shankly arrived that December in 1959, a quick read of the paper would have revealed much about the state of Liverpool. The local council was urging the government of the day to consider Liverpool for a new Ford plant that was to be located in the UK. They would eventually be successful with the plant built at Halewood, saving Merseyside from even greater economic decline. For entertainment, you could go to any number of cinemas downtown. There was Audrey Hepburn starring in *The Nun's Story* while at the Forum Victor Mature was exciting the punters at the classy Futurist in *Demetrius and the Gladiators* and at the Scala Maurice Chevalier was wooing them in *Gigi*. These were the days of city centre cinemas, long queues and Saturday nights in the back row. And, if your taste was for something more refined, there was always the Playhouse Theatre or the Royal Court where Beryl Reid, Bill Maynard and Ivor Emmanuel were starring in *Fun and Games*.

Television was still in its infancy, but you could watch any number of shows that would in time become classics. Little Charlie Drake had his own show, while 'Professor' Jimmy Edwards starred in *Whack-O*. Then there was *Dixon of Dock Green*, a far cry from *The Bill* or *NYPD*. And for a little light relief there was *Spot The Tune*, *The Beverley Sisters* or *What's My Line*. Cars were still relatively expensive: a new Austin A40 would have set you back £700, an A55 a £100 more. There was something comfortable about that age. It was called innocence.

1959/60 began as a poor season for Liverpool. It had opened with defeat at Cardiff and, after seven games, the team had already been beaten four times. Then in October came defeat at Swansea, followed by four consecutive draws. By the time autumn was over, Liverpool were clearly out of the running for promotion.

Phil Taylor had been manager of Liverpool for three years, taking over from Don Welsh in 1956. Taylor was a former player, who had joined the club before the war. He had been a wing half, winning a championship medal immediately after the war and he was captain of the side when Liverpool met Arsenal in the 1950 Cup Final. He also won three England caps, but had retired from the game as Liverpool crashed into the Second Division in 1954. He then joined the backroom staff, rising from chief coach, to acting manager and finally manager. But Taylor was undoubtedly the least successful of all Liverpool managers. Try as he might, he could not inspire the club to success.

Year after year, they failed narrowly to make the jump to the First Division. He made some useful captures in the transfer market, bringing in the England international half back Johnny Wheeler from Bolton and Scottish international goalkeeper Tommy Younger from Hibernian. He also enlisted Jimmy Harrower from Hibernian to add fire to the Liverpool attack but the fire never blazed. When he went scouting to Hibernian, everyone had assumed Liverpool were interested in Joe

Baker, a Liverpool lad who was attracting attention with his goals. But no, it was Harrower, not Baker who interested them.

It was indicative of the times: Liverpool had little ambition. Baker would eventually play for England and in 1961 was transferred to Italian giants Torino. As for Taylor's other signings, Wheeler was already past his best when he joined, as were so many in that team. Even the great Billy Liddell was well over 30. Taylor had little option but to try and build a new young side. The old hands had to go. Former England centre half Laurie Hughes was phased out along with Roy Saunders, Geoff Twentyman and Louis Bimpson.

There was more hope with the youngsters. Alan A'Court was a winger in the Liverpool tradition: quicksilver feet, direct, and a goalscorer to boot. He even won England honours. And there was Ronnie Moran at full back, who was tireless and determined, shouting at his team-mates even in those days. Taylor also encouraged Jimmy Melia who would go on to win England honours. And in early September, Taylor had given a debut to a twenty year-old blond-haired lad called Roger Hunt who would soon become an essential cog in the Shankly side. Standing in for Billy Liddell, Hunt opened his account in the 66th minute.

There would be other less successful products such as Tony Rowley, plus a bunch of honest journeymen: players like Dick White, John Molyneux and Brian Jackson. But somehow Taylor could never get the mix right. He liked big, powerful players. Liddell was the one player still capable of scoring goals but, by the late fifties, injuries were beginning to interrupt his career. Melia could also hit the net but never with the consistency of Liddell. And so, as Liverpool slumped out of the promotion race in the winter of 1959, the board began to think in terms of a new man at the helm.

The beginning of the end for Taylor had effectively arrived the season before, when Liverpool travelled to non-league Worcester City in the third round of the FA Cup. It was a tricky tie but still well within the capabilities of Liverpool. Instead, they lost 2-1 in what was undoubtedly the biggest cup shock in the club's entire history. It was a humiliating moment that emphasised how low Liverpool had sunk.

From that moment on, Taylor was living on borrowed time. Had he been able to steer Liverpool to promotion that season, all would no doubt have been forgiven, if not forgotten. As it was, they wound up in fourth spot.

When the season ended, the murmurings in the boardroom grew louder. But Liverpool have always been a club prepared to give anyone a second, even a third chance. The club prides itself on patience. And so Taylor was given a stay of execution.

The Liverpool chairman Tom Williams had been at Anfield since the club began. His earliest memories, so he claimed, were of sitting on his father's shoulders watching Everton at Anfield before the split that sent Everton to Goodison and created Liverpool Football Club. At the time, he would have only been two-years-old, so perhaps his recollections have to be taken with a pinch of salt. But it was certainly true to say that he had been around Anfield for most of its existence. He was a de Gaulle-like figure: tall, lean and unshakeable. In his younger days, he had worked in the cotton exchange but now his time was devoted to Liverpool.

Williams had been impressed with Bill Shankly when he appeared before them for an interview back in 1951. Manager George Kay had just quit through ill health, and Shankly had applied for the job. Williams wanted to appoint him but others were less keen, fearing that he would want to interfere too much in team selection. He was clearly the most impressive of the bunch they had interviewed, but then someone suggested they approach Don Welsh who had been a favourite at Anfield during the war.

Welsh had never applied for the job but, when they approached him, he snapped up the chance. Even then Shankly had seemed a determined character, a man who preferred to be out on the pitch training with his players rather than stuck behind a desk. These were days of change. In the fifties, the manager was more of an administrator than a coach. Training was usually left to the expertise of the coaching staff. The manager might choose the team but it was usually with the assistance of the board rather than his coaching colleagues. There would often be a sub-committee that would convene on a Friday evening – consisting of a couple of board members, the manager and maybe the secretary. The typical stereotypes were men like Tom Whittaker, Major Buckley and Arthur Rowe. Fine managers in their own right, but hardly ever found in track suits.

All that was beginning to change. Matt Busby had pointed the way. There were others such as George Raynor, who had managed the highly successful Swedish World Cup team in 1958, and Joe Mercer at Aston Villa. They were a new breed, never far removed from the dressing room, still young, approachable and with fresh ideas. They had a rapport with the players that was proving crucial. They believed in motivation.

What's more their new style was proving successful. The emergence of this breed was putting a spotlight on the manager's role. The time when a manager could shift the blame to his playing staff was fast disappearing. The manager was no longer an adjunct of the board. More money, and more responsibility meant added responsibility to succeed. If the team failed, it was the manager who now carried the can. Since the war, the manager's job had been comparatively secure; but now heads were rolling everywhere. Success was at a premium. If you wanted a successful side, then first you had to look at the man in charge.

When Tom Williams looked at Phil Taylor, he saw one of the old breed, a gentleman: quiet, respectable and submissive, not the kind of man who would bawl out his players. He was the sort of manager the board liked. They could run him. He never gave them trouble; they could choose the team, decide who to buy and so on. That was all very well, but Williams knew times were changing. A man like Taylor might have been fine for the fifties, but he was not the man for the sixties. Williams had kept an eye on Shankly's progress. He had followed his rise up the ladder at Leeds Road and had read the headlines about Law and the young team he was developing. He liked what he had read and heard.

As the 1959/60 season wore on, Taylor was feeling the strain. He was only 42-years-old but as football entered a new fiercely competitive era he wondered if he was equipped to meet its challenges. Taylor's deteriorating health and Williams' ambitions for the club brought matters to a head in the autumn of 1959. The two met privately.

Williams asked him if he was well enough to carry on. 'Mightn't it be better if you stepped aside,' he suggested. 'We'll look after you.' Taylor agreed to consider it. A few days later, Taylor met again with Williams, and two other senior directors, Robson Roberts and Lawson Martindale. The answer was yes: Taylor had agreed to accept their offer and stand down. The club was thus saved the embarrassment of sacking him – he resigned on the grounds of ill health. It was a neat compromise.

Taylor formally resigned to the board on the evening of Tuesday 17 November. He issued a statement. 'The club has in my opinion enjoyed reasonable success,' it read. 'My three years resulted in a third and two fourth positions. But the strain of it all has however made me very tired at times and I have decided, great as my love is for Liverpool, to resign.

'I made promotion my goal,' he continued. 'I set my heart on it and strove for it with all the energy I could muster ... such striving was not enough and now the time has come to hand over to someone else to see if they can do it better.'

Few tears were shed. The *Liverpool Echo* had no regrets. It had been a troublesome few weeks for Taylor. At the beginning of the month, he had placed Louis Bimpson, Alan Arnell and Gerry Byrne on the transfer list. It hadn't been easy, and it was ironic that Byrne, who had made only a couple of appearances, would soon become a hero under Shankly and carry on to win international honours.

Then there had been the wrangle over Dave Hickson. Taylor, ever aware that the club desperately needed a goalscorer, had done the un-thinkable by trying to buy the popular Hickson from Everton. Taylor was attacked from all sides. The Evertonians were outraged that their club could ever conceive of selling the great man, while Liverpool sup-porters were equally concerned about buying an Evertonian who had been the butt of their jokes for years.

There hadn't been a deal between the two clubs since before the war and, with Everton in the First Division, rivalry was bitter. When news leaked out, it hit the front pages. But Everton wouldn't sell at Liver-pool's price.

For a full week, the two clubs haggled over the deal while the letters poured into the *Echo*. Taylor was villified. In the end, he got his man, paying out £12,000. Taylor might have angered many, but on Hick-son's debut against top of the table Aston Villa, 50,000 turned up to watch him score a couple of goals as Liverpool won 2-1. That same day Everton lost 8-2 at Newcastle. But the strain of it was all too much for Taylor.

With Taylor out of the way, Williams could now pursue his secret plan, though first of all he and fellow director Sid Reakes journeyed to Scotland to sign left half Tommy Leishman from St Mirren.

Williams had been busy taking soundings about Shankly. He'd talked to Geoff Twentyman who had been with Shankly at Carlisle. 'I told him he'd be getting a good man,' says Twentyman. 'I was never surprised when Shankly was appointed.'

What Twentyman told him was enough to persuade Williams to

approach Shankly himself. He soon had an indication that the Scotsman would be interested in the job. But there were formalities. The board agreed that regardless of anyone's interest, the job should be advertised, and that only those who applied would be considered. The newspapers were touting their own lists of names, as well as suggesting that the new manager would have £60,000 to spend, a story that proved to be far from the truth.

Shankly was also top of the *Liverpool Echo*'s list with sports editor Leslie Edwards reporting that he'd been told by someone with good connections at the club, back in the October, that Phil Taylor would be leaving within the month and that Bill Shankly would be the new manager. But the *Echo* was putting forward other names as well. Harry Catterick at Sheffield Wednesday was a favourite, along with Jimmy Murphy, Busby's assistant at Manchester United. Peter Doherty at Bristol City also came in for a mention, as well as Bert Tann at Bristol Rovers and Jimmy Hagan at Peterborough.

But there was only ever one genuine candidate. Nevertheless, the board went through the formalities and interviewed each of them, though in fact few people had applied, an indication perhaps of the status of Liverpool Football Club at the time. And so, on the evening of Tuesday 1 December, the board formally announced that Bill Shankly had been offered the job and had accepted. He would be taking over as manager on 1 January 1960.

'It seems like a good way to be starting the new decade,' said Williams. The salary was £2,500 a year, £500 more than he was receiving at Huddersfield. Liverpool were in tenth spot in Division Two; Huddersfield were sixth.

10 Boys From the Bootroom

ON THE MORNING OF MONDAY 14 DECEMBER, Shankly pulled his Austin A40 into the small car park at the back of the old gabled main stand at Anfield. He'd driven over from Huddersfield that morning, leaving Nessie and the family behind. He parked the car, straightened his tie in the mirror and walked through the main door. He was his usual smart self, in two-piece suit, shirt collar and tie. 'I'm the new manager,' he announced. 'I've come to see Mr Williams and Mr McInnes.' He was shown upstairs to Tom Williams' office. The three men shook hands. 'Maybe we should show you around the place,' suggested Williams. 'That's hardly necessary,' replied Shankly. 'I was here on Saturday to watch the reserves.' Williams and McInnes were taken aback. Neither had been there on Saturday, and neither had heard that Shankly had been around. They were slightly embarrassed.

'The reserves had a good win,' said Shankly. 'They've got some useful players though City were so poor you couldn't judge too much.' The reserves had won 5-0. The first team had also chalked up a victory, winning 2-0 at Bristol Rovers. Williams suggested a photograph to mark the occasion of his arrival. A man from the *Echo* was there. They'd got hold of Liverpool backroom boys Reuben Bennett and Bob Paisley.

After the photographs and a few words with Bennett and Paisley, they took Shankly around Anfield to meet his new colleagues. In those days, the club only employed a handful of staff – a receptionist who doubled as a secretary, a few other secretaries, some cleaners, a groundsman and various ticket administrators – nothing compared with the hundreds employed today.

And there were always a few old-timers: ex-players, well past the age of retirement, but still part of the Anfield furniture. They'd turn up most days, do a few odd jobs on a voluntary basis. Occasionally, someone would slip them a few pounds. They just wanted to remain part of the club. And of course, on top of that, there were the coaching staff, Shankly's lieutenants.

Chief among them was Bob Paisley, a former Liverpool wing half who had played in the post-war championship team, but who had been overlooked for the Cup Final side of 1950. In the semi-final, Paisley had put Liverpool ahead with a looping shot that deceived Burnett in the Everton goal. But when it came to the final, Paisley was asked to stand down in favour of Laurie Hughes who had recovered from injury.

Paisley took the decision with typical stoicism. He was a canny character, from Hetton-le-Hole in the North-east. He'd played his early football with Bishop Auckland, winning an amateur FA Cup winners medal with them in 1939. Almost immediately after that, he joined Liverpool and went on to play more than 250 games for the club before retiring in 1954 as the club slipped into the Second Division.

During the war, Paisley had served with the army in the Western Desert and had earned the nickname 'Gunner', a name that was to stick with him. He had then been part of the liberating army that swept through Italy. When he arrived in Italy with Liverpool for a European Cup Final decades later, he was asked if it was his first visit. 'No,' he replied. 'The last time I was here I rode into Rome on the top of a tank.'

Shankly and Paisley had played against each other on many occasions. 'He was a similar type to me,' remembered Paisley. 'Whatever our faults, we'd run until we dropped and never knew when we were beaten.'

It was an attitude that was to become a hallmark of the Liverpool set-up in the future. The two men were obsessed by football, though Paisley shared with Shankly another obsession – boxing – and was always fond of reminding Shankly that he had seen the great Joe Louis and Sugar Ray Robinson fight.

Shankly would tell him that he had once spotted Joe Louis while he was riding through Glasgow on a bus. He immediately raced down the stairs, jumped off the bus, caught up with the great man, shook his hand and got his autograph. There had to be an element of doubt about the story, but Shankly and Paisley would re-enact fights and talk boxing for hours on end.

When Paisley had hung his boots up, he was offered a job on the Anfield coaching staff and, in August 1959, when Albert Shelley retired, Paisley moved up to become first team trainer. Paisley was the perfect number two: never a threat to Shankly, but always offering wise counsel. He was more than happy to play second fiddle, though his influence – even in the Shankly era – was far more crucial than has ever been acknowledged. Shankly was to become the great motivating force behind Liverpool, but it was Paisley who was the tactician.

Paisley had however been warned by a friend at Huddersfield to expect problems with Shankly. Paisley was told he'd find him impossible to work with. 'You won't be able to stand the strain,' he was advised and was given two years. But it was never the case. 'From the moment he arrived, we got on like a house on fire,' recalled Paisley.

Also on the coaching staff was Joe Fagan, a rubber-faced character, as Liverpudlian as the Liver Bird. Fagan was the psychologist, the genial scouser, full of Liverpool humour and always grinning. Fagan knew when to kick backsides, or when to put an arm around a player. As a youngster, he had somehow escaped the Merseyside scouting net and ended up a Manchester City player. In a fairly undistinguished career, he later played with Bradford, Altrincham and Nelson before enlisting as trainer at Rochdale under Harry Catterick.

Shankly had of course played against him and had even tried to sign him in the days when Fagan was playing for City and Shankly was managing Grimsby. But he had been rebuffed by City. Fagan eventually returned to his roots, joining Liverpool in 1958 and he was to remain a stalwart of the bootroom for the next 27 years.

'I have never met a nicer, more straightforward fellow,' remembers Ronnie Moran of Fagan. 'He was what the bootroom was all about. He was never interested in the fancy side of football and never looked for the glamour and the glory.'

During his whole Anfield career, Fagan lived in the same modest house, even though he would eventually become manager and lead the side to a fourth European Cup triumph. It was typical modesty. Like Paisley, he preferred to be away from the glamour, never really wanting to be number one but realising sometimes you had to be.

When Shankly arrived, Fagan was responsible for the reserves. It may not have been as important a job as Liverpool struggled in the Second Division, but in time it would become one of the most critical jobs around Anfield when Shankly transformed the reserves into a kindergarten for his future stars.

Then there was Reuben Bennett, a fellow Scot, who had played most of his football north of the border. Shankly knew of Bennett from his brother Bob at Dundee. Bennett had been recruited to Anfield following Liverpool's disastrous defeat at Huddersfield the previous season. He was as tartan as they come, always stoking the English/Scottish rivalry at the club. Yet, he would always come out with some far-fetched excuse if Scotland lost an international – it was too hot, someone had been injured, bad refereeing and so on.

Bennett had played his football with Hull City, Queen of the South and Dundee before retiring in 1950 to take over as trainer at Dens Park. After that, he had a spell at managing Ayr United before joining Motherwell as coach. In 1956, he had moved to Third Lanark and two years later was recruited to the Liverpool cause by Tom Williams. Bennett was put in charge of training and given the task of redeveloping the entire programme. Bennett has long been one of the unsung heroes of the Liverpool bootroom, a man whose influence far exceeded his fame.

Bennett and Shankly were close, 'peas from the same pod', remembers Alan Kennedy. No doubt their Scottish ancestry helped a little as well. Every morning, Shankly would pick Bennett up in his car and drive him to Anfield. They would also drive miles together looking at opposing teams, a shared experience that drew them together over the years.

And finally there was Albert Shelley. Shelley had been around Anfield as long as anyone could remember. By the time Shankly arrived, he had retired but he still turned up every day. There was always a job to be done: a room to be swept, a dressing room to be tidied, or a boot to be sent for repair. He did it gladly, never looking for payment.

After all, Anfield was a family and they had all known each other for years. Even the club secretary, Jimmy McInnes, was a former player, a wing half who had been succeeded in the Liverpool side by Bob Paisley. McInnes came from Ayr and had played with Third Lanark prior to joining Liverpool in 1938. He'd retired shortly after the war, becoming assistant secretary and then secretary, as well as studying for a degree at Edinburgh University.

There was something about each member of the bootroom that helped cement the relationship with Shankly. From Paisley's supporting role and tactical knowledge, to Fagan's psychology; from Bennett's Scottishness to Shelley's loyalty: all of them, including Shankly, had been forged in the same hard knocks school of life. They were all familiar with depressed areas and meagre wages of working-class life, where adversity bred backbone. But they had also learnt the lessons of common decency, honesty and pride.

Shankly, although he might not have recognised it at first, was joining a family, a community whose sole interest was the fortunes of Liverpool Football Club. But it was a family that lacked a father figure. They needed someone like Shankly. Neither Paisley nor Fagan was the kind of man to stand up and shout the Liverpool message. They were too phlegmatic, too concerned with the details. They might have had visions of their own, but they could never have voiced them in the way that Shankly would. In a word, they needed a leader, someone who could put into words and actions their own feelings and commitment.

On that first day, Shankly made the wisest decision he was to ever make in his entire Anfield career. He began by taking the bootroom staff aside and guaranteeing them their jobs. 'Now normally, managers come into a club and bring their trainers with them,' Shankly wrote years later in his autobiography. 'Well, I'm not going to do that. You fellows have been here, some of you, a long time. I have my own training system and I will work in co-operation with you. I will lay down the plans and gradually we will all be on the same wavelength.'

But there was a price. 'I want one thing,' he added. 'I want loyalty. I don't want anybody to carry stories about anybody else . . . if anyone tells me a story about someone else, the man with the story will get the sack. I don't care if he has been here for 50 years. I want everyone to be loyal to each other. Everything we do will be for Liverpool Football Club.'

It was a plain and surprisingly simple message. It was the foundation on which any family is built. Shankly saw Liverpool as his new family. He was to be the father figure, whom they would all respect. In return, he would be loyal to them. Over the years, he was to remain true to his word. No bootroom member or anyone remotely connected with the bootroom was ever sacked from his job.

'He made no bones about it,' remembered Paisley. 'He was the boss . . . there was a lot wrong with Liverpool, but the staff was alright and he was keeping it.' Paisley found the deal straightforward. 'There was no way that you could not work for him . . . You can sense when people have a bit of respect for you, and you could feel that Bill had respect for us, and we for him.' It was as simple as that.

Club captain Ronnie Moran also received Shankly's backing. Shankly wrote him a letter, just telling him what he expected and what he wanted Moran to do. It was only a simple note but it meant a great deal to Moran. 'It showed a bit of thought,' he says. 'I learned more in the first three months than I'd done in the seven years that I'd been a pro. I wish I'd have been five years younger.'

But while the staff were clearly to the liking of Shankly there was much else about the place that was not. Shankly was soon to wonder if he had made the right decision in coming to Merseyside. He knew that he had been taking a risk in joining them, a club that were lower down the division than Huddersfield, but he was still in for a surprise or two.

On his second morning, with Paisley, Fagan and Bennett in tow, he set off for the club's training ground at Melwood. It was the first time he had ever visited the training set-up and he was in for a shock. Melwood is situated in West Derby, a leafy suburb a few miles from Anfield. But there was little that was welcoming that morning. Shankly could barely believe his eyes.

It was a ramshackle place, made more depressing by the December weather. There was an old wooden pavilion, like the typical village cricket clubhouse. It was used mainly as a changing facility for the A and B sides when they played their games at Melwood. First and second team players changed at Anfield before arriving at Melwood.

It was a good job as well because Melwood was in no way equipped to cope with 30-odd players. There was no heating, the paint was peeling off the walls and the washing facilities were a disgrace. It was as bad as Workington. The pitch was little better either. It was full of bumps and bare patches. Where there was grass, it looked as if it had not been cut for a season. To make matters worse, there were trees.

It might have looked pleasantly rural but as far as Shankly was concerned this was a football ground, not a cricket pitch. The attitude was clear when he asked someone what the smaller pitch was used for. 'Cricket,' he was told. 'Not any more,' he replied. 'That's now a five-a-side pitch.' Shankly could barely believe what he had seen. It was a bitter disappointment. He returned to Anfield that afternoon to bang a few heads and make changes. Within weeks, repairs were carried out. The old pavilion was given a lick of paint, and the Anfield groundsman, Bert Riley, was dragged down to do a job on the Mel-wood pitch.

Nessie Shankly remembers her husband coming home and complaining about everything. 'It was all in a terrible mess,' she says. 'He was so upset.' Anfield was just as bad. 'There was barely any running water with only one sprinkler tap for the pitch. The toilets were a disgrace as well. Most of them didn't flush.'

One of Shankly's proudest achievements was to have toilets installed that flushed. One player remembers him showing people around Anfield, proudly flushing the toilet and telling them that there was no water not so long ago. 'The place was a dump,' says Nessie.

Tarting up Melwood might not have seemed crucial but it was important to Shankly. It was important that his home was spick and span, reflecting the cleanliness and decency of the family. It was all part of his working-class culture – loyalty, cleanliness, honesty. At Carlisle and all his other clubs, he had insisted that his teams turn out as smart and trim as possible. At times, it had been difficult. At Carlisle, he had to go out and buy a team strip out of his own money. But it was fundamental to Shankly that you try to look your best. He himself always turned up for work in a suit and tie, looking more like a well-scrubbed Scottish doctor than a football manager.

To the surprise of many, Shankly opted out of selecting the side for his first game, against Cardiff City. Instead he chose to wait until he had fully settled in and knew the players and their capabilities. A selection committee of directors, coaches and other executives chose the side, which showed only one change from the team that had beaten Bristol Rovers the previous week. Nineteen-year-old Alan Jones came in to make his debut, replacing John Molyneux at full back. It was a disaster. Cardiff were a useful side and gave Liverpool a thrashing, winning 4-0 at Anfield. Liverpool were a couple of goals down by half time. During the interval, Shankly reorganised the formation and in the second half they looked a far sharper outfit. 'Whatever Mr Shankly said to them during the interval,' wrote Michael Chateris in the *Liverpool Echo*, 'livened them up beyond belief.'

It was not an encouraging start, but Shankly was not about to begin screaming at anyone. Back in the dressing room, everyone looked towards the new manager expecting the worst. Instead, he simply told them, 'You can learn as much from defeat as victory.'

'We all looked for the reaction,' says Paisley, 'but it was a sensible one. You wouldn't have known from it whether we'd won 4-0 or lost 4-0. He wasn't going to shout the odds that early.'

Jimmy Melia even told Shankly that they were so anxious to please him that they had tried too hard. They had enjoyed themselves so much with the change of routine and the new training. 'It was wonderful,' he added, 'but we were over-anxious.' It was music to Shankly's ears.

The arrival of a new manager hardly seemed to have set the city alight. A crowd of only 27,000 turned up, a far cry from the 50,000 who had watched Hickson's first game six weeks earlier. At least Shankly knew the worst. It wasn't much better the following week either as Liverpool travelled to Charlton for a Boxing Day fixture. They made two changes, bringing in Jimmy Harrower for Fred Morris, with Molyneux also returning.

Liverpool lost 3-0. Shankly had only been in charge for two games and his side had conceded seven goals without scoring. They had now slumped to ninth in the table. There may have been a few panic signs elsewhere, and one or two letters had been dashed off to the *Liverpool Echo*, but Shankly was not too concerned. Two days later, Charlton were the visitors to Anfield and, in front of 25,000, Shankly notched up his first victory in a fairly shapeless game. But Shankly was delighted, dancing around the dressing room as if he had just won an FA Cup semi-final.

Shankly's impact on the players was instantaneous. 'There was a terrific change when he joined,' remembers Dave Hickson. 'There was a great transformation about the place. The basic routine of arriving at Anfield, changing and then going to Melwood was already in place but suddenly he started coaching us. We were playing football rather than just doing exercises. We'd not had that before.'

Other players also remember those early days. 'We were all aware of the reputation Shankly had earned at his previous clubs,' recalls Roger Hunt, then a 21-year-old who had just broken into the first team. 'Obviously, we didn't quite know what to expect, but once it was announced that he would be our new manager we were all looking forward to his arrival.

'He brought with him new training methods. The training was hard for the first month but, once we were fit, it was all based on speed and training with the ball.'

Phil Taylor had never been one for encouraging ball practice but Paisley, Fagan and Bennett were delighted to implement Shankly's new ideas. The five-a-side game was also instituted and in a short time would become an Anfield institution. Shankly also began to give the youngsters a little more respect.

Early on in his Anfield days, Shankly spotted one young lad hanging around as the players were about to board the team coach to Melwood. 'What's your name?' asked Shankly. 'Chris Lawler,' replied the nervous teenager. 'Where are you going? Why aren't you getting in the coach?' he demanded. 'Well, we work here during the day,' explained Lawler. 'And we do our training at night.' 'You work here, cleaning the place up, and then train at night?' asked a shocked Shankly. 'Well, you go now, son and get all the groundstaff boys together and get on that bus. You're here first and foremost to play football, and secondly to clean up.'

It was indicative of the kind of attitude that had existed around Anfield for years. Shankly soon changed that although not without an argument or two. Taking the lads off to Melwood during the day upset not only the routine but quite a few officials as well. But it had to be done.

Liverpool were already out of contention for promotion by the time Shankly arrived – by the beginning of 1960, they had already lost nine matches. But it meant that Shankly could at least experiment without fear of jeopardising any promotion hopes. Like most clubs, Liverpool had a huge staff of players, with just over 40 on their books. In those days, clubs could afford such luxuries, paying most of their players the £20 maximum wage of the time. It did not take Shankly long to realise that many were simply not up to the job in hand. Some would have to go.

Shankly was beginning to resolve a few basic questions. He always maintained that, within a month, he had made a list of 24 players who would have to go. Shankly reckoned all 24 had gone within the year.

Everyone was fearful that they might not survive. But one of the first to be given a vote of confidence was Roger Hunt. 'I had only been playing in the team for six months when he arrived, so obviously I was worried about my place and I was nervous to make a good impression,' he says. 'But one day in training shortly after his arrival, he pulled me to one side and more or less told me that I fitted in to his plans and that gave me a lot of confidence.'

Hunt was one of the lucky few. Others soon found themselves facing the dole or a move to another club – only a handful of players would eventually survive through to the championship team. But the clearout was never as dramatic or swift as had been feared. Of those who played first team football that season, only a few would have left by the beginning of the 1960/61 season.

Geoff Twentyman and Louis Bimpson who started the season with the club had already gone before Shankly arrived. Others to leave were Barry Wilkinson, who went to Bangor, and Reg Blore for Southport. All three left during the 1960 close season. Veteran South African goalkeeper Doug Rudham decided to retire and return to Johannesburg with the old England warhorse Laurie Hughes also calling it a day. Other players in the reserves and A team also moved on, but only four first team players left.

The story that Shankly came in and cleared out the club within months is simply not true. There was indeed a clearout but it took time. Billy Liddell was to survive another season but would only play one more game for the first team before retiring. John Nicholson and Willie Carlin would also remain at Anfield but would never play for the first team again. Within a few years, they too would be gone.

At the end of the season, free transfers were granted to six players – Des Palmer, John Best, Reg Blowers, Bob Early, Stan Woodall and McCarthy. Two other players, Barry Wilkinson and winger Fred Morris, were placed on the transfer list. In all, 27 players were retained.

There was only one new recruit that first season. Shankly's first attempt at a major signing had been to flirt with the idea of stealing Denis Law from Huddersfield. Nobody knew the value of Law better than Shankly. He approached the board not long after his appointment but was hardly surprised when they said 'No.' They had almost laughed at the suggestion. Law was the kind of player for Arsenal, Tottenham and Manchester City – not Liverpool. In March 1960, Law signed for City for a British record fee of £65,000.

He also made a bold attempt to sign Jackie Charlton, the Leeds United centre half. He'd watched Charlton many times and was impressed by his authority and courage. But Leeds were staving off relegation and were not really interested in selling one of their few prize assets. They quoted him an unrealistic £20,000 plus.

But it did not deter Shankly. He reckoned Charlton was worth every penny and immediately approached the Liverpool board with a proposal to buy the young man. But the board were barely interested. Fine, they agreed, but we can only sanction a fee of £18,000. Shankly returned to Leeds with his offer, knowing full well that they would turn it down. Shankly sensed though that they might sell if the price was a little higher. He raced back across the Pennines and dashed in to see Tom Williams. But Williams was adamant. 'We can't go any higher than £18,000,' he told him.

And so the opportunity of bringing Jack Charlton to Anfield was lost. Shankly was annoyed and began to wonder how he was supposed to build a promotion side if the board would not allow him to spend more than £18,000 on a player. He'd been told there would be money available to buy players, but when it came to asking, the money did not seem to be there. It was to be the first of a number of clashes with the board.

Although Shankly was to become renowned for his dealings in the transfer market, particularly at the bargain end, his first Liverpool recruit turned out to be something of a disaster. With his limited resources, Shankly was forced to lower his horizons. The search had been on for a winger and when twenty-year-old Sammy Reid of Motherwell became available, Shankly snapped him up. The price was right – a mere £8,000 – and the board gave him the go-ahead. But it was to provide a salutary lesson for everyone: usually, you get what you pay for. In the case of Sammy Reid, it was not very much. Reid failed to make even one appearance for Liverpool and was eventually offloaded back north. Liverpool, and in particular Shankly, had wasted £8,000. It did not go unnoticed with the board.

Shankly's next signing however was to prove more successful. The failure of Reid still left the problem of a winger unresolved. Shankly turned next to Kevin Lewis, the Sheffield United winger who seemed to fit the bill. During the close season, he persuaded his directors to dig into their pockets again and fork out a record fee of £13,000. Even at that price, the directors cringed at the cost, cross-examining Shankly vigorously over their outlay.

Was Lewis really that good, they asked, and if he was so good, why is nobody else interested at that price? They reminded Shankly of the £8,000 lashed out on Reid, who had yet to play a game. Shankly assured them that Lewis would be worth it and that the club needed a replacement for Billy Liddell. They could not argue with that assessment. Liddell was now 38-years-old and at the end of his career. And so they agreed to the signing of Lewis, though for not a penny more than £13,000.

That season, there was an early test for the new Liverpool side when Manchester United visited Anfield for an FA Cup fourth round tie in late January. United, champions in 1956 and 1957, had been wiped out a year later at Munich but were still a formidable force. The Busby Babes may have gone but they could still boast players of the calibre of Charlton, Quixall, Viollet, Setters and Foulkes.

The match also meant a reunion for Shankly with his old Scottish team-mate Matt Busby and Jimmy Murphy, who had been tipped by more than one newspaper for the job at Anfield. A huge crowd turned out, more than 56,000, one of the biggest gates for years. But there was little to cheer. The masterly Charlton, back in world-class form, grabbed a couple of goals and Liverpool went down 3-1.

But Liverpool had shown plenty of fight with one newspaper at least noting that 'Shankly's drive and fear-nothing characteristics had been injected into his players.' Unfortunately for Liverpool, United had cleared off the line in the first minute and had then gone on to give a display of quality attacking football.

Liverpool finished Shankly's first season in third spot, eight points adrift of Cardiff City in second place and nine points off Second Division champions Aston Villa. Shankly could at least take pride in having reorganised the side. Since the beginning of the year, they had lost only three games, won ten and drawn five. It was championship form.

If only they had not tossed away so many points early in the season, they might have been able to pitch in a realistic challenge. But it was an encouraging start, and there was clearly much to be optimistic about. Young Roger Hunt had grabbed the headlines as well with 21 goals in 36 outings. And with his new signing Kevin Lewis raring to go, Shankly could look forward to the 1960/61 season with genuine hopes for promotion.

The new season kicked off with a stiff challenge, the visit of Leeds United, just relegated to the Second Division. Among their ranks was Jackie Charlton, much coveted by Shankly and, although Leeds were to be beaten that day, it did little to dim Shankly's enthusiasm for the lanky defender. More than 43,000 spectators came and Liverpool's bright start offered plenty of encouragement for the days ahead. Unfortunately, they could not sustain it and, in their second game, away at Southampton, they crashed 4-1. Southampton would also knock them out of the league Cup. They drew their third game at Middlesbrough and then lost again to Southampton, this time at Anfield. Four games gone and only three points to show for it. It was not the kind of start Shankly had been anticipating. There were obvious weaknesses in the side.

What Shankly really needed was a strong motivator, the kind of player who could carry his orders and enthusiasm on to the field. He needed a man at the heart of the defence, a player who could become the backbone of the team. He looked again towards Jack Charlton, still in his early twenties.

Now that Leeds had been relegated, manager Jack Taylor was willing to listen to offers. But the price had been upped to £30,000. It was too high. Shankly approached the board again. Again the board shook their heads. 'We don't have that kind of money,' they told him. 'You'll have to be less ambitious.'

As usual Shankly was on the phone to Horace Yates, the *Echo*'s man covering Liverpool. 'We'd be sitting in the office and, from where we were, we could hear him ranting and raving,' remembers Yates' successor Ian Hargreaves. 'He was always threatening to resign. You could hear him all over the office.'

Rebutted, Shankly's attentions turned instead towards his old club Preston North End and Gordon Milne. Shankly had known the Milne family for years. They had even lived in the same street, Lowthorpe Road, near to Deepdale. He had played with Gordon's father Jimmy at Preston. When Gordon was born, Shankly and Jimmy had wet the baby's head and Shankly had watched young Gordon grow up over the years.

Milne was not the powerful centre half he was looking for, but he was a gutsy half back who could pass the ball with some ability. He would be a useful asset. A deal was quickly concluded. Milne arrived at Anfield for £16,000 in late August 1960, another record fee for the club. Over the next seven years, he would become an integral part of the Liverpool side, winning championship and FA Cup honours as well as fourteen England caps.

But the arrival of Milne failed to bring immediate relief. Milne made his debut against Southampton at Anfield. Liverpool lost, but won comfortably the next week. That was to be followed by a draw and a couple more defeats. By mid-September, Liverpool had tasted victory in only two of their eight matches, with four defeats.

The gloom was spreading beyond the dressing room. Gates had fallen to little over 20,000 and Shankly was in despair. Upstairs though they did not share his mood. They simply could not understand why he was so depressed. They were in the top half of the table, gates were over 20,000. What was the problem? 'The problem,' Shankly told them bluntly, 'is that I want this club in the First Division, and to do that I need money to sign new players.'

Gloom was also top of the agenda at the annual shareholders' meeting. Nobody was happy, though thankfully most of the vitriol was aimed at the directors rather than the manager. Shankly wasn't happy either. He could sense the potential. Liverpool was a big club, capable of drawing crowds of 50,000 to each game. You only had to walk around the city and meet the people: all they wanted to talk about was football. On Monday mornings in the offices, factories and schools, the conversation was soccer. He felt sorry for the fans.

Over at Goodison, there seemed to be considerably more appetite for success. Big money was being splashed on stars like Roy Vernon, Billy Bingham, Alex Parker and Alex Young. Goodison smacked of ambition.

At Anfield, they looked on in envy at their counterparts across Stanley Park. Everton manager Johnny Carey seemed to have the kind of money Shankly needed. So far, Shankly had spent £37,000 on three players. Carey had spent £27,000 on Vernon alone and, by the end of the year, he would have splashed out a staggering £55,000 to bring Alex Young and George Thomson from Hearts.

In March 1960, Littlewoods boss John Moores had become a director of Everton, promising an interest free loan of £56,000 to the club 'to enable star players to be secured'. That was the kind of attitude Shankly envied. At the Everton shareholders' meeting that year, the chairman had talked about 'visions of greatness for Everton next season'. It was in stark contrast to what was going on at Anfield.

'It was fight and argue, fight and argue, fight and argue until I thought "Is it worthwhile all this fighting and arguing?"' That was the way Shankly summed it up. He'd been promised money when he was appointed, £60,000, but only a fraction of it had been forthcoming. Shankly was furious, convinced that he had been lured to Anfield under false pretences. The side desperately needed new blood. He was slowly ridding the club of its older and less able players, but they needed to be replaced.

In truth, what had really attracted some of the Anfield directors to Shankly in the first place had been his ability to run a club on a shoestring. He had had plenty of experience of doing just that at Carlisle, Grimsby and Workington, all penniless clubs, and they could see how successful he had been.

Even at Huddersfield, a far wealthier club and a club with a great tradition, he had coped on a small budget. He had only signed a couple of players for a paltry outlay of £10,000 while bringing in three times that amount of money. The Liverpool directors liked that kind of arithmetic. Instead of dealing in the transfer market, they reckoned he would be better grooming youngsters. They were cheap and such a system might throw up a Law, a Wilson or an O'Grady, just as it had at Huddersfield.

Shankly was losing patience. He had had enough. The directors might be perfectly happy, but he wasn't. Squeezing more than £20,000 out of the board looked to be a hopeless dream and finding quality players for less was practically impossible.

To make matters worse, the board were still interfering with team selection. They would have a word with him about certain players and let their views be known. The interference was blatant. At board meetings, when Shankly presented his report, heavy hints were made about who should be in the team.

'Those early days were very difficult for him,' remembers Nessie Shankly. 'The directors wanted to choose the side and they wouldn't let him have any money to buy players. I don't know how they expected to get out of the Second Division. I sometimes wonder if Bill didn't regret leaving Huddersfield. I never asked him, and he never said, but I could sense that maybe he was beginning to regret it.'

Shankly complained to his friend Matt Busby, half seeking advice. He told Busby that he was going to resign. 'Somebody had rubbed him up the wrong way,' remembered Busby in his book *Soccer at the Top*. 'I asked him if he had a job to go to but he hadn't.' Busby counselled caution. 'I said, "Bill, things are bound to break for you." Whatever the trouble was, he felt strongly and the fact that he would not have a job, and therefore would not have any wages would scarcely have entered his head. There was something he didn't like and he would go. It was as simple as that.'

Fortunately, Shankly accepted his friend's advice. He had the highest respect for Busby. Most weeks, he would drive over to Manchester just to see his old friend and chat about football. 'They were like brothers,' remembers former player Phil Chisnall who witnessed their relationship, 'Busby the admiring elder brother, Shankly the respectful younger brother.'

'He loved going to see Matt,' says Nessie. 'There was a tea lady at Old Trafford. He was very fond of her. They'd greet each other like long-lost friends. She would make a cup of tea for Matt and Bill and they would just sit and natter about football.'

Further help however would eventually be forthcoming and from a surprising source, the board itself. But for the moment, it was back to the task in hand. Over the autumn, results picked up. The next four-teen games produced eleven wins and three draws, before their next defeat.

There were plenty of encouraging signs. Roger Hunt was continuing to score goals while Kevin Lewis was looking a bargain buy. On Box-ing Day, Liverpool stood well positioned but by mid-January, following three consecutive defeats, they had lost all the ground they had gained.

Liverpool lad Gerry Byrne, who had been transfer-listed by Phil Taylor, was quickly settling into the defence and beginning to look a bright prosect. Byrne had managed to put the ball into his own net on his debut back in 1957. Not surprisingly, his confidence had gone downhill. But Shankly built it up again, giving him his opportunity a few weeks after his arrival. Byrne was in the side from the start of the new season and would go on to serve the club with distinction as well as winning a couple of England caps.

Another future England international to be thrown a shirt that sea-son was Ian Callaghan. The young Liverpool-born lad made another appearance in the early-season win over Brighton and performed well enough to earn the applause of his colleagues as he left the field. Back in the dressing room, Shankly shook him warmly by the hand. A star was in the making. Callaghan made only three more league appearan-ces that season but he had given notice that he was hungry to play for Liverpool. He would go on to make a record 843 appearances for the club.

There had also been a problem with Dave Hickson. The big, popular striker, who had joined Liverpool in a whirlwind of publicity when he crossed the city from Goodison, soon hit the front pages again as he was sent off for the third time in his career.

Shankly had faced the problem of Hickson at Huddersfield and had soon unloaded him to Everton. Hickson was a fiery character:

a powerful striker but one who could easily be distracted from his task. He was famed for going in search of trouble and against Sheffield United at Anfield in mid-January he found it. It wasn't altogether Hickson's fault but, with his experience, he should have learnt how to avoid problems.

It all began when Hickson was flattened by a United player. The incident went unnoticed by the referee, as did Hickson's retaliatory flattening of Joe Shaw. Incident followed incident, until Hickson's name finally wound up in the referee's book. But even that warning was not enough to deter the centre forward who moments later lunged in on United full back Coldwell. The referee, Mr Pickles, had little option but to send Hickson packing.

The Liverpool centre forward had become his own worst enemy. Liverpool were leading 3-0 at the time and, with just six minutes remaining, it was all so unnecessary. As if that was not enough, the Kop then bayed for the referee's blood, with one irate fan sprinting half the length of the pitch to have his say. After the game, referee Pickles had to be escorted by police from the pitch.

Outside the ground, there were unprecedented scenes with bottles being hurled and police reinforcements called in to disperse the angry crowd. Shankly was not amused, especially when he discovered that Hickson was being charged by the FA with violent conduct. Privately, he was furious with Hickson who was reduced to tears. Publicly, Shankly argued that Hickson had been victimised. Hickson was indeed a marked man. Players knew that they could wind him up and take his mind off the game.

The club decided to ask for a personal hearing, and weeks later Shankly was giving full support to his man. But at the hearing in the Midland Hotel in Manchester, Shankly ended up infuriating his old pal Matt Busby and Derby manager Harry Storer. During the hearing, Shankly alleged that certain players and clubs deliberately set out to provoke Hickson. He named two clubs – Derby County and Manchester United.

Much to Shankly's embarrassment, the allegations hit the front pages producing swift responses from Busby and Storer. 'He has let his emotions run away with his reasoning,' snapped Storer, while Busby, denying any truth to the allegations, argued that his remarks 'do football no good at all'.

A couple of days later, the FA's Disciplinary Committee delivered its verdict, accepting Hickson's arguments. Instead of a lengthy suspension, Hickson was simply cautioned. Shankly was delighted when he heard the news, and mightily relieved not to be losing his man. Hickson was being given another chance, but the whole affair only underlined the liability of having a player like Hickson in your team. Hickson played just one more season for Liverpool.

In the end, Shankly's first season at Anfield was to prove yet another frustrating season for Liverpool as they wound up in third place, eight points off promotion. Aston Villa were champions, nine points ahead of Liverpool, with Cardiff also promoted. Had Liverpool beaten Cardiff twice instead of the other way round, then Liverpool and not Cardiff might have been promoted. It seemed that Liverpool were destined to remain in the Second Division forever. Since 1955, they had finished eleventh, third, third, fourth, fourth, and third again; time and again missing promotion by the narrowest of margins. They were becoming the nearly club, always the bridesmaid never the bride.

Shankly was depressed. He had seriously hoped for promotion that season and a couple more points might have done it but needless points had been thrown away at Anfield. Year after year, the club had stood on the threshold of the First Division, only to crash out of the race in the final month or so. Against Aston Villa at the end of March, they had astonishingly given away a four-goal lead with 30 minutes remaining and then in the final minute Villa had missed an open goal that would have given them a 5-4 win. Their defence was as vulnerable as any in the Second Division.

Doubts were also being voiced by fans. One long-standing supporter remembers heated discussions in the pubs at the time about Shankly's qualifications for the job. Many were privately pointing out that Shankly's record elsewhere was not all that it had seemed.

When you examined the evidence, what had Shankly achieved at Carlisle, Grimsby, Workington and Huddersfield? His record was highly questionable. None of his sides had ever been promoted. He'd never tasted management in the top flight. All that he had done was to give Denis Law his first break in football. He hadn't even signed him in the first place. Maybe they had all been fooled, taken in by Shankly's silver tongue.

As far as Shankly was concerned, the club simply had to buy new players if it was to ever make that final push for promotion. The weaknesses in the side could still be detected particularly down the backbone. They had used 26 players that season. Upfront, Hickson remained a favourite but he was 30-years-old and a constant worry. He could still manage 16 goals in 33 appearances and had passed on much valuable advice to young Roger Hunt. But it was time to search for a new partner for Hunt.

Others were also ageing. Johnny Wheeler was now 32, close on 33, while centre half Dick White was almost 30. Both would survive just one more season. John Molyneux was also 30 and, although he had played in most games that season, he was about to be eased out. Others would also find their days numbered.

Billy Liddell bowed out at the end of the season after 16 years of unstinting service. Others had already gone. Alan Arnell, never a regular, joined Tranmere Rovers in February 1961, while Bobby Campbell elected for a move to Wigan Athletic later in the year. Shankly was slowly shaking out the club, ridding it of its older and less able players.

The youngsters such as Hunt, Byrne and Callaghan had grabbed their chances while new players like Milne and Lewis had been sensibly drafted in. Shankly now had the nucleus of a First Division side. A little more experience and one or two more signings and he felt sure that they could win promotion and hold their own in the top flight. The problem lay in convincing the board of the validity of these ambitions.

For many years, John Moores, boss of the multi-million pound Littlewoods empire, had been a major shareholder in Liverpool Football Club. Oddly enough, Moores was also the principal shareholder in Everton where over the past year or so he had begun to exercise the authority that came with his stake in the club.

Moores had been elected to the board at Goodison in March 1960, taking over from Colin Ashkam, a Littlewoods employee who had been the company nominee on the board.

Moores had decided that, after years of supporting the club, he wanted to play a more active role in its affairs. With his election to the Goodison board came the promise of interest-free loans, blank cheques and so on. It was only a matter of months before the club chairman Fred Micklesfield gracefully retired and John Moores was elected chairman. Everton's return to glory was about to begin.

Over at Anfield, John Moores had retained only a nominal interest in the club. He was a bridge-playing chum of chairman Tom Williams. The two lived not too far from each other, and Moores, as principal shareholder, was kept informed of any exceptional happenings on the board.

Moores was more than content to steer his efforts towards Everton which at the time, as he no doubt guessed, had a brighter future than Liverpool. It would never have been possible for him to have sat on the board of both clubs, and anyhow that would hardly have gone down well in the soccer-mad city of Liverpool.

Moores had made his choice and he was stuck with it. But given his substantial shareholding at Anfield, he was at least entitled to place a nominee on the board. He had never taken up that opportunity, but with his new interest in Everton he decided at roughly the same time to activate his interest in Liverpool. His chosen nominee was Eric Sawyer.

Sawyer was an accountant, an executive in charge of finance at Littlewoods. Moores had a high regard for him and decided to place him on the board at Anfield with a view to 'sorting out their finances'. It was generally acknowledged that the club was in something of a 'mess' as he described it.

Average gates had fallen to below 30,000 and it did not take much knowledge of football to see that the club could easily spiral into decline, in much the same way as, say, Huddersfield Town.

Luckily, Sawyer was astute enough to realise that the club simply had to buy new players. Shankly had an ally. Without him, Shankly might not have lasted at Anfield much more than another year. Shankly found that he could talk to Sawyer more easily than any of the other directors. They seemed to talk the same language.

Shankly had never had much time for directors. He always felt insecure in their presence. At Anfield, it was probably as difficult as any other club he had been at. They belonged to another world, the world of freemasonry, finance and high politics. He had little in common with them; even their love of football was questionable.

But Sawyer was different. Round-faced, and with a broad smile, he was prepared to come downstairs and have a cup of tea with Shankly and mull over the problems without telling him how to run his business. But he let Shankly know that he would back him if he wanted players. 'You find the players, I'll do the rest,' he promised him.

Shankly had already begun a clear-out at the club. So far, it had not brought in much money but in 1961 his unloading began to pay a return. Alan Arnell was one of the first to go that year, sold to Tranmere Rovers for a nominal fee. Then in March, Jimmy Harrower was sold to Newcastle United bringing in a massive £15,000. Money was also being saved on wages. Shankly was playing his part in making savings and raising money. Now the club had to reciprocate.

11 A Colossus and a Saint

ONE SUNDAY MORNING towards the end of the 1960/61 season, sitting at home in his lounge, Shankly was glancing through the back pages of the Sunday newspapers, as he had every Sunday since he had become manager, when something caught his eye. Oddly enough, it was in one of his favourite papers, the *Sunday Post*. There, he spotted a story that had him reaching for the telephone. Ian St John, the Motherwell striker, was looking for a move. He was set to slap in a transfer request, predicted the *Post*.

St John was the man Shankly had watched three years before and had wanted to sign for Huddersfield Town. Born in Motherwell, he had been playing for his local club since 1956. Shankly had never forgotten him, always assuming that the price would be either too high or Motherwell would not sell. But St John was now determined to leave and, what's more, reckoned the *Post*, he was looking for a move to an English club.

Reading between the lines, it seemed as though Motherwell would not stand in his way. As Shankly read the story, he became excited. The asking price was reported to be around £35,000, a not inconsiderable amount. It was more than twice the amount Liverpool had ever paid for a player. In August 1960, Shankly had paid £16,000 for Gordon Milne. It was even more than Leeds United had been asking for Jack Charlton and his own board had turned him down when Shankly expressed an interest in signing the gangly centre half.

That summer, Shankly had also been keen on signing Brian Clough. Clough wanted to leave Middlesbrough and it seemed that Middlesbrough might finally relent and let him go. Everton were interested, but so too were Sunderland. The asking price was over £40,000.

Liverpool's offer had been derisory. They could come nowhere near that kind of money. In July, Clough finally signed for Sunderland for £45,000. Shankly was furious that the board were not prepared to go any higher and told them that they had missed out on one of the best centre forwards in the game. He felt like quitting again. If he was ever to drag Liverpool out of the Second Division mire, he needed to sign a quality centre forward.

Now St John was available. It would be a gamble, but there are moments in life when you need to follow your instincts – this was one such moment. St John had his critics. He was only small for a centre forward, just under 5ft 8 inches, but he was strong and could outjump far taller men. He'd just been capped at Under-23 level and he had proved that he could hold his own in the best company.

Shankly needed to act quickly. Within minutes, he was talking to the Motherwell chairman and immediately arranged to see him the following evening. Next, he was on the phone to Eric Sawyer, arguing that Liverpool simply could not afford not to sign St John.

'He's the best centre forward in Scotland,' he told Sawyer. 'We have to sign him. Hickson has to be replaced. Hunt needs a partner.' That was enough for Sawyer. If Shankly was so convinced, then he assured him that he would back him all the way and argue it out with the board.

The next day, Shankly made his way to Glasgow with Tom Williams and another director Sid Reakes and that evening they watched Motherwell playing Hamilton Academicals. By half-time, they had lost interest in the game: St John had done enough to convince them that he was an outstanding prospect, and Shankly was rightly worried that other clubs might snatch the young Scot from under their noses. First Division Newcastle United had been alerted and the prospect of challenging for honours at a First Division club, not too far from the borders, would have its appeal.

There was no time to lose. At half-time, the Liverpool contingent had a word with the Motherwell chairman and, rather than watch any more of the game, they retired to the board room to open discussions. It took some hard bargaining, and more than three hours, but by midnight they had shaken hands on a deal. Liverpool could have their centre forward for £37,500. All that remained now was to convince the player that a move to Liverpool was in his best interests. St John was informed and by the following morning was on his way down to Merseyside.

'He gave me the Shankly sell,' remembers St John. 'He told me Liverpool were about to become the greatest club in England, that they would soon be league champions, and that I was a vital part of his plan. He soon convinced me. It was difficult not to believe him.'

St John was impressed at the prospect of playing for Liverpool and quickly agreed. By the late afternoon of Tuesday 2 May 1961, St John was a Liverpool player. Joe Baker of Hibs had also just come on to the market that weekend, a player linked with a possible move to Liverpool for some time. 'No,' snapped Shankly. 'We're not interested in Baker, we've already got the best centre forward in Scotland.' The fact was that Baker's price was way beyond Liverpool's reach.

It was Shankly's first big money deal and undoubtedly one of the most significant transfers he was ever to be associated with. But if the truth be known, Shankly was just as nervous as Williams or any of the club's directors. He was never happy himself at having to pay out huge fees, a fact which no doubt reflected his spartan upbringing. And as transfer fees spiralled, so too did Shankly's nervousness.

Fortunately, in his Anfield career he was to make few mistakes in the transfer market. Those that did fail tended to be at the bottom end of the market. His only big-fee failure was Tony Hateley, signed for £96,000, who lasted little more than a season. But at least in that instance he recouped most of his money by selling him on to Coventry for £80,000.

Ian St John duly made his debut for Liverpool a week later against Everton in the Liverpool Senior Cup Final, a game that was little more than a friendly, if such a thing was possible between Everton and Liverpool. More than 50,000 turned up at Goodison. Everton won 4-3 but St John marked his debut with all three Liverpool goals. The Liverpool directors grinned like Cheshire cats. Within the year, there would be even broader smiles.

The signing of St John also resurrected memories of Ron Yeats, the tall Dundee United centre half Shankly had coveted for Huddersfield. Yeats was still playing with United, and had helped them to promotion from the Scottish Second Division in 1960, but was not actively seeking a transfer and nor were United looking to sell him.

Yeats was in the army, stationed in the south of England, and seemed to be content with his lot. But Shankly had other ideas. He needed a strong, powerful presence in the heart of his defence, a general who could lead the side on the field. Yeats matched the job description. At 6ft 3 inches, he towered above everyone, a giant in defence. But having just lashed out so much on St John, Shankly knew the club directors would balk at paying out another huge fee. But Shankly was again determined to pursue his man.

In June 1961, he put in a call to the Dundee United manager. Much to his surprise, he was not immediately rebuffed. Yeats was not available and Dundee United did not want to sell, but the manager figured the club probably needed the money and that his directors might not be averse to an offer. It was enough of a hint to encourage Shankly to see Eric Sawyer and Tom Williams. 'With this lad in the side,' he told them, 'we could win the Second Division. It's an investment.'

Within days, Shankly, Sawyer and Reakes were on the train to Dundee. But the Liverpool board had set a limit. They could go no higher than £20,000. Shankly and his directors met with the Dundee United officials that evening but came away with little satisfaction. Their meeting had been nothing like as fruitful as they had hoped.

Yeats was not for sale, certainly not at the price they were offering. If he was for sale they'd be talking £40,000. They'd just had a good season back in the Scottish First Division, finishing in the middle of the table and wanted to build on that. The Liverpool contingent had drawn a blank. Feeling like the poor relations at a funeral, they shook hands and were driven to the station by United director Duncan Hutchinson. But as they stood on the station awaiting their train, Hutchinson casually leaned over to Shankly and whispered in his ear, 'I'll bet you could get him for £30,000, maybe a little more.'

Shankly stared at him. 'Thanks,' he said. 'I think we'll be back soon.' With that, they boarded the train. On the journey, Shankly kept his counsel. He didn't want to discuss what he'd been told with Sydney Reakes. He wanted instead to talk it over privately with Eric Sawyer. But he was in no doubt that they should continue pursuing Yeats. Shankly duly rang Sawyer when they were back in Liverpool and told him of Hutchinson's hint.

Sawyer suggested that Shankly should follow his instincts and told him to keep in touch with Dundee United. 'When the time is right, make them an offer they can't refuse,' he told him. 'I'll try to persuade the board to go to £30,000. I'll sort things this end.'

In the meantime Shankly pursued other options. Frank Upton, the 26-year-old Derby County half back was set to sign for £14,000. He arrived at Anfield, took a look around Liverpool but then changed his mind, citing 'personal domestic reasons'. His child was ill and his wife wanted to stay in Derby. Then there was Tommy Knapp of Leicester. But that deal fell through before it had even taken off.

The failure to lure either Upton or Knapp to Anfield upset everyone. The mood was changing and so too was the mood in Dundee. Sawyer gave the board some advice learned from running Littlewoods. 'Football is like running a shop,' he told them. 'You need first-class products and attractive premises. It's no good having a nice shop if you don't have the right stuff on display.'

His argument was persuasive. The board could only agree. Sawyer told Shankly to put in a call to United. 'Ask them to name their price,' he said. Shankly was delighted. Back came the answer; £30,000. That afternoon, Tom Williams grabbed as many of his directors as he could. They agreed the price and on Saturday 22 July Williams, Reakes and Shankly were on their way to an Edinburgh hotel to finalise the deal.

Yeats was not fully convinced about the move. Had Dundee United offered him a £2 a week rise, he would have stayed. But inevitably it was Shankly who made up his mind for him. 'I asked him where Liverpool was, meaning whereabouts in the country,' said Yeats. 'We're in the First Division, son,' Shankly replied. 'But that's not true,' snapped Yeats. Quick as a flash came the reply from Shankly, 'Ah but they will be with you in the team!'

Later that afternoon, Yeats signed and they were all back home on Merseyside by midnight. Yeats was a Liverpool player. The big Scot flew into Liverpool the following day, sailed through his medical and duly signed on the dotted line. Shankly had the final piece in his jigsaw. Alex Young of Everton, an army friend of Yeats, reckoned Liverpool had got 'a great deal'.

Shankly introduced his new player to the press. 'Just walk round him,' he told the gathered journalists. 'He's a colossus!' He was too, as one journalist remembered. 'He was as big as anyone we had seen. I just wondered if he could play football as well. Sometimes, big fellas are a bit slow on the ground, especially at turning. But I need have had no worries with this guy. He soon proved himself.' Shankly promptly installed Yeats as club captain.

With new players at Anfield, Shankly could now safely unload more of his surplus staff – and pick up some money in the process. Off went John Nicholson to Port Vale for £6,000 and Alan Banks to Cambridge City, bringing an eventual return of £3,000. In July, Dave Hickson also went, teaming up with Banks at Cambridge, while Bobby Campbell joined Wigan Athletic. It said something about the quality of those he sold that most of them ended up with non-league sides.

In all, Shankly had raised some £20,000, which went some of the way to paying for St John and Yeats. As part of the deal to squeeze more money out of the board, Shankly had also agreed to dispense with the B team. It was an unnecessary expense. Liverpool were carrying surplus players, which created an astronomical wages bill. A full-time B team was something of an anachronism. It was largely the disappearance of the B team that brought down the overall numbers of players at Anfield to around 30 full-time players.

Shankly also instituted a new wages policy at the club, designed to reward players for success. Basic wages were low, but players earned bonuses for every point with promotion as the ultimate big payday. It was a system that would be refined, but it worked extremely effectively and was to remain in force for many more years.

As the new season kicked off, Shankly was sounding bullish about Liverpool's promotion chances now that Yeats and St John had been installed. 'I told Mr Reakes,' he wrote years later, 'these players will win us promotion – they will win us the cup as well.' They were to win more than that.

That season, Shankly decided to have all his opponents watched by a member of his staff shortly before they were due to play them. Often it was Shankly himself making long mid-week journeys around the country. But it was a tactic that would give Liverpool a significant edge over opponents. Although today it is the usual practice, in 1961 it was revolutionary, especially in the Second Division. This time, Shankly was taking no chances. He wanted to know everything about Liverpool's opponents.

You could sense the excitement from the word go. The signings of St John and Yeats had ignited the red half of the city. A crowd of just under 50,000 greeted Liverpool in their opening home game against Sunderland. What's more, it was a Wednesday evening match. Liverpool had kicked off their campaign with a 2-0 win at Bristol Rovers but nobody could have guessed that such a huge crowd would roll into Anfield for the next game.

It was the biggest gate for a league game at Anfield since the arrival of Dave Hickson, just before Shankly had joined the club. Liverpool promptly put on a display fit for such a crowd, winning 3-0. Roger

Hunt scored a couple with Kevin Lewis adding a third. Three days later, another 42,000 turned up at Anfield as Liverpool thrashed Leeds United 5-0. Hunt hit a hat-trick and the Kop went wild.

A few days later, Liverpool visited Roker Park and gave Sunderland another drubbing in front of a huge crowd. In three games, Liverpool had been watched by almost 140,000 people and scored 12 goals with Roger Hunt hitting seven. Ian St John also opened his account at Sunderland with a couple of well-taken goals. Liverpool shot to the top of the table. They were on their way and would remain at the top until the end of the season.

The win over Sunderland was followed by wins at Norwich and Anfield. The visitors in the latter game may only have been Scunthorpe yet 46,600 turned out to see the Reds. Liverpool had notched up six wins in a row. They then dropped a point at Brighton before embarking on another winning sequence. This time, it was a run of four wins with 13 goals scored, including a couple of wins over mighty Newcastle. Hunt and St John were devastating. Hunt had netted four more goals. 52,000 spectators were there to urge them on against Newcastle at Anfield.

It was not until the twelfth game of the season that Liverpool suffered their first defeat, against Middlesbrough at Ayresome Park. But they came back with a vengeance, winning 6-1 at Anfield against Walsall. Hunt struck another hat-trick.

'Roger Hunt impressed me the first time I saw him,' wrote Shankly years later. 'You could see he was a good player. He could control the ball; he could shoot; he had all-round ability. But I think he became a better player with the change of routine and the arrival at Anfield of Ian St John, Ron Yeats and Gordon Milne. The team became better organised and the system suited Roger.'

Hunt felt much the same way. The arrival of St John had not only created space for him but had given him a partner he could play off. St John with his flicks, his guile, and his heading ability was laying on the goals for Hunt. By the end of the season, Hunt had scored a club record of 41 league goals, a dramatic improvement on his 15 the previous season.

By the halfway mark, Liverpool had stretched their lead over the trailing pack to eight points. Promotion was almost a foregone conclusion. Over the next couple of months, they hit five against Norwich in an exciting 5-4 win, and another five over Middlesbrough. Shankly's only doubt concerned goalkeeper Bert Slater. At 5ft 8 inches, Slater was undeniably on the short side for a goalkeeper, and Shankly was on the lookout for someone bigger, more commanding. He eventually settled on Jim Furnell, the 6ft 1 inch Burnley custodian. With gates regularly exceeding 30,000, Shankly had little trouble in persuading the board in February 1962 to lash out £18,000 on him. Furnell immediately took over from Slater. In the summer of 1962, Slater was offloaded to Dundee.

But if the Liverpool attack was scoring goals almost freely, the defence was proving as mean as a fox on a winter's night. Dick White had started the season by dropping back to accommodate Yeats with Gerry Byrne partnering him at left back. Late in the season, Ronnie Moran would take over from White before White left the club to join Doncaster Rovers.

There were still one or two weaknesses. Leishman was never the best passer of the ball, relying instead on his natural speed. His presence didn't always suit the side, and especially the passing style Shankly was trying to instil in his players. In Second Division football Liverpool could camouflage Leishman's weaknesses, but once they were in the First Division they would become glaringly obvious. Kevin Lewis also had his limitations. Before Christmas, he had lost out to Ian Callaghan, a young Liverpool lad who had made only a handful of appearances for the club. Callaghan would eventually play more than 800 games for Liverpool.

Liverpool also enjoyed a good cup run in the 1961/62 season, beating First Division Chelsea 4-3 at Anfield in the third round. Liverpool had led 4-1 at half-time in front of a near 50,000 crowd. In the next round, they faced Oldham away, winning 2-1, and then met up with Preston North End, Shankly's old team. They drew the first game at Anfield 0-0 in front of 55,000. The replay ended the same way but, in a second replay at Old Trafford, Preston edged their way into the quarter finals with the only goal of the game. 135,000 had watched the three games.

Promotion was finally clinched on Saturday 21 April 1962 with five games still remaining. The visitors were Southampton, the crowd topped 40,000 and the atmosphere was festive. In the mist and steady drizzle, Liverpool were two ahead within half an hour, both goals coming from Kevin Lewis. At the end of the game, the two sides trooped off the field, with Southampton forming a guard of honour to applaud the jubilant Liverpool team.

The Liverpool players waved triumphantly to the crowd and disappeared down the tunnel towards their dressing room for their own private celebration. But now something was about to happen that was to inspire a generation of exploits that would sweep Liverpool Football Club and English football into a new era. The crowd simply refused to go home. They stood there in the pouring rain, repeatedly demanding the return of their heroes.

Eventually, Shankly appeared in the directors box to join Tom Williams in addressing the crowd. Williams told the crowd they had won the hardest thing in football, the Second Division championship but the rest of his remarks were drowned out by yet another chant of 'We want the reds'. Williams then announced that the players were in the bath but that they would come back out on to the pitch in a few minutes. When they finally reappeared, a roar went up from the Kop. Half the players were in a state of undress: some were shirtless, others bootless but in the end it became a fight for survival as they were mobbed by supporters. St John and Yeats were both hauled into the crowd by ecstatic fans and had to be rescued by the police. 'It was frightening, I'd never seen anything like it before,' says Yeats.

The telegrams poured in. Matt Busby was thrilled for Shankly. 'A club like Liverpool deserve to be playing in the highest class,' he said. Even local MP and Evertonian Bessie Braddock was forced to admit that it was good for the city to have two First Division sides. Local actress Rita Tushingham, star of *A Taste of Honey*, confessed that she was 'already excited at the prospect of the two real local derbies we shall have next season'. Liverpool had recently played a friendly with Everton that had attracted a crowd of 60,000 to Goodison.

By the end of the season the statistics told their own tale. Liverpool had lost only seven games and had been undefeated at home for the first time since the 1905/6 season, winning eighteen of their 21 home fixtures. They had scored just one short of a century of goals and ended the season eight points ahead of runners-up Leyton Orient. They had led the table from start to finish.

The fans at Liverpool had always been known for their fanaticism but suddenly that fanaticism was about to reach new heights. In particular, the Spion Kop at Anfield was renowned for its vocal support, but even that fame would be surpassed over the next few years.

The Kop was a mighty terrace behind one of the goals at Anfield. It was built in 1906, as a reward to the fans after Liverpool had clinched their second league championship. It was an enormous structure, capable of holding as many as 25,000 supporters. The name came from a small hill in South Africa known as Spion Kop where in January 1900, during the Boer War, a terrifying battle had left hundreds dead. Many of the British soldiers who had so needlessly died came from Lancashire regiments with a strong contingent from Liverpool.

Ernest Edwards, then sports editor of the *Liverpool Echo* was the first to suggest calling the new structure the Kop. The name, he thought, would keep alive the memory of those Liverpool soldiers who had died. It was a vast expanse, extending ever upwards with 100 steps, and towering over the Walton Breck Road behind the ground.

Other similar terraces would be built at football grounds around the country, some almost as enormous, and would similarly be christened the Kop. But there was really only one Kop. Shankly was very much aware of the Kop before he joined Liverpool. He'd played in front of it many times as a player with Preston, and knew that the noisy support it generated was worth a goal start to Liverpool.

Twenty-two years after it had been built, the Kop was extended, and roofed as well, taking its capacity to 27,000. The new steel roof also gave it added acoustics as the roar of the crowd swelled and reverberated inside the steel dome. It was like a cathedral with its echoing sound. Above all, it was an impressive sight as thousands swayed and fought to stay on their feet in the vast throng.

The Kop was at its height immediately after the Second World War when huge crowds flocked to English football grounds, getting their first taste of leisure after years of war and fierce austerity. Liverpool won the first championship after the war playing regularly in front of crowds above 50,000. In 1952, a cup tie against Wolverhampton Wanderers produced a record gate of 61,905 as Liverpool beat their famous opponents. With relegation in 1954, came a fall in Liverpool's attendances.

For years since then, there had been ominous silence at Anfield – the Kop rarely stirred into passion, other than for the occasional cup tie when a First Division side might be the visitors. In Shankly's first month at the club, a crowd of more than 56,000 watched Liverpool lose to Manchester United in the fourth round of the FA Cup. And in the same season, when Liverpool won promotion, a crowd of almost 55,000 had seen Liverpool draw with Shankly's old team Preston.

Those games had shown Shankly the kind of passion that could be

Shanks leads out the Scotland
international team in a wartime
match *(Steve Hale)*

Fifty years later, Bill and wife Nessie
outside Buckingham Palace with his
OBE *(Press Association/Steve Hale)*

Shankly (at left) as a Preston
North End player, parading the FA
Cup in 1938 *(Steve Hale)*

Shanks deals with Arsenal's
Lishman in one of his last games
for Preston, 1949 *(Steve Hale)*

Shankly looks over Denis Law's shoulder as he signs for Huddersfield Town, 1957 *(Steve Hale)*

Shanks (third from right) being typically competitive in a dads' and kids' kick-about on an open field, Huddersfield, 1957 *(Steve Hale)*

Shankly (second from right, bottom row) looks on as Liverpool pose with the Second Division Championship trophy, 1962. It was his third season in charge *(Steve Hale)*

1965: Shankly leads out Liverpool at Wembley to face Don Revie's Leeds United. Liverpool won 2-1 after extra time *(Steve Hale)*

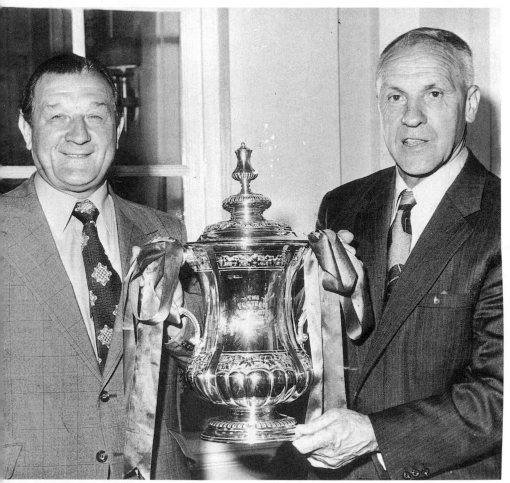

Manager Shankly shares the 1965 FA Cup with future manager Bob Paisley. Between them they made sure that Liverpool's name was rarely missing from it for fifteen years *(Steve Hale)*

Two very differen[t]
generations of Sc[ottish]
football managers[:]
George Graham a[nd]
Shanks prior to th[e]
1971 FA
Cup Final
(Hulton Deutsch
Collection)

Although he lost the '71
Cup Final to Arsenal,
Shankly was still greeted
as a hero when the team
returned to Liverpool
(Steve Hale)

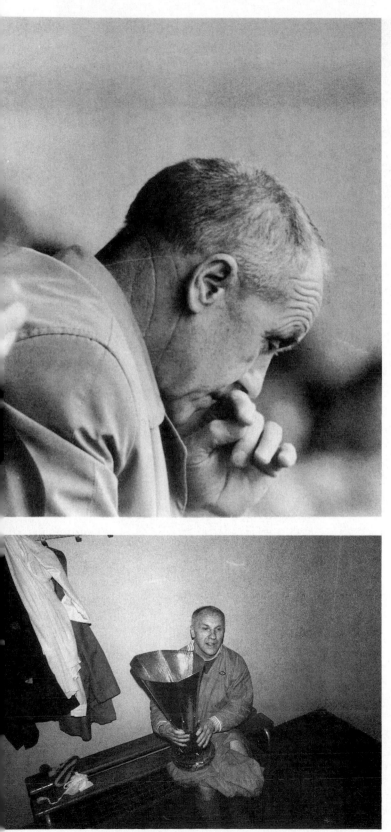

The two sides of
football:
deep in thought
during a match
and in the
changing room
with the UEFA
Cup, 1973
(Steve Hale)

Dynasty. The famous
Liverpool bootroom staff at
Anfield, just prior to
Shankly's retirement in 1974:
(left to right) Bill Shankly,
Bob Paisley, Ronnie Moran,
Joe Fagan, Reuben Bennett
(Steve Hale)

Always a cut above the rest.
Current Newcastle United
manager Kevin Keegan with
friend and mentor Shankly in
1979. Doubtless Shanks is
telling his former charge to
get a haircut *(Popperfoto)*

generated at Anfield. If only he could build on it, he knew that such support would drive the club to even greater heights. 'In all sincerity, I can say that they are the greatest crowd of supporters in the game,' he was telling the *Liverpool Echo* by the end of that season. And he meant it.

As Liverpool strode towards promotion, the Kop broke into song. For the first time, spontaneous singing was heard at the ground. In the past, there had been community singing, particularly in the post-war years when a podium would be placed on the pitch and a conductor would lead the band and the crowd in a selecton of music hall favourites. The Kop however was well-known for its anarchic tendencies, usually preferring to sing some number of its own. It always amused everyone and usually ended with the conductor having to revise his songsheet to include the number the Kop wanted. But it was always singing of an organised fashion.

In the early 1960s, the Kop began to sing spontaneously, without any accompaniment. At first, it was clapping and chanting. Ian St John had quickly become a favourite with the Kop and his name was soon chanted in unison accompanied by a rhythmical clapping of hands. The inspiration for this came from a hit of the time by the Routers called 'Let's Go', released in 1962. But instead of chanting the words 'Let's Go', the Kopites substituted the name 'St John'. It would soon become the talk of the football world and, once Liverpool were in the First Division, chanting would be taken up by fans everywhere. But it all began at Anfield, and it all began in that season as Liverpool pushed for promotion.

The inspiration was undoubtedly the pop scene that had invaded the back streets and clubs of the city. A new popular culture was emerging, the likes of which had never been seen anywhere before and, for that matter, had rarely been witnessed since. Pop music and football were about to merge and produce a new synergy.

Outside Liverpool, nobody had yet heard of the Beatles, yet on Merseyside almost every seventeen-year-old was in a pop band and on a Saturday they carried their lyrics from the clubs to the terraces. From the Kop, they chanted and sang. Shankly and the Beatles were their inspiration. The city of Liverpool was about to burst on to the world stage.

12 King of the Kop

BACK IN THE FIRST DIVISION after eight seasons, the first thing every Liverpool fan did was to check the fixture list for the derby date, the day Liverpool and Everton would once again play each other in a league match.

Over the years there had been umpteen friendlies between the two sides but they had not met in genuine competition for some years. The last time was in the FA Cup, in January 1955 when Liverpool, then in the Second Division, had surprisingly beaten their First Division neighbours 4-0 at Goodison. But with Everton also having spent some years in the Second Division, the two sides had not met in a league encounter since January 1951. Saturday 22 September 1962 was the date everyone pencilled into their diaries.

But before then, Liverpool did their neighbours an almighty favour. In August, they sold Johnny Morrisey to Everton for a giveaway £10,000. It was a deal that was to spark off a furious boardroom row. When Everton approached Liverpool with an offer for Morrisey, it seemed a good idea to the directors. Alan A'Court was the automatic choice for the left wing spot, and Morrisey's appearances had always been intermittent. In fact, he had never featured at all during the previous season, and had made just 30-odd appearances since 1957. But Shankly was furious. He did not want to sell him and put up a stubborn fight against the board. In the end he was forced to accept the deal, but not before he had warned them if they ever did anything like that again he would leave. Ironically, Morrisey would be clutching a league championship medal by the end of the season, coming to fruition in Harry Catterick's emerging side.

Liverpool kicked off their first season back in the top flight with a visit from Blackpool. A crowd of 51,000 showed up at Anfield, but despite the glamour and the excitement it was Blackpool who took the points. That defeat was followed by a 2-2 draw at Manchester City and a 1-0 defeat at Blackburn. Liverpool were finding it hard – the problem was that they admired teams like Tottenham, United and Arsenal and envied players such as Greaves, Law and Mackay.

They finally made the breakthrough when Manchester City came to Anfield and were the first victims of a more committed Liverpool. Sheffield United were also beaten 2-0 at Anfield, and Liverpool notched up their third win of the season against West Ham, again at home. Liverpool then drew at home to Ipswich to leave them lingering in the lower reaches of the First Division. They had played nine games but had only eight points to show for their endeavours.

Next in line was the real challenge, the game everyone had been anticipating – Everton at Goodison. The match was a 73,000 all-ticket sell-out. They could have sold three times the number of tickets as well. It was the game all Merseyside had been waiting to see for years. Nobody would be disappointed. Everton stole the first goal through a Roy Vernon penalty, but Kevin Lewis equalised shortly before half-time.

In the second half, Johnny Morrisey outwitted his former clubmates to put Everton ahead but then, with the referee poised to blow for full time, Roger Hunt snatched a late equaliser for the Reds. Honours were even though by the end of the season Everton would be league champions. A couple of weeks later, the Beatles released their first record, 'Love Me Do'. It topped the charts on Merseyside but in the *NME* Top 30 it could only make number 28.

Liverpool's last-minute equaliser against Everton might have given them encouragement but it hardly lasted. They went down 3-2 at Wolves in the next game. After a 1-0 win over Bolton at Anfield, they then lost three successive matches and looked to be heading back where they had come from – the Second Division. It was a serious situation that called for drastic action. Without it, Liverpool were doomed.

Fortunately, Shankly had the answer. Liverpool were simply not good enough. The team needed new blood, beginning at the back. First to be introduced was a fresh face between the posts. Goalkeeper Jim Furnell, signed from Burnley by Shankly, had served his purpose but he was not really good enough as far as the manager was concerned.

Tommy Lawrence may have been stagnating in the third team when Shankly arrived at Anfield but the manager had spotted some potential in the youngster. Like Shankly, Lawrence came from Ayrshire, but had joined the club via Warrington as an amateur, turning professional in September 1957. Lawrence had been picked for promotion under Shankly and was given his chance in the 1-0 defeat at West Brom. It might not have been the most auspicious of starts but it was some years before anyone displaced him in the Liverpool side.

Above all, Liverpool needed a creative midfielder. Tommy Leishman, for all his pace and unquestionable popularity, was out of his depth in the First Division. Speed and sheer power might have been formidable attributes in the Second Division, but in the top flight more guile was needed. Shankly scoured the market for a quality midfielder, someone who could pass the ball and drive the team forward.

His search ended with Willie Stevenson of Glasgow Rangers. Stevenson had been languishing in the reserves at Ibrox, ousted by new signing Jim Baxter, and looked set for a move to Australia when Shankly swept in with a £20,000 bid. Stevenson was soon on his way to Anfield although it would be some time before he convinced everyone of his pedigree.

The ex-Ranger was a different breed to Leishman, nowhere near as fast or flamboyant, nowhere near as muscular, but he epitomised the style that Shankly was creating at Anfield – neat passing, thoughtful football, players always chasing into open space. 'Pass and move,' he told them. It was to become the Liverpool motto.

The changes did the trick. Liverpool knotted nine consecutive wins together over the winter months as they climbed out of the danger zone and towards respectability. People began to sit up and take notice. 'This is a useful side that could go on to win something,' noted the *Manchester Guardian*.

Liverpool's impressive run came to an end against a fine Leicester side, rated the best side in the league by Shankly. But after that mini run, Liverpool ran out of steam winning only four of their remaining 17 fixtures, and drawing six. Sandwiched within this sequence was the visit of Everton to Anfield before a capacity crowd of 56,000. Honours were even yet again, though this time neither side managed a goal. They even beat Tottenham 5-2 at Anfield, after trailing 2-0, but three days later were on the end of a 7-2 hammering at White Hart Lane. It was the biggest defeat Liverpool had suffered in many years. Disappointing though their late form had been, they still managed to finish in eighth spot, 17 points behind champions Everton. Roger Hunt was again top scorer with 24 league goals, while Ian St John backed him up admirably with 19.

But if the league brought only moderate satisfaction, there was much to cheer in the FA Cup as Liverpool raced to the semi-finals before falling to Shankly's team of the season, Leicester. On their way, they had disposed of Wrexham, Burnley, Arsenal and West Ham but against Leicester at Hillsborough they went down to the only goal of the game. 58,000 watched them beat Burnley at Anfield, while 65,000 had made the journey to Sheffield for the semi-final. The crowds that Liverpool were attracting both home and away that season were a good indication of re-emerging passion. Liverpool would soon be contenders for honours and the fans as much as the players had their part to play.

By the end of the season, it was obvious to Shankly that, while Liverpool could hold their own in the upper division, they would need to strengthen their squad if they were to become serious challengers for any silverware. Alan A'Court on the left flank had been a fine servant to the club, but he would play only one more game in a red shirt.

His chosen replacement was Peter Thompson, a young whippet of a winger from Preston. Thompson although only 20-years-old cost the club £37,000 but the days of questioning such deals was now gone. Shankly had proved his pedigree and, with more cash flowing through the turnstiles than the club had ever known, nobody was going to refuse him another signing.

Years later, Shankly called the Thompson deal 'daylight robbery' adding, 'he'd be worth £10 million today'. Shankly had also brought cash into the club through the sale of a number of surplus players that season and he was not far off showing healthy profits on his transfer dealings. It was good housekeeping and kept him in favour with the board.

Thompson was a winger in the Finney/Matthews mould. He could twist and turn defenders, creating chaos as full backs backpedalled towards the by-line. He was the natural replacement for former Kop hero Billy Liddell. Often an unsung hero, Thompson was to play a major part in the pursuit of honours over the next few seasons. With Thompson operating on the left flank and Ian Callaghan conniving on the other, Liverpool were capable of cracking even the most uncompromising of defences.

Perhaps more fundamental was a growing optimism in the boardroom, where directors were now beginning to share Shankly's determination to challenge for honours. The Morrisey affair had been forgotten. Now the board were becoming just as swept up in the passion that seemed to have gripped Anfield. The complacency of past years had been consigned to the dustbin by Shankly's enthusiasm, and no doubt nudged along by the success of Everton.

John Moores at Goodison had undoubtedly pointed the way, demonstrating that an ambitious chairman prepared to spend money can achieve much. Everton had spent heavily in the transfer market signing top-quality stars such as Roy Vernon, Alex Young, Tony Kay and Alex Scott – players that cost a fortune. But it had reaped dividends. Everton were league champions and had set extravagant standards for others, in particular Liverpool, to follow.

In comparison with their neighbours, Liverpool would spend little in their pursuit of glory. And with Moores' nominee Eric Sawyer on the Anfield board, there was a feeling of intense rivalry to put Merseyside on the footballing map. If Tom Williams had once balked at spending money, he was now forced to concede that Shankly was usually right. What's more, he was basking in the glory and as keen as anyone else at Anfield in pursuing the quest for honours.

The city of Liverpool had come alight. Early in the New Year, the Beatles had released their second record, 'Please Please Me'. Within weeks, it had swept to the top of the charts. Beatlemania was about to take off. With Everton as champions, Liverpool semi-finalists, and with Bill Shankly hovering in the background, things were beginning to happen in Liverpool.

Kevin Lewis was eased out at the end of the season. Lewis, who had been one of Shankly's first signings when the club paid a record £13,000 to Sheffield United, was offloaded to Huddersfield for £18,000. Shankly was especially pleased to show a handsome profit which paid in part for the signing of Thompson. Leishman, the man Tom Williams and his fellow directors had bought shortly before Shankly arrived, had been sold earlier in the season to Hibernian for £10,000. Veteran Johnny Wheeler also left joining New Brighton while Alan Jones went to Brentford for £6,000. The clearout was almost complete. Only a handful of pre-Shankly players remained at Anfield, and most of those would be on their way by the end of the following season.

The club's success was also recognised at international level with four players capped by England during the season. They were Gerry Byrne, Roger Hunt, Jimmy Melia and Gordon Milne, while there were Scottish caps for Tommy Lawrence and Ian St John.

With Everton as champions and set to enter the European Cup,

Liverpool began the 1963/64 season in the shadow of their neighbours. They kicked off with a 2-1 win at Blackburn but then lost at home to Nottingham Forest. They also lost their next game, again at home, this time with Blackpool the visitors. After four games, Liverpool had a mere three points and looked hopeless challengers for Everton's crown.

There was still a lack of belief in the side. Chins would drop and shoulders droop when they went a goal down. Shankly decided to call them together to talk it over. 'What's the problem?' he asked them. 'We want to do well,' the players told him. 'Perhaps we try too hard, especially at Anfield where the crowds expect so much.'

Shankly could excuse the pressures but he could not understand their lack of confidence and self-belief. 'You're better than any side in the division,' he told them. 'And as for players like Greaves, you're as good as any of them. I bought you because you are the best. Now go out and play like the best.'

It did the trick. They immediately beat Chelsea and Wolves 3-1, both games away from home, but then slipped up again at Anfield. They had now lost all three home games. But as they faced Wolves for their fourth home game, Shankly decided to have a quiet word with each player as he left the dressing room.

One by one, he went up to them, leaning towards them and reminding them of their qualities. 'Remember you're the best,' he whispered. 'Wolves are just a name, a team of the past. We're the team of the future. You're an international. That means something.' Wolves were thrashed 6-0. But against Sheffield United five days later Liverpool slipped up again, losing 3-0.

With nine games played and four defeats already, nobody but the most ardent Kopite would have put money on Liverpool to win the title. Yet they were about to embark on a five game run of victories, starting at Anfield against neighbours, and champions, Everton. Liverpool won 2-1, courtesy of a couple of goals from Ian Callaghan. To defeat the reigning champions, even if it was at Anfield, was a tremendous spur. Suddenly, all the confidence came oozing back. Willie Stevenson, after a quiet start that had its critics on the Kop, was now beginning to look a formidable signing. Over the next few weeks, Aston Villa, Sheffield Wednesday, West Bromwich Albion and Ipswich were all soundly beaten before Liverpool lost at home to Leicester City. Four more wins followed before a draw with Arsenal and a fifth home defeat, this time by Blackburn.

Over Christmas, Liverpool began to emerge from their shell, slamming six goals past Stoke, while reaping handsome revenge on Sheffield United with a 6-0 victory at Anfield. They would also thrash Ipswich 6-0 in early March.

'We were the fittest team in the country,' Roger Hunt told one journalist. 'In game after game, we took control because even if our opponents could match us for skill, they could not match us at producing it right at the end. Invariably, they ran out of steam in the second half, whereas we managed to keep going.'

There was also a good run in the FA Cup, a competition Liverpool had never won. They began their assault on the cup with a 5-0 win over Derby County at Anfield, then overpowered Port Vale in a replay before defeating Arsenal in the fifth round. In the quarter finals, they were drawn at home to lowly Second Division Swansea. Liverpool looked odds-on favourites to reach the last four, but on the day Swansea goalkeeper Noel Dwyer gave the performance of a lifetime, saving a penalty from Ronnie Moran and keeping Liverpool at bay to hold out for a shock 2-1 win. Yet again, the Cup continued to evade Liverpool.

Back in the league, Liverpool also lost 3-1 at Goodison and 1-0 at Fulham but then a run of seven victories with only two goals conceded ensured them the title. Shankly told his team, 'Go out and get it going.' They did and clinched the title at Anfield with a 5-0 hammering of Arsenal. By 5 pm, they were on another lap of honour around Anfield, this time parading a mock trophy. Everton had refused to hand over the original.

After that, the season fizzled out with a couple of defeats though Roger Hunt added three more goals to his tally to take his season's total to 31 league goals. His partner, Ian St John, had notched up 21. It had been a bizarre season. Liverpool had lost 11 games, including five at Anfield, yet had still wound up champions, collecting a mere 57 points.

And yet, despite their defeats at Anfield they still managed 60 goals in front of their own crowd. Shankly was ecstatic. It was the first time he had ever been associated with a championship side. Even the great Preston team of pre-war days had never achieved as much. Chairman Tom Williams also basked in the glory, visiting the dressing room to congratulate the players, talking excitedly to journalists and urging Shankly to take the plaudits of the crowd. 'This is my greatest moment in football,' Shankly told the papers.

Williams might have been a reluctant spender, taking Shankly to the brink of resignation on more than one occasion, but he was now a convert to the Shankly school of soccer. Not that Shankly was a spendthrift. He was just as reluctant to spend money as he had been at Huddersfield. Ray Wilson, the former Huddersfield and England defender, once suggested Shankly 'was the only manager in the world who might spend his own money to buy players'. But it was never true. Shankly hated dishing out huge sums to buy players. It was anathema to him. Six figure fees were way beyond his financial horizons. He could never have existed in today's multi-million pound market where even second rate defenders cost mind-blowing millions.

Shankly would simply have refused to pay out such vast sums even if it did make long-term financial sense. It was undoubtedly for that reason that he placed emphasis in the years ahead on unearthing talent in the lower divisions that cost a fraction of the price of a First Division star. Although at times he did spend heavily, it was always reluctantly. There was always nervousness. Was the player worth that amount of money? What if he turned out to be a failure?

Shankly would worry, chew it over with the bootroom staff, watch the player in question on countless occasions, have just about everyone in the club watch him as well, and still not be convinced. In his entire Anfield career, he only brought in expensive ready-made stars on a handful of occasions. Almost all his signings were from the lower divisions or the middle ranks of the First Division. Only Tony Hateley, Alun Evans, John Toshack, Peter Cormack and Ray Kennedy were expensive imports. And of those, Hateley and Evans, for one reason or another, failed to make the grade at Anfield.

That season he tried to sign Freddie Hill, the Bolton Wanderers and England inside forward. Shankly rated him 'the best player in England'. Hill was always slapping in transfer requests and Bolton finally grew weary of trying to appease him. Eventually, they decided to let him go. Shankly was quick off the mark and agreed a £60,000 fee for the England man. Hill was immediately despatched to Anfield for a medical. He arrived one Monday lunchtime. 'Have you trained Freddie?' asked Shankly. 'Yes,' replied Hill. 'Then go down and see the doctor now,' suggested Shankly. Hill went down and an hour later the doctor asked to see Shankly. 'He's got high blood pressure,' the doctor told him. 'I've tested it a number of times and it's still high,' he said adding ominously, 'I don't like the look of it.'

That was sufficient for Shankly. If he was going to spend that amount of money, then it had to be right; the player had to be 100% fit and well. The Bolton manager Bill Ridding was shocked. 'Oh, he'll be alright,' he argued. 'He's fit enough.'

'He may be fit enough for Bolton,' thought Shankly, 'but is he fit enough for Liverpool?' Nevertheless, Shankly agreed to take a second opinion. Another medical was arranged but again Hill's blood pressure was unusually high. Shankly called the deal off. Of course, there was never anything really wrong with Hill. Bolton took him to a specialist who quickly affirmed that there was no problem and Hill went on to play plenty more years in football although never as successfully as Shankly had predicted. Years later, there would be a similar incident as Shankly tried to sign another coveted inside forward.

With the title under his belt and with average Anfield gates of 50,000, Liverpool FC was in a healthy enough financial position to dip into the transfer market almost at will. But for the moment, Shankly did not see much need to strengthen his squad. He made just one signing, bringing in Phil Chisnall, the Manchester United striker in April 1964. Manchester-born Chisnall had been an England schoolboy star and had been snapped up by United but, in an era when Charlton, Law and Best were plying their trade for United, Chisnall never got a look in. At £25,000, it looked an intelligent buy but it never worked out for Chisnall who was to make even fewer appearances for Liverpool than for United.

Chisnall however was in a unique position to compare the two top clubs in the land, the only man to have played for both in more than half a century. When he arrived at Anfield, he was staggered by the training routine. 'There was nothing like that at Old Trafford,' he remembers. 'The training there was much lighter but at Anfield it was back-breaking.'

Chisnall remains convinced that Liverpool were by far the fittest team in British football and that this was fundamental to their success, but adds, 'In time, other clubs adopted similar routines and caught up with Liverpool.'

Styles on the field were also remarkably different. 'At United, Busby simply let us play our own game. He encouraged individualism; he let us do what we wanted. He had signed players because they could play football. But at Liverpool everything was done collectively. You were playing for each other.'

Besides new signings at Anfield, there would also be departures. Earlier in the season, in November 1963, Jim Furnell had been offloaded to Arsenal for £15,000. Ever since Tommy Lawrence had taken over the goalkeeper's shirt, Furnell had rarely featured, making only the occasional appearance when Lawrence was injured. Then, as the season drew to a close, Jimmy Melia was transferred to Wolverhampton Wanderers for an amazing £55,000. Shankly was reluctant to let Melia go. He still featured in the side, having played a couple of dozen games that season but £55,000 was a sizeable amount of money and too tempting an offer to ignore.

Another veteran, and pre-Shankly Anfield man, to leave was Alan A'Court who moved on in October 1964, joining Merseyside neighbours Tranmere Rovers for £4,500. A'Court had been at Anfield since the early fifties. He had even played for England in the 1958 World Cup finals but he was no longer quick enough to turn First Division defenders.

'Shankly did not force me to go but I wanted to play regularly,' remembers A'Court. 'In my days, substitutes did not play but, after I left, bigger squads were needed and I probably could have played more if I had stayed.' But A'Court decided on a move and took the ferry across the Mersey.

The transfers of A'Court and Melia meant that only five of the pre-Shankly era players now remained at Anfield. They were Lawrence, Byrne, Moran, Hunt and Callaghan. Some twenty players had been sold from that era, bringing in not far off £150,000 while another seventeen had either retired, quit the game or disappeared on free transfers. In the process, Shankly had won the Second Division championship and the League title. What's more, he had spent just over £150,000 in bringing in new blood. It was good housekeeping, the sort the board liked, and the sort Shankly could justly be proud of.

13 'Ee-Aye-Addio, We've Won the Cup!'

AS LEAGUE CHAMPIONS, Liverpool were entitled to a crack at the European Cup, a trophy that no British club had ever won. Hibernian and Manchester United had both reached the semi-finals of the competition, but so far no British side had yet made the ultimate breakthrough.

Like Busby, Shankly now shared a dream of proving that English football was the best in the world. Yet, he had not always been so enthusiastic about European soccer. He was a naturally suspicious person. The war years had left their scars and he simply didn't trust the continentals.

Shankly had played for Scotland against Hungary in 1939 and that had hardly been an inspiring occasion. The Hungarians had taunted the Scots with their cynical tactics. As far as Shankly was concerned, Scottish and English football were far superior to anything on the continent and they did not have to prove it. The war years only reinforced that attitude.

But with the arrival of Puskas and the magnificent Hungarians in the early fifties and Matt Busby's brave assault on Europe in 1957, Shankly began to recognise that perhaps sides like Real Madrid and Hungary really did have something to teach British teams.

Like most converts, he soon became a zealot, always keen to tell his players how he had met Puskas and Hidegkuti on a train one day. But Shankly's enthusiasm for continental football was restricted only to those sides who played genuine football. He had no appetite for the negative football of Inter Milan, effective as it was, and he certainly had no taste for some of the cynical football that came out of South America. He called it 'cheating' and above all he didn't believe in that.

What Shankly delighted in were tough, honest sides, like Real Madrid, Brazil, Anderlecht and the Hungarians of the mid-fifties. 'I'll hurt you,' he was fond of saying, 'but I'll never cheat you.'

Even when England won the World Cup in 1966, Shankly greeted the achievement with his usual brand of scepticism. 'I thought the World Cup was played in a negative sense and England won with negative football,' he told readers of the *Liverpool Daily Post*. He argued that few of the teams had been entertaining, with the honourable exceptions of Brazil, Portugal and Hungary, and that English fans wouldn't pay to watch that kind of football week after week. But perhaps that was just his way of arguing that Scottish football was as good as any in the world.

Shankly's assault on Europe began with a trip to Iceland, to face the Icelandic champions Reykjavik. Liverpool had little to fear and ran out comfortable 5-0 winners. Young Gordon Wallace, given his chance in the first team, hit the net within three minutes and later added a second, while new boy Phil Chisnall, also given an early run out, hit Liverpool's third.

The trip to Iceland brought with it a new set of complex logistics. Flights had to be booked; essential equipment had to be taken; food had to be packed. The problems were not at first apparent, and it was only with time and good organisation that these tiresome details would be worked out. Wolves, Chelsea, Arsenal and Manchester United were far more used to playing on the continent than Liverpool. For Liverpool, it was a new experience.

'Most of us didn't even know where Reykjavik was,' remembers Ron Yeats. 'It was a terrible journey and we got there by the most circuitous route. We flew from Speke to London, then from London to Prestwick in Scotland and finally caught a flight from there to Iceland. When we got to Scotland, we had four or five hours to kill, so Bill Shankly said "Come on, we'll go on a tour of the area, and see some of the local landmarks." So we piled into the bus and off we went. He decided to take us to a Butlins camp, would you believe? When we got there, Shankly got out and said to the man on the gate, "We are Liverpool Football Club, on our way to play a European tie in Iceland." "Oh aye," replied the man, "Well, you're on the wrong road here, mate!" '

Back at Anfield a few weeks later, Liverpool completed the job against the Icelanders winning 6-1. St John scored a couple, while Motherwell-born apprentice Bobby Graham was given his first outing. The blooding of youngsters in the early European games was to become a hallmark of the Shankly era that would be carried on by later managers. Against teams of the calibre of Reykjavik there was little fear of slipping up and Shankly was able to test his youngsters in genuine competition. It also offered a chance for experimenting with new tactics.

Shankly had realised that, with so much always at stake in league and domestic competitions, there was rarely opportunity to put his younger players, or any new signing, in the team. Liverpool would always be looking to win domestic trophies and could ill afford to gamble.

Even facing Fourth Division opposition in the FA Cup or the League Cup was no foregone conclusion. But in Europe, where the first round usually meant facing third-rate opposition home and away, there was less likelihood of slipping up. Such experiments involving new faces didn't always work but, in the next round of the European Cup, a young Tommy Smith would make his debut and go on to play more than 600 games for the club.

It was clear almost from the outset that season that Liverpool would make little headway in the league. They opened with a win at Anfield over Arsenal, but then crashed to Leeds and Blackburn. A couple of weeks later, they lost three more league fixtures including a 4-0 drubbing from Everton. Five games lost and it was only mid-September. Part of the problem was an injury to St John. Chisnall and Wallace were both given their chances in the league but with little success: Chisnall stepped aside after two games, while Wallace lasted a few more.

In November 1964, Shankly decided to step into the transfer market, snapping up Arsenal's Geoff Strong for £40,000. Strong was to prove a fine utility player, although he was initially acquired as a striker with a record of 69 goals in just 125 outings for the Gunners. It was to be Shankly's last major signing for some years.

The jigsaw was virtually complete. In goal, Tommy Lawrence, despite occasional criticism, proved a capable custodian, and was already recognised as such with a Scottish cap. In defence were twin scousers Chris Lawler and Gerry Byrne. Neither had cost a penny. In the centre of defence were Ron Yeats and the precocious Tommy Smith, while running the middle of the park were the creative men, Gordon Milne, Willie Stevenson, Ian Callaghan, and Peter Thompson. Finally, upfront was the twin spearhead of Ian St John and Roger Hunt. In reserve,

Liverpool had Geoff Strong, Bobby Graham and Ian Wallace. That was the formation that would remain for the next two years.

Shankly reckoned that, at full strength, this side was invincible. During the seventies, he looked back and boasted that it had been 'the best team seen in Britain since the war'. It was Shankly's first great Liverpool side, a team that would serve him well. It was also the first Liverpool side to bring the FA Cup back to Anfield.

Stepping aside at the end of that season was Ronnie Moran, the burly enthusiastic scouser who had made his league debut in 1952. Moran had survived Shankly's purges, though injury had kept him sidelined for long periods. But he had returned as Liverpool headed for the First Division, bringing vital experience and steely determination to the defence.

Moran had gone on to pick up a league championship medal, but in the 1964/65 season at the age of 0 he stepped aside to be replaced by another Liverpool youngster Chris Lawler. It wasn't quite a straight swap. Byrne moved into Moran's left back role and young Lawler took over on the right. Lawler had made his league debut back in March 196 and had played half a dozen games in the championship season. Lawler went on to become one of the pillars of the Liverpool defence, clocking up more than 500 first-team appearances.

Shankly liked Moran. He was straightforward. Like most scousers, he spoke his mind and was a trier on the field. You could always hear him bellowing, even as a player; urging the side on, trying to organise those around him. Shankly and Paisley would chuckle to each other about him.

Towards the end of the 1964/65 season, it was obvious that his playing days were numbered. Moran could probably have carried on a while longer but injuries were repeatedly catching him out. Shankly decided to offer him a job on the coaching staff as a way of harnessing all that energy. When he put it to him, Moran jumped at the chance. He wouldn't be earning as much money, but it was a unique opportunity. The bootroom welcomed a new member.

With a second league championship looking a hopeless dream, Shankly found himself concentrating on Europe and the FA Cup. To battle for all three trophies was impossible, although subsequent Liverpool sides would regularly pick up two trophies a season, even three on one occasion. In the league, too many points had been thrown away. They lost four games at Anfield that season and eleven away from home. The problem was that Europe and the FA Cup were sapping their concentration.

Liverpool began their FA Cup run with an away tie at West Brom. When the two sides had met at the Hawthorns in October, Liverpool had been on the end of a 3-0 pasting. The omens did not look good, but in the event Liverpool came away 2-1 winners, thanks to the goal-scoring partnership of Hunt and St John, plus a missed penalty by the Midlanders.

Next in line was a home tie against Stockport County. Shankly reckoned he could afford to miss the game and instead decided to go on a scouting mission to watch Liverpool's next European opponents. Bob Paisley was left in charge. There seemed little chance of any upset.

When Shankly returned to England late that evening, he asked an airport official if there had been any shocks in the FA Cup. 'None,' came the reply. But then Shankly caught sight of a newspaper headline. Stockport County had pulled off a draw at Anfield. 'If that's not a shock, then I don't know what is,' he spluttered, hailing a taxi to take him straight to Anfield.

In truth, it was just one of those things. Lowly Stockport had risen to the occasion in front of almost 52,000 at Anfield, battling with commitment and honesty. And Liverpool, for all their endeavours and obvious superiority, had been unable to find the key to unlock their defence. The match finished one-apiece. Shankly gave his players a roasting when he got hold of them. A few days later at Edgeley Park, they made amends, perhaps more afraid of another roasting from the manager than of exit from the Cup. So far, it had been an uphill battle and it would not get any easier. In the fifth round, Liverpool faced Second Division Bolton at Burnden Park, with Ian Callaghan's lone strike five minutes from time settling.the tie.

Liverpool were now into the quarter finals and also going strong in Europe. The league continued to bring mixed fortunes, Everton having the better of them home and away, although they had put together a fourteen-match unbeaten run over the winter months. But by March, they were out of contention in the league race. When Liverpool drew their old bogey team Leicester away, it looked like the end of their cup run as well.

Leicester had twice beaten them that season and had got the better of them at Anfield the previous year. The season before, they had beaten them twice in the league and in the semi-finals of the Cup. In three years and seven games, Liverpool had lost six times to Leicester, winning just once themselves.

Shankly was determined to end the Leicester curse. He had no secret formula; he just used a bit of Scottish cunning. He told his players their name was on the trophy, and that Leicester were not fit to tie their bootlaces. It was the kind of psychology that had now become a staple part of the Shankly team talk at Anfield. But even though Shankly might have told them that Gordon Banks in the Leicester goal had his weaknesses, they were not apparent that day as Liverpool flung every-thing in his direction. Banks held out and the two sides made for Anfield and a replay.

It was proving to be another titanic struggle, worthy of all their previous encounters. But in the 72nd minute with extra time looking likely, Hunt struck to send Anfield's 52,000 crowd home smiling, and working out how to get semi-final tickets. The hoodoo had been bro-ken – never again would Leicester hold the same sway over Liverpool.

The semi-final surprisingly turned out to be the easiest of all the ties Liverpool had so far faced. Tommy Docherty's young Chelsea were the opposition, Villa Park the venue and almost 68,000 were in attend-ance. Chelsea held out until the second half, but then Peter Thompson grabbed control, bursting down the flanks and firing in Liverpool's first. With ten minutes remaining, Liverpool were awarded a penalty. Willie Stevenson stepped up and Liverpool were on their way to Wem-bley.

Never have so many chased so few tickets for a Cup Final. They were like gold dust, and the race was on to track them down. Seven shillings terrace tickets were changing hands at £10, while 63 shillings seats were going for £25 on the black market.

Liverpool's chief scout Norman Low happened to be in the office a few days before the final when the phone rang.

'Bill picked it up and I could hear the fellow on the other end. He had a strong Birmingham accent. Bill says, "Yes, yes, what do you want sir?" The fellow said, "Did you get my letter?" "What letter," asks Bill, "Would it be after tickets?" "Yes, I wrote to you from Bir-mingham." "Birmingham, Birmingham?" exploded Bill, "I wouldn't give a drop of my blood to Birmingham. You know what sir, you know what? I've got a hundred relatives and there's not one of those beggars getting a ticket. They're going to the boys on the Kop, any tickets I've got. By Christ, Birmingham, Birmingham." "But Mr Shankly, sir," came the pleading voice from the other end of the phone, "I was born in Liverpool." "Were you by Christ! Well by the sound of your voice you've been away a long time. You'll get no tickets here!" '

And that was the end of the conversation. Shankly was uncompromising when it came to handing out Cup Final tickets. They had to go to real fans. And it would always be the same for any Cup Final. Shankly loved the Kopites. They were the heart and soul of the club. He realised their importance.

'When the ball's down the Kop end, they frighten the ball' he once said. 'Sometimes they suck it into the back of the net.' Shankly knew that with the Kop behind them Liverpool could achieve anything and he was not going to let the ordinary fan down. This was when Shankly was at his most generous.

A few years later, James Logan wrote to *The Kop* magazine with another story of Shankly generosity over tickets, although in this instance it was not Cup Final tickets. 'On Monday 19 February, a friend of mine went to Anfield to buy tickets for the Walsall–Liverpool Cuptie. After standing for three hours, she fainted and was carried to Mr Shankly's office. When she came to, she found that the two pounds that she had for the tickets had been taken from her hand. Mr Shankly sent someone out to look for the money, but as you might guess, it wasn't there. He then gave her the two pounds she had lost, plus two ten-shilling tickets for the match, and had her driven home.'

Hundreds of letters dropped on Shankly's doormat over the weeks before the Cup Final. Bill and Nessie sat down every evening and answered each one. For weeks, the phone never stopped ringing and there was always someone knocking on the door. They were forever answering the door: Shankly was always polite, always understanding, always ready to listen. 'Bill was very upset at the ticket business,' admitted Nessie at the time. 'If he had had his way, everyone on the Kop would have had a ticket.'

The final was to turn out to be one of those rare events, full of pathos and everlasting memories. Thirty years on, few who were there have ever forgotten the occasion. Liverpool have played in so many Wembley finals since, that many of them have become blurred. But not 1965 – that was different and its memory will never fade.

Leeds United turned out to be the opposition. They had just been pipped to the league title, losing out to Manchester United on goal average. Jackie Charlton remained at the heart of their defence, still much revered by Shankly, although on the day of this game he was being talked into the usual rubbish bin by a bullish Shankly.

Reaney, Bremner, Hunter, Giles and Sprake were all in the team, as they would be over the next decade, though there were to be one or two more vital additions before they became the Leeds United we all remember. Don Revie was in charge and, like Shankly, he had taken his side from the Second Division back into the first.

For a decade, Shankly and Revie would be the fiercest of opponents, caught in a bitter annual battle for league and cup honours. Shankly was to be the winner on more than one front, coveting more trophies, but more importantly capturing the affection of football lovers everywhere. Revie, trapped in scandal and intrigue later in his career, deserted England for foreign riches and became a much despised and abused character. Even his death failed to resurrect much affection.

But at Wembley on May Day 1965, the two sides that were about to dominate English football had their first major tussle. London was awash with red though by tea-time it would be even redder. This was an occasion for Liverpool fans. They had only been to Wembley once before, for the 1950 final when they lost to Arsenal, a defeat masterminded by Arsenal captain and ex-Evertonian Joe Mercer. Years earlier, they had also played in the 1914 final as war drums sounded around Europe. They lost that day, at the Crystal Palace, to Burnley by the only goal of the game, scored appropriately by another ex-Everton man, Bertie Freeman.

In 1965, as the two sides limbered up for the final much was being made of the fact that Leeds had an ex-Evertonian in their ranks, little Bobby Collins. He would be the man to undo Liverpool predicted the press. But he wasn't. Collins was by then some way past his impish best.

On the morning of the game, Shankly was introduced to Signor Sorti, general manager of Inter Milan, Liverpool's opponents in the European Cup semi-final. Sorti was on a spying mission. Shankly was in one of his special bullish moods. 'Are your team used to hearing a lot of noise?' Shankly asked the Italian. 'Ah yes,' replied Sorti. 'We have a lot of noise in Milan.' 'Not like the noise we have at Anfield,' Shankly came back. 'Yes,' replied Sorti. 'We visited Goodison Park last year. We know what it is like.' 'That's nothing,' snapped Shankly. 'You haven't heard noise until you've heard our supporters.'

Liverpool's chief pre-match worry was Gordon Milne who was

never a realistic candidate for the game. Instead, his place was taken by Chris Lawler. But Shankly had every faith in the young lad and his team. 'If we win today,' he told them in the dressing room, 'we will win the European Cup as well.' Outside Wembley, thousands who had arrived in the hope of picking up a ticket, had to make do with transistor radios.

In truth, it was a dour game: the pitch was heavy and greasy from the morning's rain. Neither side was keen to be too adventurous and after 90 minutes it came as no surprise that nobody had scored. Indeed, scoring opportunities had been rare. Extra time was needed for the first time since 1947.

The only remarkable event in the first 90 minutes had been an injury to full back Gerry Byrne who had fallen stiffly on his shoulder in a tackle with Bobby Collins. Trainer Bob Paisley raced on, immediately realised that Byrne had broken his collar bone, but said nothing. Substitutes were not allowed in those days. Byrne was strapped up and told to get on with it. And, to his everlasting credit, he, unflinchingly, did just that.

Paisley returned casually to the bench and leaning across to Shankly whispered in his ear that he thought Byrne had a broken collar bone. They decided to reveal nothing and let him play on. Shankly was full of admiration for Byrne and would forever be grateful for his undoubted courage. 'Gerry's bones were grinding together,' he remembered, 'but he stuck it out and should have had all the medals to himself.' That was the kind of character Shankly liked, a player with heart.

Three minutes into the first period of extra time, the devilish Peter Thompson slipped a ball to the injured Byrne overlapping on his left. Byrne burst down the flank, but rather than attempt a shot himself, sensibly slipped in a centre for Roger Hunt to head home. Eight minutes later, with Wembley still celebrating, Billy Bremner stole in to equalise for Leeds.

The two sides turned round and, with a draw and a replay looking odds-on, it was Ian St John who was to cover himself in glory. With nine minutes remaining, Ian Callaghan broke on the right, stroked in a cross and the little Scot flung himself forward to head the winner. Wembley erupted as it had never done before. The Cup was coming to Liverpool.

As Ron Yeats lifted the FA Cup a deafening chorus of 'Ee-Aye-Addio, we've won the Cup' echoed around the famous old stadium. Nothing quite like it had ever been heard before. There had been celebrations from past winners but never fanaticism like this. Supporters sang their hearts out and chanted the names of all the players.

Live on television for everyone to see and hear, Liverpool Football Club had arrived. They were different, driven on by a fanatical following. 'That was the greatest day,' remembered Shankly years later. 'Of all the days, that is the one I treasure the most.' Liverpool had won the FA Cup for the first time in their 73-year history.

In London that night, they painted the town red, even pouring red dye into the fountains around Trafalgar Square. They climbed the statue of Eros in Piccadilly Circus and tied their scarves around his neck before descending on Soho. From the West End to the East End, Liverpool supporters celebrated as they had never celebrated before. Liverpool players and officials also toasted one another in style, the only note of disharmony coming from Billy Liddell, who refused an invitation to the party because his wife had not been included. The club claimed there was not enough space for everyone, but it was typical of Liverpool, parsimonious to the last.

Kopite Jim Hartley remembered the occasion vividly. 'I think that Cup Final brought the power of the Kop home to everyone. People knew there was singing up at Anfield, but nobody realised quite how incredible it was until that game, when millions watching on television had their first experience of the Kop choir. It was after that, that singing really took off at football grounds. All the papers were full of it, and the commentators were saying that Wembley had never seen or heard anything like it before.'

Another Kopite, John Doig, returned home from Wembley that Saturday night, slightly the worse for wear, and went straight to the hotel where his girlfriend worked as a receptionist. 'Right that's it,' he told her jubilantly. 'We're getting engaged.' She'd only known him six months but she accepted readily. It probably wasn't the only proposal that Saturday night. Everyone was in a state of jubilation.

But if the celebrations around Wembley and in the West End had been exuberant, they were to be nothing compared with what happened the next day as Shankly and his team carried their prize back to Liverpool. Even Shankly was not prepared for it.

When Shankly and his entourage arrived at Lime Street station, they were warned by the police that a huge crowd was awaiting them.

Outside the station itself, there were 50,000. They climbed aboard various buses and coaches and slowly drove out into Lime Street.

The sight that greeted them had never been seen on the streets of the city before or since. Not even VE Day or the Relief of Mafeking had brought such a crowd out on to the streets. It was phenomenal. The crowd had been gathering in the early spring sunshine since the late afternoon and by five o'clock it was estimated that as many as 250,000 people were hemmed into the city's streets.

As the coaches came out of the station, a mighty roar erupted. Dozens of teenagers had swarmed all over the massive billboard hoardings outside the station, keen to be the first to give the signal that the Cup was coming. They were perched dangerously on top of hoardings and as the coach drove into view, they began thumping the wooden hoardings with their heels, setting up a rhythmical chant of 'Liv-er-pool'. Within moments, the entire city had taken up the chant.

The coach drove the short distance from Lime Street to the Town Hall. Shankly was in tears. He had never seen so many people, so deliriously happy, and all because his Liverpool had brought some happiness and pride into their lives. Even when he had brought the Cup home to Preston as a player in 1938, there had never been scenes quite like this.

'The reception in the city centre was unbelievable,' he wrote years later. 'The emotion was tremendous. When we came out of the station, we couldn't see anything but buildings and faces. People were climbing up the walls of shops and banks to get a better view. They were in dangerous places. But their name was on the Cup at last, and that was all that mattered.'

Outside the Town Hall, it seemed the streets were even more densely packed. It was impossible to move. The Cup was taken on to the balcony where Shankly and his players showed it to the vast crowd swaying below them. Later that evening, the St John ambulance reported more than 250 injuries. The following morning, the *Liverpool Daily Post* estimated the crowd at a quarter of a million. 'It seemed the entire city of Liverpool had turned out to greet them,' it reported. 'It made the recent Beatles reception look like a vicarage party.' There had never been a homecoming quite like it.

'It was the greatest feeling any human being could have to see what we had done. There have been many proud moments. Wonderful, fantastic moments. But that was the greatest day,' claimed Shankly with his usual tendency towards exaggeration, as well as an assumption that the response of others were identical to his own. But there was no doubt that, from the historical perspective of Liverpool Football Club, winning that first FA Cup ranked one of their greatest achievements.

What is also true is that winning the Cup changed perceptions of Liverpool Football Club. They suddenly assumed star status with their fans fittingly accorded their own role in the process. As for Shankly, he was now well on the way to becoming a living legend. But there was still one more great occasion to come.

Liverpool's progress in the European Cup had so far been impressive. After their early stroll past Reykjavik, they faced tougher opposition in the Belgian champions Anderlecht. Shankly had been as confident as ever until he went on a spying mission to watch the bulk of their team playing for Belgium against England at Wembley.

Just for once, Shankly was overawed by a side other than his own Liverpool. Belgium gave England a hard time and, although they drew 2-2, all the papers admitted that England had been given a football lesson. Shankly returned home to consider his options though he was not of course going to admit that he had in any way been impressed by the Belgians. What made it worse for Liverpool was that the first leg was to be played at Anfield, giving the Belgians a slight advantage. It wasn't going to be easy.

It turned out to be the first great European soccer night for Anfield. A crowd of 44,500 showed up, although had Shankly hyped Anderlecht up a little more, no doubt Anfield would have been bursting at the seams. Shortly before the game, Shankly decided to give young Tommy Smith his debut. Alf Arrowsmith and Gordon Wallace were both injured and new recruit Geoff Strong was ineligible.

Smith was still only nineteen but Shankly reckoned him man enough to face the Belgian champions. Shankly had tired of Smith knocking on his door demanding a place in the side, even when he was only eighteen. Eventually he relented, Smith was to become a typical Shankly favourite: full of determination, a never-say-die attitude and full-blooded tackles. Even then, he wasn't altogether sure about playing the youngster.

'He had a word with Ron [Yeats] and me on the quiet,' says St John. ' "What do you think?" he asked. "Don't worry, he won't let you down," we told him. Smith was a man when he was eight-years-old . . . and he didn't let anyone down.'

Gordon Milne was given the specific job of marking Belgian international Paul Van Himst, the man who dictated the pattern of Anderlecht's play. But Milne was also told that, when Liverpool had the ball, he could ignore Vam Himst and push forward himself. It was a tactic that was to confuse the Belgians.

Prior to the Anderlecht game, Shankly had also been playing around with the idea of making a slight alteration to the Liverpool strip. For years, Liverpool had played in red shirts and white shorts with white stockings and red hoops.

A day or so before the Anderlecht match, Shankly decided to experiment. He found Ron Yeats and Ian St John sitting in the dressing room. 'Come here, lads,' he shouted to them. 'I've had an idea. I thought we might try playing in red shorts. I think it'll make us look even more frightening.' He threw a pair of red shorts to Yeats. 'Here, try these on. Let's see what you look like in them,' he suggested. Yeats tried them on. 'Christ he looks like a giant, he's frightening, isn't he, Ian,' he said turning to St John.

'Why don't we go the whole hog?' suggested St John, 'and wear all-red socks as well.' 'Christ that's a good idea,' replied Shankly. 'Go find some red socks, son,' he ordered. St John immediately went rummaging around the dressing room and reappeared clutching a pair of red socks. Ron Yeats duly pulled them on and stood there. 'Perfect,' muttered Shankly. 'Just perfect. We'll frighten the hell out of them. Real Madrid play in all-white; Liverpool in all-red.'

Before the match, Shankly was up to his usual tricks, rubbishing the opposition. 'Nothing any good ever came out of Belgium,' he told them. 'You name me one famous Belgian footballer. You'll take them apart,' he added, knowing full well that Anderlecht really were a side that could play football.

From the moment they took the field against Anderlecht, the crowd loved the new strip. They looked fierce, the only side in Britain then playing in all red. 'I think the Kop was a bit shocked when we appeared in this new rig-out,' says St John. 'But it seemed to make them roar us on even more and after that we stayed in red.' It was another Shankly masterstroke although in fairness St John's vital suggestion undoubtedly improved the new image.

Shankly's various ploys were soon working. Within ten minutes, Liverpool were a goal ahead through St John. Hunt made is 2-0 shortly before half time and, minutes into the second half, Yeats headed Liverpool three goals in front. It had been a magnificent performance and gave Liverpool a comfortable advantage to take to Brussels.

After the game, Shankly became a little less dishonest about Anderlecht. 'You've just beaten one of the greatest sides in Europe,' he told his players as they trooped back into the dressing room. They could barely believe it. Here was the man who two hours earlier had been telling them that Anderlecht were bereft of ideas and trapped in a footballing cul-de-sac. Now he was telling them that they were not just one of the finest sides in Europe but one of the best he had ever seen. They shook their heads in disbelief. But then that was the Shankly way.

Full back Chris Lawler remembers it as one of Liverpool's greatest games. 'We were tremendous that night,' he says. 'I guess there have been greater nights since, but I felt that Liverpool Football Club really arrived that night. It was a coming of age.'

In the return leg, Liverpool were even more commanding, winning 1-0 in Brussels in front of 60,000, with Roger Hunt scoring in the last minute. Shankly had told them to sit back and soak up the pressure, let the opposition do the running and not to take any unnecessary risks. 'They'll eventually get frustrated,' he predicted. He was right. Even to this day, Ian St John reckons Anderlecht were the best side they ever faced. 'They played brilliant football,' he remembers. 'Sometimes it was beautiful. They were better even than Inter Milan.'

It was a result that had Europe sitting up to take note. Liverpool's tactics may not have been pretty to watch but they were effective. Liverpool were into the quarter finals where their next opponents were the West German champions FC Cologne, another side brimming with internationals.

This time, the first leg was away, giving Liverpool the slight advantage although in the previous rounds it had been of little consequence. Expectations were sky-high, especially after Liverpool returned home following a goalless draw in Germany. But it had been a dour battle with defences dominating.

The return leg was scheduled for 3 March. On Merseyside, it had been a bitterly cold morning; a light sprinkling of snow had fallen across the city but in the afternoon the thermometer edged upwards and the snow virtually disappeared. As a precaution, the French referee was called in. He inspected the pitch and announced the game could go ahead.

Then an hour or so before kick off, the snow began to drift down again, gently at first but soon turning into a blizzard. Within an hour, the city was shrouded in a blanket of snow. By then, the Kop was full. Shankly didn't like the look of it but the Cologne players were already changed and making their way out to warm up.

Shankly huffed and puffed around the corridor. He was never one to shirk a game just because of the conditions, but he realised that with the scores level it would only need one silly mistake to eliminate either side. And with the snow still falling, mistakes would be numerous. Cologne, more accustomed to playing in snow, also knew that this was their best chance of success and were eager to get out and get on with it.

Behind the scenes, a row was raging. The German officials, egged on by Cologne manager George Knopfle, were pleading with the referee to let the game go ahead, and pestering the Liverpool officials to clear all the snow from the touchlines.

Ian St John remembers it well. 'Bert Trautmann, then the boss of Stockport County, was acting as interpreter for the Germans. He was in the passageway outside the dressing room conducting some sort of argument between Bill Shankly and their boss. It was quite amusing really. If we'd said we wanted the match played, then they would have said it should be called off.'

The groundstaff had already cleared the lines once and had painted in new blue lines, but they had disappeared almost as soon as the paint was dry. The Germans had deliberately changed early and ventured out to test the conditions as a ploy to convince the referee that the match was playable.

Shankly was trying to act the diplomat. He wanted the game called off but with thousands of Cologne fans having made the long journey and thousands more Liverpool fans piled into the ground he was in something of a dilemma. Others were less reticent, urging the referee to inspect the pitch and postpone proceedings.

By the time the referee did venture out on to the pitch, the snow was tumbling down even more heavily. It was clearly impossible to play football and the referee was left with little option but to call the game off. The Cologne players threw their arms up in disbelief and shrugged their shoulders. The subsequent deterioration in conditions proved the referee's decision right, but as the Germans stormed off the field, there was much abuse being hurled at Shankly and other Liverpool officials, all accused of trying to influence the referee's decision. In the end, the referee's decision was to cause as much of a headache for Liverpool as for Cologne. First, they had to clear the stadium and give out vouchers for the rescheduled game. And with no proper procedures in place, it resulted in memorable chaos. Thousands were trapped on the Kop. They couldn't simply open the gates as everyone needed to be given a voucher and the problem with the turnstiles was that they were one-way.

Evacuating the Kop was a long painful process that took most of the evening. The fans frustrated by the long wait finally resorted to a snowball fight on the pitch. Gangs of Kopites tore from their end of the ground to launch a snowball attack on the Anfield Road end. Then they retreated, only to be assailed by a similar invasion from the Anfield Roaders. It was hilarious.

Shankly was as taken with the events as anyone, standing in the directors' box along with the players laughing at the antics of the Kopites. There may have been no football but it was a memorable night, one of those moments of togetherness, that helped bond players, fans and manager.

The rematch eventually took place a fortnight later and, in front of almost 50,000, the two sides fought out another bruising goalless draw. With their fixture list piling up, it was the last thing Shankly wanted. In those days, away goals did not count and with no penalty shoot-outs either, a third game was required.

The replay took place a week later, on neutral territory, in Rotterdam with an astonishing crowd of 45,000 turning up, mostly Germans but with enough Liverpool fans to give an early indication of the fanatical following they would carry across the continent in the years ahead. This time, the two sides drew 2-2 after Liverpool had swept into a two-goal lead in the first half. Again there was no penalty shoot-out rule, and the match was decided on the toss of a coin.

The two sides gathered in the centre circle; players craned their necks to see which way the coin would fall. But on the first toss, the coin unbelievably stuck on its side in the mud. It seemed the tie would never be decided. The referee tossed the coin again, and this time Ron Yeats called out correctly. Eleven red-shirted players in the centre circle leapt with joy. After 300 minutes, the tie had finally been settled.

Liverpool were only the second Football League club to have ever reached the semi-final of Europe's most prestigious cup competition, a competition still to be won by an English club. But in the draw for the semi-finals, Liverpool found themselves paired with the current holders and world club champions, Inter Milan. It was hardly the draw Shankly had hoped for. Inter Milan had knocked Everton out of the competition the previous year on their way to winning it.

Three days after lifting the FA Cup, Liverpool lined up against Inter Milan at Anfield. After the euphoria of Wembley and a tumultuous return home, the reality began to sink in. On the Monday morning, Shankly drove to Melwood and began to size up the problem. Gerry Byrne may have battled on grimly at Wembley with a broken collar bone but he clearly had to be ruled out of the Milan game, while Gordon Milne's injury still made him unavailable. Byrne with his gutsy determination would be sorely missed but in Ronnie Moran Shankly had an experienced campaigner he could rely on. There were no other serious injuries, just bruises and a few sore heads from the celebrations. Nothing another 24 hours would not mend. The side more or less picked itself and, after the FA Cup victory, they were itching to get at the European and world champions.

By the Tuesday evening, the excitement had reached fever-pitch. The entire city of Liverpool seemed to be floating on a cloud of euphoria. It was a four-day period the likes of which Liverpool Football Club and its supporters had never experienced.

The game against Inter Milan could not have come at a better moment. It seemed that almost everyone in the city, with the exception of a few die-hard Evertonians, was champing at the bit to see this game. It was the ultimate test for Shankly's young team. When he arrived at the ground early that afternoon he could barely believe the scenes.

There were thousands already queuing outside the Kop with the roads around Anfield jammed with cheering crowds. By 3.30 pm, the streets were so packed that the police asked the club to open the turnstiles straight away in order to relieve the congestion. By 5.30 pm, the gates of the Kop had been closed with 25,000 on its terraces. Thousands were locked out.

Shankly could already sense that this was going to be an occasion. And as the evening wore on, it became clear that the crowd would play as much a part in this contest as the players themselves. Sitting in his bunker beneath the old Main Stand that evening, Shankly and the players could hear the crowd outside bellowing. Within an hour of opening, the turnstiles had been closed, with the Kop crammed to capacity with 25,000 fans. Even the stands and other parts of the ground, not normally filled until near kick-off time, were packed long before 7 pm.

There seemed to be only one thought on everyone's mind. On the Kop the chant said it all: 'Ee-Aye-Addio, we wanna see the Cup,' they sang. Hearing this, Shankly had an idea. All day long, he had been wondering about sending the FA Cup out for the crowd to see. Now a plan began to take shape. Why not let Gordon Milne and Gerry Byrne take the cup out? The noise would be deafening. At first, he was inclined to send them out some ten minutes or so before the teams emerged, but the more he thought about it, the more he came to the conclusion that to send the Cup out alongside the teams would produce such a deafening noise that there would be a huge psychological impact on Inter Milan. It was a cunning plot.

Bob Paisley agreed and was sent off in search of Byrne and Milne. When they all returned, they began to refine the plan. Paisley chipped in with an idea. Rather than bring the Cup out before the team, why not wait? There would be an enormous cheer anyhow when Liverpool emerged, so why not let the team appear, take their applause and then have Milne and Byrne appear with the Cup? That way there would be even more noise.

But as Shankly, immediately pointed out, if the plan was to really work effectively, they needed to have Inter Milan out on the pitch first, then Liverpool, and the Cup could appear. It was no good having all this happen if Milan were still sitting in the dressing room.

'I'll invite them to go out early,' suggested Shankly, wandering down the corridor and spotting Helenio Herrera, the Inter Milan manager, talking to the press. The Italians gratefully accepted the offer and Shankly returned to the Liverpool dressing room to bide his time. But as the minutes ticked away and kick-off time approached, Inter Milan had still not appeared from their dressing room.

Shankly was getting anxious. At this rate, Liverpool would have to go out first and his plan would be wrecked. The dressing room doors were open, the players all eager to get outside. Milne and Byrne hid behind the door clutching the Cup, not wanting anyone from Milan to spot what they were up to. Even the referee and linesmen had appeared. But still no Milan.

'I'll go see if I can hurry them along,' Shankly told Paisley and went storming down the corridor. The door to the Italian dressing room was open with the players milling around but not appearing keen to leave.

Shankly spotted Herrera and began pointing to his watch, smiling and beckoning them to go out. Herrera eventually took the hint, shouted at his team and within minutes had them running out on to the pitch.

The old actor Shankly now held his own team back, though unknown to him Inter Milan had immediately sprinted down to the Kop end of the ground for their pre-match kickabout only to be greeted by a wall of whistles. Realising their error, they had turned tail and raced down towards the Anfield Road end. They might just as well have raised a white flag.

Still Shankly bided his time. He gave his players a last minute instruction. 'You've won the cup, lads, so just go out and enjoy yourselves.' With the Austrian referee looking anxiously at his watch, he finally gave Ron Yeats the nod to lead the side out. The blast was phenomenal. Then out of the dressing room, hobbling down the corridor came Milne and Byrne with the FA Cup. And, as they emerged out of the players' tunnel, the most fearsome sound erupted.

'The noise was unbelievable,' remembered Shankly years later. 'People were hysterical. It was the greatest night in the history of Anfield.' Milne and Byrne slowly walked around the perimeter of the pitch, and the noise grew louder as they approached the Kop. Shankly and his lieutenants watched in awe: Inter looked on in horror.

On the Kop, grown men were in tears, young boys leapt up and down and the crowd spilled forward like a giant wave. Everyone wanted to touch the Cup. Sitting in the Kemlyn Road stand that night was another youngster who would one day finally hold the European Cup aloft for Liverpool.

That night, more than any other, turned Phil Thompson into a Liverpool fanatic. It was his first visit to Anfield. 'My Mum got us tickets,' he remembers. 'I was eleven. I always remember we were in the front row of the Kemlyn Road stand. We'd just won the FA Cup, and Gerry and Gordon came round the ground just before kick-off with the trophy. The Kop was great that night, probably the greatest I've ever seen. The whole night, my eyes were fixed on the Kop. I couldn't believe it. I was mesmerised. The steam was rising; the noise was incredible. "Go back to Ital-ee," they were singing, to the tune of "Santa Lucia".'

Chief Inspector Ian Thompson of the Merseyside Police was on duty that night, a young officer policing one of his first-ever matches. He was standing right in front of the Kop. 'When that Cup came out, I'll swear the earth was vibrating,' he recalls. 'I've never experienced a noise like it; your head was just buzzing. We could have beaten anyone that night, including Pele and Brazil.' Under the Anfield floodlights that evening, young Phil Thompson and many more were converted to the cause of Liverpool Football Club.

Their conversion was helped not just by Shankly's pre-match tactic but by one of the finest displays ever given by a Liverpool side. The Italians were visibly shaken by what had happened. Within four minutes, Roger Hunt had capitalised on the mood, firing Liverpool into an early lead with as spectacular a goal as any he ever scored. It was a fierce volley that simply flew into the net.

'That was not a British goal,' groaned Herrera later. 'It was a continental goal.' Hunt rated it one of his top six goals ever. But the euphoria did not last long. While Anfield was still celebrating, Mazzola stole in to equalise.

But Liverpool were far from finished. In the 34th minute, Callaghan added a deserved second to give Liverpool a 2-1 lead at half time. Then in the second half Ian St John made it 3-1 to send the 54,000 crowd home deliriously happy. The Italians trooped off the field visibly shocked by the onslaught, the anguish and pain showing in their eyes.'

Nessie Shankly was also there that night, the first time she had ever seen a match at Anfield. In the four-and-a-half years they had been on Merseyside she had not seen Liverpool play until the Cup Final. She was so swept up by the occasion that a few days later she was watching them again. 'I wanted to hear the Liverpool supporters on their own ground,' she said. 'It was a night I shall never forget.'

Inter manager Helenio Herrera was distraught. 'We have been beaten before,' he told pressmen, 'but tonight we were defeated. The enthusiasm of the Liverpool fans stunned my players. Liverpool are a great team.' Herrera had paid a number of visits to Anfield to watch Liverpool and became something of an admirer of Shankly and the passion he instilled into his side. Pulling back a two-goal deficit would require an almighty effort, maybe more.

But the following afternoon came an incident that left Shankly and everyone else at Liverpool Football Club bewildered and shaken. Jimmy McInnes who had been secretary at the club since 1955 was found hanged in a turnstile attendant's box in the Kemlyn Road entrance to the Kop. Nobody could believe it.

McInnes who was only 51 had joined the club as a player in 1938.

After the war, he had joined the coaching staff, later moving into administration. McInnes had been a good friend to Shankly. He may have been autocratic, even downright rude to some at Anfield at times, but he was always straight with Shankly. If they did have words, they were soon forgotten.

Shankly was deeply upset by McInnes' suicide, brought on almost certainly by the team's phenomenal success that season. The intense workload involved in dealing with Cup Final tickets and organising Liverpool's travels throughout Europe had taken their toll. Shankly felt as much to blame as anyone. It was little wonder that many of the team travelled to Italy the following week in a state of shock and gloom.

Quite what happened a week later in the San Siro stadium is open to debate. Even before the game kicked off, there were ominous signs. Liverpool had not done their homework. They stayed at Lake Como, a quiet, relaxed spot over the mountains from Milan. Or at least it seemed peaceful enough, but nobody had reckoned with the church bells. You tended not to hear them during the day but at night in the stillness of the valley they tolled forebodingly, echoing around the village.

The players were soon complaining that they could not sleep. Shankly was furious. He grabbed Bob Paisley and the two of them went off in search of the local priest to get them stopped. 'We've come here for the most important football match in the world this year,' he told the Monsignor. But although he was sympathetic there was little he could do. The bells struck automatically.

Shankly even suggested Paisley go and tie some bandages around them. What's more, he was serious. Paisley could hardly beieve what he was hearing. It was one of the rare occasions when Paisley said 'No' to Shankly. Fortunately, the Monsignor also said 'No' and a potential split was averted. They simply had to put up with the noise.

But if they thought the noise of the bells was bad, it was nothing compared to the sound that greeted them when the gladiators entered the San Siro stadium. The Italian press, and in particular the local Milan papers, had been running something of a hate campaign against Liverpool, accusing the club of foul tactics in sending the Italians out first at Anfield and then bringing out the FA Cup. The Italian club had even considered an official complaint to UEFA but in the end decided against.

And so the barrage of abuse and accusation went on. The message was simple: get out and support your team. And so they did. If Anfield had been a cacophony of noise, the San Siro was like a bomb going off. For a start, there were almost twice as many fans – 90,000 at least – carrying klaxons, trumpets, smoke bombs and anything else likely to leave an impression on the minds and eardrums of Liverpool.

Liverpool were visibly shaken. They had never been on the receiving end of this kind of din. Goodison, Old Trafford, even Wembley, might have been cauldrons of sound but the San Siro was in a different league. It was even noisier than Hampden admitted Shankly, somewhat reluctantly.

As if the noise was not bad enough, Liverpool then had to put up with a succession of dubious refereeing decisions. Within eight minutes, they were a goal down. The referee had awarded what some assumed was an indirect free kick. Up stepped Corso and slammed the ball beyond Tommy Lawrence into the goal. The Italians jumped for joy as the referee pointed to the centre spot. Liverpool protested but it was of little use. Inter were off to a dream start.

A few minutes later came another disputed goal. Tommy Lawrence with the ball safely in his hands was bouncing it in preparation for a big kick upfield, when in stole Peiro, the long-legged Spanish international, to toe-poke it out of his hands and into the net. Lawrence glared angrily at him only to see the referee point astonishingly to the centre circle. Two goals down, and the game had barely begun. It seemed they were playing against more than Inter and its fans. Liverpool would never recover and, when Inter added a third in the second half, the game was effectively over. Inter just retreated into defence and soaked up the pressure. By then, the stuffing had long been knocked out of Liverpool.

Shankly was furious with the referee. 'Inter's second goal was a disgrace,' he roared. After the game, he spotted him laughing and joking with Inter officials. It was enough for him to remain convinced that there had been some questionable dealings. Years later, *Sunday Times* journalist Brian Glanville uncovered enough evidence to suggest that Shankly might have had some cause for anger. Although Inter would march on to lift the European Cup for a second time, there remains much that is questionable about that period of their history.

Yet when you carefully examine the video replay of the two incidents, it is clear that Liverpool's case for having been hard done by is barely justifiable. The referee does not fully raise his arm to indicate an indirect free kick. It is raised horizontally for a brief second but is clearly not raised to indicate an indirect free kick. If Lawrence was so convinced, then we might ask why he makes every attempt to save the ball, instead of just leaving it.

As for the second goal, Lawrence was indeed bouncing the ball preparing to kick it, but Peiro did not kick the ball while it was actually in Lawrence's hands. Admittedly, an English referee in the Football League might well have disallowed the goal but there was nothing illegal about Peiro's goal. Shankly however quickly convinced everyone that Liverpool had been robbed.

It was a bitter lesson for Liverpool. But Shankly and his entourage were ready to learn from it. 'All the time we were learning,' said Shankly. 'Taking a particle from here and a bit from there, building ourselves up just like a hydrogen bomb.' Herrera had at least paid Shankly's side the respect they deserved, admitting that Liverpool were indeed one of the finest sides in the world.

Shankly was phlegmatic, always ready to turn defeat into something positive. 'All right, we've lost,' he told players as they drove through the noisy streets back to their hotel. 'But see what you've done. Inter Milan are the unofficial champions of the world, and all these people are going mad because they are so pleased that they have beaten Liverpool. That's the standard you have raised yourselves up to.'

14 The Centre of the Universe

BY 1965, THE CITY OF LIVERPOOL had become the centre of the universe. The phenomenal success of the Beatles and Merseybeat music had swept the name of Liverpool across Europe, the Atlantic and as far as Tokyo and Australia. The world was Liverpool-crazy.

Besides the Liverpool musicians, there were Liverpool poets, Liverpool comedians and Liverpool writers. Suddenly, Liverpool was an artistic centre. It was Soho, Greenwich Village and the Left Bank all rolled into one. It was on the front cover of *Time* magazine, packed into the pages of *Paris Match*, and featured in just about every major newspaper in the world.

Wherever you turned, the sound of the Beatles, Gerry and the Pacemakers, Billy J. Kramer and the Swinging Blue Jeans seemed to reverberate. Even the recently elected prime minster, Harold Wilson, had a Merseyside connection: he was educated at Wirral Grammar School, and elected by the Liverpool constituency of Huyton. And it wasn't just music and writing that drew the world's attention towards the city. On top of all that, Merseyside boasted the best football in the land. The sixties might have been only half-over, but Everton and Liverpool had already picked up the league, with Liverpool adding the FA Cup to the growing collection of trophies. By the end of the 1965/66 season, the city's teams would have totally dominated English football with Liverpool picking up another league trophy, while Everton stole the FA Cup from under the noses of Sheffield Wednesday in a memorable Cup Final.

In May 1964, on the back of the league championship triumph and the Beatles success, Liverpool FC had toured America, even appearing on the famous *Ed Sullivan Show*, an acknowledgement, if ever one was needed, that Liverpool had arrived. Everything connected with the city of Liverpool was hot. Shankly and the team must of course know the Beatles, the Americans assumed. So they were invited on to American television, dressed in their smart blazers and club ties.

But Shankly never really took to America. For once, he was lost for words when he came across someone who had never heard of Tom Finney. 'Never heard of Tom Finney,' he gasped. 'But everybody's heard of Tom Finney.' That was too much for him. Perhaps more to the point, nobody seemed to recognise Bill Shankly or his famed Liverpool players. They might have appeared on the famous *Ed Sullivan Show* but, in the land of American football, soccer counted for nothing. If America did not want to know Finney, then Shankly didn't want to know America. He had arrived late, part way into Liverpool's five-week trip, missing the appearance on the *Ed Sullivan Show*, and after the Finney incident he was off again, back home to watch some Highland League football in Scotland. He only stayed a week.

Shankly's eccentricity seemed to touch new levels that trip. On an internal flight in America, he rolled up his sleeves to reveal half-a-dozen wrist watches. Each had been carefully set to a different time zone. Shankly was taking no chances: he wanted to know the precise time in New York, Chicago and back home in Liverpool, no matter where he was. Throughout the trip, he operated on UK time, even to the extent of handing out team sheets at 3 o'clock in the morning.

Compensation could be found in the boxing, and of course the gangsters. When the team was in Chicago, he and Paisley went off on their own to Soldier's Field. Shankly went in search of the groundsman demanding to know the exact spot where Jack Dempsey had fought Gene Tunney for the world heavyweight title. When the spot was pointed out to him, off came the coats and out came a ball and the pair of them proceeded to have a kickaround on the precise spot where the famous fight had taken place.

They were like a pair of kids, each as bad as the other, though there can be little doubt that it would have been Shankly encouraging Paisley. His appetite for the sporting occasion knew no bounds. But Shankly was also able to indulge his love of gangsters. He'd wear his trilby hat and a flashy tie, pretending to be James Cagney. Sometimes before matches, he would stride into the dressing room and throw a bundle of photos on the table. There would be pictures of James Cagney, Bugsy Moran and Eliot Ness. 'These were hard men,' he'd tell the players, 'real hard men. When they did anything wrong, they'd get shot. You think you're hard men. This is a hard man.'

Friday evenings were also planned around *The Untouchables*, then a television series. It was Shankly's favourite programme. If Liverpool happened to be playing away, then the departure of the team coach would be planned, so that they arrived at their hotel in time to watch Eliot Ness and his men.

Shankly was an unworldly character, xenophobic even, who could never have coped on his own in a foreign country for more than a day. Every trip he made was organised by the club and usually in the company of club officials. Filling in a form at a hotel once, he entered his occupation as 'football' and his address as 'Anfield'. 'No, that's not right,' someone said. 'They want to know where you live.' 'That is where I live,' he answered stonily.

On the trip to Italy to play Inter Milan, Shankly was astonished by the number of vans carrying the VW sign. He was convinced the vans belonged to the Woolworths company. 'It's one of the biggest companies in the world, Woolworths,' he was telling his players, 'their vans are everywhere.' The players tried to explain to him that VW stood for Volkswagen and was a make of car. But he would not have it.

'He was totally serious,' remembers Phil Chisnall, 'and we could not convince him.' It was part of his innocence. Yet nobody ever laughed at him behind his back. There was far too much respect. People simply put it down to his eccentricity.

Shankly was also renowned for his driving, the butt of much humour. He rarely drove people anywhere: they usually hurriedly volunteered to take the wheel themselves. You could hear him miles away, revving up his car, foot flat down on the clutch. He had little idea about mechanics.

One afternoon, he went downtown in the car and parked it just outside the Mersey Tunnel on a double-yellow line. A police officer came up and told him he couldn't park there. Shankly was having none of it. 'You take the car then,' he told the policeman. 'It's not mine; it's a club car.' And with that, he walked off and caught the bus.

On another occasion, as he was driving near Bellefield he spotted Everton's Mick Lyons driving in the opposite direction. Shankly stopped his car and wound down his window. Lyons did likewise and, for the next five minutes, they sat there chatting about the game. 'There's 20 cars behind me round the corner,' remembers Lyons, 'and about 20 cars behind him, and I'm looking embarrassed. "Aye," he says. "This is life we're talking about, son. Ignore them. They don't know what it's about." '

After the cruel defeat by Inter Milan in the European Cup, Liverpool might have been forgiven had the after-effects lingered for a season or so. But, on the contrary, coming so close to winning Europe's most prized trophy, seemed to make the team all the more keen to have a second crack. But that meant qualifying for the European Cup first, which meant winning the league title again. From the start, Liverpool set out with a determination to regain their crown.

They kicked off with a vengeance beating their old bogey team Leicester 3-1 at Filbert Street. They then lost their opening home game 1-0 to Sheffield United but did not lose too much more that season. They were soon firing five past West Ham at Upton Park and, despite a 2-1 defeat at Tottenham, slammed another five against Everton at Anfield in their next game. Anfield went wild; it was their biggest derby win in decades. The size of the victory was attributed to Shankly's tactics.

Days before the game, he had been telling Bob Paisley how he had been spying on Everton from the bedroom of his house which over-looked the Everton training ground at Bellefield. 'Get the best odds you can on a Liverpool win,' he urged Paisley, knowing that his assistant liked a flutter now and then. 'You can't fail,' he added in a deliberately loud voice so players could overhear. 'I've been watching them and Catterick's got them running lap after lap around Bellefield. They'll be knackered by Saturday.'

Paisley of course knew what he was up to and the both roared at Catterick's supposed heavy training schedule, a routine totally alien to the one at Anfield where there was little running or heavy training.

On the day of the match, Shankly sneaked out of the dressing room to have a peep at the Everton players as they arrived. He returned a few moments later and informed anyone who cared to listen, in his best mocking Scottish voice that the Everton players could barely walk.

'They look shattered,' he said. 'It's all that racing around Bellefield.' It's hard to imagine that anyone seriously believed him but the Liverpool players took it all in and duly went out and ran Everton ragged. It was 1-0 at half-time, but as the second half progressed Everton grew all the more weary conceding four goals in 45 minutes.

After the game, Shankly went in search of Harry Catterick. The

Everton manager looked stunned, particularly as Liverpool had lost at Tottenham in their previous match. 'Nah,' Shankly told him, 'we were brilliant last week. We should have won 6-0 at Tottenham. We gave them the drubbing of their lives. So this was coming to somebody.' He was always believing his own exaggerations. He called them his 'little white lies'. Catterick nicknamed him Rob Roy.

In successive matches in November, Liverpool slammed five past Northampton Town and Blackburn Rovers. Victory in the FA Cup had assured Liverpool of a place in the European Cup-Winners Cup. And when the draw for the competition was made, it seemed as if Liverpool might not progress beyond the preliminary round as they had been pitted against the crack Italian club Juventus.

Now here was a real test. Had Liverpool learnt anything from their bitter experience in Milan only a few months earlier? But at least on this occasion the opening leg was in Italy, so that Liverpool would know precisely what they had to do at Anfield. Liverpool were quickly absorbing the tactics of European football; containment away, attack at home.

It didn't matter if you lost away, as long as the deficit could be recovered. Defeat by a single goal was not the end of the world; it was easily recoverable in the heady atmosphere of Anfield but a two-goal deficit was more difficult if not impossible. A three-goal deficit though was the end of the world.

Juventus were still one of the most respected club sides in the world, holding a special affection for English fans because of their association with John Charles. With the Inter Milan experience still fresh in their minds, Liverpool went to Turin to defend. Hold the line, don't go recklessly looking for goals, warned Shankly.

Much to their surprise, Juventus were being told the same in their dressing room. The result was a gaggle of players congesting the midfield, all afraid to commit themselves. Liverpool held on, barely troubled, until with nine minutes remaining Gianfranco Leoncini swung a speculative boot at the ball from 30 yards. But even a goal up Juventus reverted to their defensive tactics. Normally that would have been a signal for an all-out Liverpool assault but they had learned a lesson.

From the touchline, Shankly urged them to hold back for fear they might commit too many men forward. They heeded his warnings and, although they left the field with stooped shoulders from disappointment at losing 1-0 Shankly was ebullient. He knew the deficit could be turned around at Anfield. Liverpool had gone out to do a job and had kept their discipline. He was proud. It was another lesson absorbed.

Shankly had few worries for the return leg although he admitted it would need an all-out assault on the Italian goal if they were to reverse the balance. With appetites whetted, 51,000 turned up at Anfield on an October evening with a distinct taste of autumn in the air. Shankly was relishing the challenge, giving his troops their usual briefing. Yet he was never one to dwell on the talents of the opposition.

'We never went in for dossiers like some managers did,' he once told the BBC, having a slight dig at Leeds manager Don Revie. 'We didn't want to frighten our players.' Dossiers were overcomplicated and, as Shankly once put it, 'Football matches are played on football pitches and not in exercise books.' But that is not to say that Liverpool ignored the opposition. On the contrary, they always paid them every respect, ever aware of the most dangerous players. It was simply that they did not concentrate on analysing and discussing them. Shankly always believed that, as long as you were satisfied with your own players, then the opposition could look after themselves.

And on that chilly autumnal night at Anfield, Shankly was proved right as Lawler and Strong fired Liverpool two goals ahead within the half hour. There were no more goals although Liverpool were hanging on at times to their slender lead. Having longed since the Inter Milan game for another European evening of breathtaking excitement, the crowd devoured every thrill. Although greater European triumphs lay ahead, those early nights of European soccer under the Anfield lights will remain in the memory for their passion, the packed Kop, the singing, and the early romance of European football.

For the first time ever, Liverpool were pitting their wits against the glamour names of the continent, playing not just the best sides in England but the finest in the world. They offered the ultimate challenge. As a club, Liverpool had neglected Europe in the past, rarely cashing in on the opportunity to test themselves against continental opposition. Others like Arsenal, Chelsea, Manchester United, and most notably Wolves, had been there from the outset. Now, ten years or so behind them, Liverpool were finally awakening to the challenge of Europe and beyond.

In the next round of the Cup-Winners Cup, Liverpool faced Standard Liege, a useful Belgian side but little better than a top quality English

Second Division club. Within two minutes, Chris Lawler had Liverpool a goal ahead at Anfield. Lawler added a second and then Peter Thompson a third, as the Reds ran out 3-1 winners. Liverpool also won the second leg, demonstrating their growing confidence away from home.

Full back Lawler was becoming something of a goalscorer in European competitions, deceiving defenders with his quiet bursts into the penalty area. Shankly encouraged him to go forward, to sneak unexpectedly into places he was not supposed to be. He was the first of many overlapping full backs at the club. Lawler was known as the 'silent knight around Anfield'. In one famous incident in a five-a-side game at Melwood, Shankly asked Lawler, who was watching from the sidelines, to judge whether his side's goal had been legal or not. 'Did you think that was a goal Chris?' he shouted to him. 'No,' replied Chris casually. 'Good God, Chris,' roared Shankly. 'This is the first time I've heard you speak to me and you tell me a bloody lie.' Lawler retreated into his shell once more, but as long as he stole into opposing penalty areas from time to time Shankly was more than happy with him.

In the league, Liverpool had stormed to the top of the table by December and would not be dislodged. They were determined to be in Europe's premier competition the following season. The only shadow was a 1-0 defeat at home by Leeds United during the Christmas period, but at least they made amends by travelling to Yorkshire the following day and inflicting a similar scoreline on Don Revie's side. They would lose only two more league games all season.

But if Shankly had any dreams of repeating the previous season's FA Cup triumph, they were shattered from the start. Chelsea were the visitors with a young side out for revenge following Liverpool's semi-final triumph over them the previous season. What's more, they got it, winning 2-1 at Anfield in front of 54,000. Shankly was philosophical. 'It means we can concentrate on the league,' he told his players.

Ironically, Liverpool wrapped up the league with a 2-1 win over Chelsea at Anfield in late April. Chelsea even acknowledged Liverpool's supremacy forming a guard of honour and applauding them as they came on to the field. As far as they were concerned, Liverpool were already champions and by 4.40 that afternoon they really were, equalling Arsenal's record seven title wins. They had been out front on their own since November.

It was another excuse for a party. A replica championship trophy was produced and the side strode out on a lap of honour, watched enviously by Chelsea's Young Turks. Celebrations were becoming a regular feature at Anfield. Shankly applauded vigorously from the touchline until he was finally dragged into the proceedings by his admiring players and demanding Kop. 'Shank-lee, Shank-lee,' chanted the Kop. He did not disappoint them. By now, the Kop had more than taken him to their hearts. Back in the dressing room, the directors were playing at being waiters as the champagne flowed.

In the quarter final of the Cup-Winners Cup, Liverpool came up against one of the glamour names of European football – Honved. The Hungarian side, which had boasted Puskas, Czibor, Kocsis and Kovacs in its line-up, in the fifties was no longer the thundering force it had been; Italian and Spanish clubs had stolen most of Honved's stars. But a name is a name and they didn't come much more exciting than Honved.

How Shankly would have loved to have pitted his Liverpool against the Honved of old that had played so stirringly under the floodlights at Molineux. But the first leg was in Budapest and the modern Honved were a pale shadow of their proud ancestors. With the Hungarian season emerging hesitantly from its winter recess, the Magyars had barely kicked a ball in months. It showed too. Liverpool comfortably held them to a goalless draw, even though they suffered relentless pressure in the second half as Honved renewed acquaintance with the ball. Shankly returned home well satisfied.

Puskas and company may have fled Budapest at the time of the Hungarian uprising in 1956, but the Honved name clearly lived on in Liverpool luring more than 54,000 worshippers to Anfield, a bigger gate than the one that had greeted Inter Milan. By now, Honved had shrugged off their hibernation and were growing more accustomed to playing football. They stroked the ball around in graceful patterns.

'I half-closed my eyes, and I could see the old masters,' wrote one reporter. In the dugout, Shankly looked worried, but then in the 27th minute came a stroke of luck. Callaghan lashed in a corner that was only half-cleared: Thompson raced on to it and struck a speculative shot that thundered against the post, rebounding to the lurking Lawler who headed in Liverpool's opening goal. It changed the course of the game. All the spirit seemed to evaporate from Honved. Early in the second period, Hunt added a second and the game was all but over.

If that had been an evening of drama and romance, the semi-finals were to produce two matches of such memorable quality that years later they are still talked of as two of the most stirring ties in all Liverpool's European adventures.

Out of the hat came Glasgow Celtic, European champions in the making, a side that would go down in Scottish footballing history. The hope had been that these two sides might meet in the final, especially as that match was scheduled for Hampden Park where the presence of Celtic and Liverpool would have guaranteed a gate of 130,000.

Shankly relished the prospect. 'It will be a semi-final to remember,' he told the press, 'a British championship decider, the best in Scotland against the best in England.'

There was little doubt that this was how everyone viewed it. Liverpool topped the Football League; Celtic the Scottish League, both sides within a handful of points of reclaiming their respective league titles. The following season both would be in the European Cup. The first leg was played at Parkhead on 14 April in front of a frenetic crowd of 80,000.

For Shankly it was a return home, back to his roots in Ayrshire. He may have played all his football in England and lived all but the first eighteen years of his life south of the border, but the Scots still thought of him as one of their own. When it came to claiming great managers, Shankly, Stein and Busby were top of their list.

Interestingly, all three were born within a few miles of each other. And of course the feelings were reciprocated. Shankly was a Scot through and through, even though he had been exiled for almost 40 years and by 1966 was an adopted Liverpudlian. His favourite five-a-side games at Melwood were, as ever, England against Scotland. When it came to choosing his favourite music, it had to be Moira Anderson and Kenneth McKellar.

Roger Hunt was missing for the Glasgow tie, injured, but Shankly was not unduly worried. He knew the likelihood was that Liverpool would be spending much of their time penned inside their own half. St John would be the lone raider. It would not be an evening for the faint-hearted, predicted the Glasgow papers gleefully and they would not be wrong. Gruelling was probably the best word to describe the game.

The first half was evenly matched but, not long after the interval, Bobby Lennox squeezed Celtic ahead. It was the signal for a Celtic onslaught. Yet, for all their possession over the next 30 minutes, Celtic struggled to convert chances into goals. The discipline that Shankly had instilled in his players was paying dividends as they gritted their teeth and held their concentration to limit Celtic's winning margin to just one goal.

The opening leg had not been a great advertisement for flowing football. The stakes were too high; the atmosphere too intense; fear was at a premium. Yet at Anfield five days later in front of 54,000, both sides produced the full repertoire of skills that had been absent from Parkhead. It was frenetic, and as memorable as the Inter Milan clash. It was aided unquestionably by the huge contingent of Celtic supporters, who had made the journey south and whose merrymaking, drinking and fanaticism would become legendary.

Fortunately, Liverpool revelled in the atmosphere. Liverpool created chances in the first half – Smith crashing a shot against the angle – but the breaks came after the interval. Smith again, this time from a free kick, hammered in a low shot that skidded off the surface and into the net. Six minutes later, Geoff Strong, still suffering from an early knock, hobbled bravely upfield to head home Ian Callaghan's cross. In the dying moments, Celtic were denied a penalty that would almost certainly have taken the game into extra-time. But it was not to be, although to this day Celtic captain Billy McNeill remains convinced that Celtic were robbed of victory.

After the game, Shankly and Jock Stein shook hands, exchanged memories and agreed that this had been one of the most exciting and dramatic games they had ever witnessed. A disputed penalty appeal was never going to stand in the way of their friendship.

And so it was back to Glasgow for the final, but instead of Celtic it was the West German cup-winners Borussia Dortmund. Hunt was back from injury but he still wasn't fully fit and, although he was to score in the final, there is little doubt that his injured ankle hindered more than one attempt on goal.

Liverpool had been hoping for a full-house at Hampden but the defeat of Celtic kept Scottish enthusiasm to a minimum. The rain also intervened. It poured all day across the north of England. Fans making the journey left Liverpool in mid-morning in torrents of rain, only to arrive in Glasgow in a deluge. It had poured the entire journey.

Hampden was almost waterlogged. The rain spilled down the terraces in floods forming glistening pools around the touchline but did little to dampen the enthusiasm of the travelling Liverpool supporters. In the event, a crowd of 41,000 was more than impressive considering the weather conditions.

But it was to be one of those nights when nothing went right for Liverpool. Try as they might, their name was clearly not written on the trophy. Borussia opened the scoring shortly after half-time but Liverpool kept plugging away and eventually Peter Thompson, busy and inventive as ever, carried the ball to the by-line and centred for Roger Hunt to tap home an equaliser.

Liverpool stuck to their task, harrying the Germans at every opportunity and mounting attack after attack. With just moments remaining, the ball fell tantalisingly at the feet of Roger Hunt in front of an open goal. But the Liverpool marksman hesitated and the moment was lost. But you could hardly apportion blame. Hunt was not fully fit; his ankle continued to trouble him and a sharpshooter needs to be at his best if he is to convert half-chances into goals. And as Shankly was fond of telling people, 'Yes, he misses a few. But he gets in the right place to miss them.'

After 90 minutes, the score was deadlocked at 1-1 and Liverpool had to face a further 30 minutes of football on the energy-sappping mud of Hampden. Liverpool's moment had come and gone. Opportunities were few and far between in extra time. Then, in the 107th minute, came the decisive moment. Tommy Lawrence raced to the edge of his area to meet a high ball but could only punch it out. The ball spun tantalisingly into the path of Reinhgard Libuda who lashed a 40-yard shot over the head of the stranded Lawrence to win the cup for Borussia.

For once, Shankly admitted that Liverpool had not played well. There was little point in denying it. 'We gave away two silly goals,' he told reporters as they crowded into the dressing room. 'The Germans got the breaks and that was it. That's what football is all about.'

It had been a cruel evening. But Liverpool had come a step closer to winning a European trophy and were still absorbing all the lessons. Roger Hunt was bitterly disappointed, agonising over his last-minute miss in normal time. Shankly had to console him, but within a couple of months Hunt would have cast disappointment aside and be clutching a World Cup winners medal. It would be more than adequate compensation and, proof if ever it was needed, of his goalscoring ability.

Hunt began the new season in the Charity Shield parading the World Cup and the League championship trophy around Goodison helped by Everton full back Ray Wilson and new signing Alan Ball. In all, four

Liverpool players had been in Alf Ramsey's England squad for the finals. Peter Thompson and Gordon Milne had also been there but had not been called upon to play. Ian Callaghan had played in the opening round against France but had then given way to Alan Ball.

Shankly was rightly proud of his World Cup players but it would be the last any of them would see of any silverware for a few more years. The truth was that his side was ageing though it would not become too obvious for a few more seasons.

Commitments in Europe and the FA Cup meant that Liverpool were playing well over 50 games a season. When they lifted the FA Cup in 1965, they had played 59 games. What's more, many of Shankly's players had international commitments on top of that. It was a gruelling schedule and one that was bound to take its toll. Indeed, had it not been for the implementation of a carefully thought out training scheme, such a high number of games might have brought innumerable injuries.

Call it luck, if you like, but Shankly would claim that his training system kept injuries to a minimum. During the 1965/66 season, Liverpool had used only 14 players and one of those – Bobby Graham – played only one game, the final match of the season. Another, Alf Arrowsmith, had just five outings. It was an astonishing record that will probably never be equalled.

When Shankly arrived at Anfield back in December 1959, training had been as haphazard as everything else. There was no system, no logic, no structure. From day one, Shankly instituted a methodical system with ideas he had already formulated and tested at Huddersfield and elsewhere. Much of it, he maintained, was derived from his days at Preston. 'We trained to be football players at Preston,' he always said proudly.

Shankly's main principle was that, above all else, training should be simple and enjoyable. Never over-elaborate was his guiding rule in football. He was always fond of telling those who tried to complicate the game that 'football is a simple game and should be kept simple'.

And so it was with training. In truth, this rarely consisted of more than a little light jogging, some hard exercises and plenty of five-a-side games. It was stamina-building. Little attention was paid to weight training, yet Shankly's teams could always outlast the opposition and were usually at their most dangerous in the final ten minutes when other sides were wilting. Shankly maintained that Liverpool were the fittest side in the First Division, and he was probably right.

The hard training would commence even before the season had kicked off. But it would begin gently. Players didn't return from their summer break to find themselves facing a ten-mile jog or a dozen sprints up the 100 steps of the Kop, as other clubs demanded. Instead, they would be slowly broken in to avoid injuries.

The object was to be as fit as possible for day one of the new season. Shankly always believed that those first few games of the season were crucial. They were important not just for morale but because it was just as important to secure vital points early in the season as it was at the end. Shankly also introduced the tradition of pre-season tours against top class opposition. Other clubs tended to go on post-season tours and maybe play a warm-up game before the season kicked off against some lightweight Scottish club.

Liverpool had often done the same during the post-war years, making regular trips to America after the season ended. European competition however convinced Shankly that there was more merit in playing the best German and Scandinavian clubs as part of the pre-season build-up, so that as soon as the season began Liverpool would already be at their best.

Some managers sneered at the 'soft approach' of Liverpool but Shankly was never bothered. 'Some people might think we are lazy,' he argued, 'but that's fine. What's the point of tearing players to pieces in the first few days? We never bothered with sand dunes and hills and roads; we trained on grass where football is played.'

Throughout the season, there was a simple routine to training. Players would make their own way to Anfield in the morning where they would change and prepare for the trip to Melwood. A coach would then pick them up and take them the three miles or so to the training ground. Once there, they would begin with a few jogging exercises, starting with a slow lap or two of the pitch, and building up to some sprints. The players would then do ball exercises but rarely anything that involved sitting around getting cold.

Everyone had to be involved. There were very few set-pieces; free kicks, corner kicks or penalties were rarely practised. Players were expected to be able to do that kind of thing. 'We didn't spend a lot of time working slavishly at things,' said Phil Thompson, 'certainly not set-pieces. We didn't need to. Our players were all well-educated in a football sense, so they knew how to react to various situations.'

Even before Thompson arrived, it was much the same. 'All the time

I was at Anfield, we never practised a corner or a free kick,' says Tommy Smith. And at times, it showed as Liverpool wasted free kicks and corners, never quite sure what they were going to do.

Light work would then be followed by some hard stamina-building exercises, particularly with what became known as 'the sweat box'. Boards would be set up about fifteen feet apart. Players would then be expected to kick the ball within these confines, running, dribbling, playing the ball from one end to the other. When a new player arrived, he could never survive more than a minute or so of this; in time a player would be able to keep it up for up to five minutes.

At the core of Shankly's training routine was the five-a-side game. The final hour of every training session would be devoted to five-a-side. They were called five-a-side games even though there might be as many as seven or even eight in a team.

Footballers enjoy training with the ball and there was no better way, reckoned Shankly, than in a competitive match. The five-a-side games, involving close control and a need for quick accurate passing, taught players the basic rudiments of Shankly's style. This was where the passing game was learnt. It was all summed up with his belief that in football, 'All you have to do is pass the ball to someone wearing a shirt the same colour as yours.' An uncomplicated philosophy, yet startlingly accurate.

Reuben Bennett would take the players initially giving them some light jogging exercises before breaking them into groups. They were always the same groups, systematically worked out before the season began, so that teams were finely balanced. Each group would then do a separate series of routines, perhaps weight training, sprinting, abdominal exercises, skipping or jumping. They would spend a few minutes or so performing each routine, then as soon as Bob Paisley blew his whistle they would move on to the next.

After that, they did a circuit of footballing exercises. These involved shooting practice, heading, chipping the ball, and so on. It would all be done at speed with the ball kept constantly in play. Players were always involved, always active, and hopefully, always enjoying themselves.

'In all my years at Anfield, I can honestly say,' argues Tommy Smith, 'that we never once practised a corner kick or a penalty or any other set-piece. Not once. Nobody ever believes me but it's absolutely true.'

As for the five-a-side games, everyone would be placed in teams of much the same ability and there would often be a competition. Shankly would always play for the staff against the youngsters, or occasionally, if he was feeling bullish, he might suggest a Scotland versus England game.

The staff team was usually Shankly, Bob Paisley, Joe Fagan, Reuben Bennett, and later Ronnie Moran, plus anyone else they might fancy. They liked playing the youngsters as it gave them the opportunity to get to know them, and in particular helped the young players feel they were important even if they weren't playing for the first team. Sometimes, the youngsters would be the club's own apprentices but often they might be a group down from Scotland or somewhere else on a week's trial.

Phil Thompson remembers rushing home to tell his Mum, 'The great man spoke to me today. I played against him.' But the exercise also allowed the staff to assess the apprentices on a regular basis, to discover just how quickly they were learning and to test them. On occasion, the staff would deliberately niggle them or harass them just to see how they coped.

Shankly wanted to know if they could stand up to the rigours of the game, whether they needed their confidence boosting or whether they needed bringing down a peg or two. And Shankly's team always won their five-a-side game. If they were losing, play would continue until they were ahead, whereupon Shankly would suddenly call an end to training.

Shankly entered into the spirit of those games as if nothing else mattered. Winning was all important. He would rub his hands in glee at the prospect, telling everyone what he was going to do to them. It was as if it was a Liverpool/Everton derby. And nobody other than Shankly took penalties.

Phil Thompson remembers how he used to carefully place the ball, then walk back, turning to swagger forward before crashing the ball into the back of the net. He never missed and, if the goalkeeper saved it, he would instantly claim that the keeper had moved before he kicked the ball and insist on retaking the kick. Just about every morning, whether it was wind, hail, rain or snow, he would slap a player on the back and say 'Great to be alive, boys, all you need is the green grass and a ball.'

The bootroom boys even tried three-a-side games on a pitch 45 yards long and 25 yards wide, all aimed at developing fitness and speed. At first, the players could barely survive more than five minutes each way but with practice they were soon playing a full 30 minutes.

Shankly enjoyed life with the youngsters. They were receptive, enthusiastic and took a fresh approach. Sometimes the older players grew weary, and just wanted to get their training over and done with. Shankly encouraged the youngsters as much as he could. He had done the same at Huddersfield where his first job had been to develop raw talent like Law, Wilson, McHale and Massie.

Passing on his experience to youngsters was a role he relished. He learnt their names and tried to treat them like adults and did his best to have a regular chat with each of them. The apprentices were given jobs such as scrubbing floors and looking after the kit. Shankly would be watching, just to see how well they did the job. Did they take a pride in their work?

Shankly reckoned that whatever job you had, you should do it to the best of your ability. An apprentice's future could depend on it. Phil Thompson maintains that Shankly signed more than a few average players, simply because they could scrub and clean, while some good footballers were lost because they did not put the effort into scrubbing.

The apprentices were often put on the famous Shankly diet of steak to build them up. If it wasn't steak, then it could be one of his special tea or coffee brews. 'I remember we had one rather weedy looking seventeen-year-old,' remembers Ian St John. 'Shanks was a bit concerned and wanted to build him up, so he and his staff had a meeting and decided to put him on a steak diet. Shanks had a contact with a butcher, so every week this lad went to the abattoir and collected a big parcel of steak which he would take home for his mother to cook. Every day, the lad ate steak. Six months later, this lad knocks on Shanks' door. "Come in, son," says Shanks. "You're looking better now, filling out a bit."

' "Well, sir," says the lad, "I've come to tell you I'm getting married." "Getting married, are you," replies Shankly. "Yes, I have to," answers the lad. "What do ya mean," asks Shankly. "Well sir, my girlfriend's pregnant." "Bob, Reuben, Ronnie, Joe, come here quick," shouts Shankly to his lieutenants. "We've created a monster." '

During training, Shankly's eyes were everywhere. And if he couldn't be watching then his spies – Paisley, Bennett and Fagan – were his eyes and ears. He wanted to know how each player was coping and developing. Some had to be coaxed; others had to be chastised. Ian

Callaghan, for instance, regularly had to be warned by Shankly to calm down.

'He worked so hard on a Saturday,' said Shankly, 'that I had to say to him, listen, son, you take it easy, just go through the motions.' Callaghan however also remembers that the following week when he did ease up he was promptly ordered to put his back into it a bit more. And on more than one occasion, Ian St John had to be told that the idea behind most of the exercises was to speed him up not slow him down.

Once the five-a-side games had finished, it signalled the end of training. Players would then board the team coach and return to Anfield where they would bath, change and eat. It was a tradition that had been in place for years, but it was refined by Shankly and Paisley. In part, they wanted to breed a familiarity with Anfield. Shankly wanted the players to know everyone, so that on matchdays they would not feel like strangers entering a hostile environment. At Goodison, they did everything at Bellefield and only turned up at Goodison once a fortnight. 'It made the experience of playing a game twice as nerve-racking,' remembered one Everton player. But at Anfield the players were more relaxed and were able to joke with the tea lady or those on the ground staff.

But there was a more important reason than simply getting to know Anfield and its staff. Above all, the system allowed players to cool down after their training and so avoided many injuries. Both Shankly and Paisley, who was a trained physiotherapist, were earnest believers in the cooling-down period. Just as players needed to warm up, so too, they needed to cool down. It takes anyone about 40 minutes to cool down after heavy exercise, they argued, and if they go into a bath while they are still sweating, their pores remain open and they will be more susceptible to chills and strains.

The short bus journey back to Anfield allowed just enough time for players to loosen up and cool down. Back at Anfield, they would bath and change. The result was an astonishing lack of injuries over the seasons. Year after year, Liverpool would field fewer players over a season than any other club, putting out just fourteen players in the entire 1965/66 season. It was fundamental to winning championships.

It was a tradition that was carried on until the early nineties, when Graeme Souness changed the long-established training patterns. It resulted in a glut of injuries, far more than any Liverpool manager had experienced in twenty years.

Shankly and Paisley themselves experienced a brief problem when the old gabled stand was pulled down and the new Main Stand was erected. During the course of construction, when the dressing rooms were unavailable, the players had to abandon their normal routine, meeting instead at Melwood where they would change, train and later bath. That season, there were more injuries than ever before.

Shankly and Paisley had few doubts that the cause of all the injuries was the loss of their cooling-down period on the trip back to Anfield. It is impossible to stress just how important the two men regarded this routine. It was part of their psyches and also a crucial superstition.

The journey back to Anfield also helped bond the players. It was good for morale. They would laugh, joke, get up to high jinks and generally get to know each other in a leg-pulling atmosphere.

By the late sixties, Shankly and Paisley had become a recognised double act inside Anfield. Outside Liverpool FC however, Paisley's contribution was yet to be appreciated. But it was always only a professional relationship; away from Anfield, the two men were not close. They never socialised.

Like all the best double acts, the magic only worked in public. Paisley had his family and friends; Shankly had his entourage. They kept their private lives apart. It was only at Anfield that they gelled as one.

Nevertheless, it was an astonishing double act. Paisley, the tactician; Shankly the motivator. Shankly the emotional extrovert; Paisley the quiet thinker. Shankly and Paisley were not unlike Matt Busby and Jimmy Murphy though with a role reversal. At Old Trafford, it was Busby who was the calmer, more reflective, while Murphy was the joker, the more emotional.

Paisley's abilities finally came to the fore after Shankly had gone, when he was free to indulge his own theories of the game, particularly his ability to outfox European defences at the highest level. In terms of honours, Paisley was to achieve far more than Shankly had ever done and, with a different side, perhaps one with more natural flair. Although Shankly applauded from the sidelines, there was to be an element of jealousy. Paisley had achieved the ultimate in winning the European Cup, the one trophy that eluded Shankly.

Paisley was always the first to acknowledge Shankly's influence on the club. 'His arrival was the making of Liverpool,' he wrote in his autobiography. 'It was a privilege and an honour to have been allowed to work with him.' But equally Shankly would have been the first to acknowledge Paisley's role alongside him. Of all his lieutenants, Paisley was the one he relied on. They came from similar backgrounds; they had similar modest tastes and similar ambitions for Liverpool.

Paisley's principal complaint about Shankly was that he stole his lines. He was forever grumbling that he had originated half of Shankly's jokes and stories. He'd sit and listen in amazement at times, while Shankly told the press some tale. 'That was my story,' he'd mutter to a journalist sitting nearby. 'I told him that the other day.' But it was never said in bitterness; it was always with a grin on his face. But perhaps he might have liked an acknowledgement.

Paisley understood Shankly. He was aware of his every whim, all his likes and dislikes. He knew what upset him, and what pleased him. In all their years together, by both men's admissions, they never once argued. There were moments however when Paisley was forced to bite his tongue. Shankly could be appallingly thoughtless and selfish.

Paisley remembers being in an hotel with him. They sat down together in the lounge where some elderly women were watching the television. Shankly suddenly jumped up. 'There's boxing on the other channel,' he announced and promptly walked over to the set and changed the channel. Everyone looked on in dismay. It had not occurred to Shankly to ask if anyone minded him switching channels. Paisley was so embarrassed he had to leave the room.

By contrast, Paisley knew how to cheer Shankly up when he was having a bad time with the press or the board. Paisley was able to shield his boss from the mounting problems of football management and ease many of the pressures on him.

If Paisley encountered a problem, he would try and resolve it before it ever reached Shankly. If a player was up to no good, he and Fagan would sort it out. There was much that Shankly never even heard about. Shankly didn't need to delegate. Paisley and his team quietly took on board the responsibilities themselves. It was perhaps for that reason that the succession was so smooth after Shankly's resignation.

Paisley had never wanted to be number one, and only accepted the role under duress. The two of them had been a double act. Paisley was not a front man. He never possessed the public persona of Shankly. Paisley could not stand up and woo an audience. He had none of the charisma of the Scot. Paisley would stumble over his words, often unable to articulate his thoughts in a coherent way. He might have been able to communicate on a one-to-one basis, but it was Shankly who would then take his words and articulate them in an unforgettable way.

There can be no doubt that, without Paisley, Shankly would not have been anywhere near as successful. Shankly might have been the man of vision, but it was Paisley who looked after the detail. It was Paisley who travelled the land spying on opponents, Paisley who dealt with the players on a regular basis. When the players had complaints, they came to Paisley first, not Shankly.

Shankly's managerial record prior to Liverpool was hardly sensational. He had never won an honour. The best he had ever achieved was to take Grimsby to within a whisker of promotion from the Third Division North. But at Anfield, the combination of Paisley, Liverpool's fanatical following and available funds, allowed Shankly's vision to be fulfilled.

The 1966/67 season marked something of a watershed for Shankly's team. By the high standards that Liverpool had set, it was not a good season. They wound up fifth in the league, twice losing at home near the end of the season. They had begun poorly, beaten twice in their first three games, with some of the team's England players showing signs of weariness after their long World Cup campaign. There were further disappointments.

In the FA Cup, they began steadily, eventually beating Watford 3-1 after a goalless draw at Vicarage Road. In the fourth round, they made heavy weather of beating Aston Villa at Anfield, but then drew Everton out of the hat in the fifth round.

It was to be a tumultuous tie. Tickets were like gold-dust. 65,000 were sold for the Goodison game alone and, with queues stretching halfway round Stanley Park, Liverpool decided to put up screens at Anfield to show the game live. Another 40,000 turned out, with the combined audience of 105,000 making it one of the best attended FA Cup games of all time. They may have only been plastic screens at Anfield, but it did not stop a packed Kop from singing and chanting at every Liverpool move. Unfortunately, the result did not go Liverpool's way with Alan Ball snatching the only goal of the game.

But if there was disappointment in the league and the Cup, there would be even greater weeping over the European Cup. After regaining their championship crown, Shankly was intent at another almighty crack at the European Cup. After reaching the finals of the Cup-Winners Cup, he had every hope that this time they would finally become the first British side to lift the major trophy. Instead, the campaign was to end in disaster.

Liverpool's efforts got off to a pretty dismal start as they puffed and groaned against third-rate Romanian opposition. Petrolul Ploetsi might have been in the middle of nowhere but they were still the kind of team Liverpool ought to have seen off inside an hour. But at Anfield, they struggled woefully, not even scoring until the 71st minute. Ian Callaghan added a second ten minutes before the whistle, but it had been a lacklustre performance.

Shankly put it down to early-season nerves and a packed Romanian defence but he could have no such excuses in the return leg. The conditions may not have been ideal: Liverpool's dressing room was plunged into darkness ten minutes before they were due out on the pitch and the hotel and food left much to be desired, but none of that could account for a shock 3-1 defeat. Had the away goal rule applied then, Liverpool would have been through but, in those days, it meant a replay. In Brussels, Liverpool finally managed to complete the job with a couple of first half goals from St John and Thompson.

That win set up a tie against Dutch champions Ajax. Nobody anticipated too much of a problem from Ajax, least of all Shankly, but they were to be horribly surprised as Liverpool experienced what would turn out to be their most humiliating defeat ever in European football.

An appalling fog descended on Amsterdam that night. It had been gloomy all day in the city but as dusk fell, smog drifted in from the North Sea. You could barely make out the other side of the pitch. From one goal, it was impossible to see the other. In fact, it was nearly impossible to see the halfway line. Amsterdam Airport was closed.

Shankly pleaded with match officials to call the game off. Indeed, by his reckoning, the game was sure to be postponed. The Italian referee seemed to agree. 'If we can see from goal to goal, okay,' he told them. 'If not, then the game is off.' But then the UEFA observer Leo Horne intervened, offering a different interpretation.

'In Holland,' he told them, 'we only need to be able to see the goal from the halfway line.' They all strolled out on to the pitch. Everyone agreed that you could not see one goal from the other, but it was possible to see one goal, albeit only just, from the halfway line. That was it, the game was on. In the event, it turned out to be a farce.

Shankly and his entourage, sitting close to the halfway line in a vast crowd of 64,000, saw little of the action. Indeed, visibility was so poor that at one stage Shankly wandered on to the pitch to talk to the players, and wasn't spotted by referee or linesmen. Liverpool were

soon trailing by two goals with Shankly urging his side to close them
down in the hope of going to Anfield with only a two-goal deficit. As
he stood in the fog that night, the only thing he could see clearly were
his dreams of lifting the European Cup fast disappearing.

It was easy to use the fog as an excuse. The truth was that Liverpool
were in decline, while Ajax were an outstanding team in the making,
guided by the inspirational floppy-haired nineteen-year-old Johann
Cruyff. Ajax would not win the European Cup that year but they
would soon be dominating world football. Cruyff, Suurbier, Nuninga,
De Wolf, and company were set to become household names.

Liverpool eventually lost 5-1 with Chris Lawler providing some relief, and the faintest of hope, with a late goal that nobody saw. It was a
depressing result, one that would rankle for years with Shankly, causing
him much soul-searching over the next few months. But for the moment, he was showing few fears or doubts about his side's ability. As far
as his public outbursts were concerned, he was blaming the fog and he
remained confident that at Anfield Liverpool could retrieve the deficit.

Shankly slammed Ajax, calling them negative and defensive, remarks
that did not go down well with the Dutch press who would remind him
of his comments many times over the next ten years. It did him little
justice. When an English journalist suggested to him that perhaps he
had underestimated the Dutch, Shankly was furious, rounding on the
reporter claiming that no amount of watching a team can tell you how
they will play against you. He was clearly rattled by the suggestion.
Ajax had not been watched enough. When Shankly went to see them,
they had given their worst display in seasons and much of Liverpool's
preparation was based on that performance.

It was remarkable that over the next few days Shankly managed to
convince the population of Liverpool, and it seemed most of the national press, that a 5-0 win for Liverpool in the return leg was far from
impossible.

Indeed, so convinced were Liverpool supporters that they were about
to see the biggest turnaround in the history of European football that
they came in their droves to Anfield. Almost 54,000 were shoehorned
into the ground to witness the impossible. It was Shankly at his optimistic best, dropping quotes to journalists, urging his players on, and
convincing them that they were supermen. Shankly conned them all
and, as the match kicked off, there was anticipation of a huge Liverpool win. But of course it was never to be.

Liverpool had an early goal disallowed in the second half which might have swung the game in their favour. Then Johann Cruyff put Ajax ahead just after half-time and there was no coming back from that chasm of deficit. Hunt levelled the score, only for Cruyff to strike yet again. Hunt equalised for a second time with just four minutes remaining and the final whistle came as something of a relief to a battle-weary Liverpool side. However, in his autobiography, Shankly was still arguing that Liverpool should have won that night. 'We threw everything to the winds,' he wrote, 'and they were lucky.'

15 All Change at Watford

FTER THEIR DEVASTATING DEFEAT by Ajax and a comparatively poor season in the league and Cup, Liverpool were being written off as a major force in English soccer. They had enjoyed their time and done Shankly proud, but now the mantle of success had passed on. Manchester United had won the league that season and in the following season would become the first English club to lift the European Cup. The spotlight was turning away from Merseyside towards Manchester.

Liverpool's humiliation in Europe had been further put into perspective by Glasgow Celtic who had become the first British club to win the European Cup. The side that Liverpool had narrowly beaten in the previous year's European Cup-Winners Cup semi-final, had subsequently beaten Inter Milan in the Lisbon final. Shankly was delighted for them, especially for his old friend Jock Stein. 'Jock,' he told him immediately after the game had ended, 'you're immortal now.' But Shankly had wanted to be the first manager to lead a British side to a European cup triumph. His dream had been stolen from him.

Instead, Shankly was having to reappraise his side, and begin the search for new players, who could continue the success he had started. By the summer of 1967, he had reluctantly concluded that the side that had won promotion, the league and the FA Cup was coming to its natural end. Many of those players were now past their peak.

Shankly always reckoned a player was at his best between the ages of 25 and 28. Gordon Milne was already 30, Ron Yeats was almost 30 while Ian St John, Gerry Byrne and Roger Hunt were all 29. Changes were necessary, but it wasn't easy for Shankly. He was a loyal man, always the first to stand by someone in a difficult time. He might have looked and sounded like a tough guy with his James Cagney swagger, but the private Shankly was very different.

Joe Mercer summed Shankly up best when he claimed that his image was really 'a myth in so many ways. They say he's tough, he's hard, he's ruthless. Rubbish, he's got a heart of gold, he loves the game, he loves his fans, he loves his players. He's like an old Collie dog, he doesn't like hurting his sheep. He'll drive them. Certainly, but bite them, never.' Shankly may have looked tough but he wasn't. Older hands like Yeats and St John had realised that. It was the younger players who lived in awe and fear of him.

And when it came to dropping players, who had served him so loyally over the years since his arrival at Anfield, it was difficult. Some continued to wear the Liverpool shirt when a more ruthless man might have taken it away from them; others still hung around the club, contributing wherever they could. Bob Paisley was perfectly positioned to spot Shankly's reluctance to upset any of his long-serving players. 'If Bill had one failing,' he claimed, 'it was the fact that he did not like to upset players that had done so well for him. He was a softie at heart.'

Though this reluctance may have been a failing when it came to moving a player on, it was a strength when a player was out of form. Shankly would stand by them, rarely dropping a player, especially one who had proved himself over the years. 'We never drop players here,' he used to say, 'we just shift things round a bit.' It was what he labelled 'the squad system'.

That kind of loyalty also stretched to the way his sides played. He called on all his teams to help each other out by running back into defence when necessary. Any player failing to lend a hand when a hurricane was hitting them would swiftly be given a piece of Shankly's mind. 'Steve, son,' he once snapped at Steve Heighway after the winger had failed to back up full back Alec Lindsay when he was under constant pressure, 'if your next door neighbour's house caught fire, what would you do?' There was only one answer to that.

But inevitably players do age and new talent has to be found. There had been several signings since the arrival of Geoff Strong from Arsenal in November 1964 but none of them had made any impact. They were all bargain basement signings, bought as cover more than anything. Only full back Peter Wall had made more than a handful of appearances. The others all disappeared without trace. It showed, at least, that Shankly was fallible and did not always get it right.

Throughout 1967, the search was on for new players. One player he really took a fancy to was Howard Kendall, the Preston half back.

Liverpool put in a bid but with Preston having already sold a couple of jewels to Liverpool in the shape of Peter Thompson and Gordon Milne, the Preston directors said 'no, not a third'. Kendall wound up at Everton, leaving Shankly furious and bitterly disappointed.

Instead, he was forced to look elsewhere and in February 1967 he dipped into the market paying Blackpool £65,000 for a young half back by the name of Emlyn Hughes. Shankly and his staff had watched Hughes for some months and were convinced that he was an England player in the making.

Shankly had spotted the potential in Hughes the day he made his debut for Blackpool at Blackburn in an end-of-season match at Ewood Park. After the game, he meandered up to the Blackpool directors and immediately offered £25,000 for the teenager. But the directors hesitated. A couple of months later, they sold their other star, Alan Ball, and any chance of them selling Hughes disappeared for the moment. But a year later, as Blackpool hovered in the relegation zone, clearly destined for the Second Division, the Blackpool directors decided to cash in one of their assets. 'You can have him,' they told Shankly, 'but he'll cost you £65,000.'

Shankly had no misgivings. It was a huge fee, larger than any Liverpool had ever paid out, especially for a nineteen-year-old. Yet by March he was in the first team. Shankly revelled in Hughes' attitude: it was infectious, if not a little irksome at times. Hughes, the son of a rugby league international, was enthusiastic, confident and overwhelmingly committed.

Shankly had never been so certain of a player's future. As he returned from Blackpool with his prize possession, he was stopped by the police. 'Do you know who you are talking to?' he warned the officer as he produced his notebook. 'It's Mr Shankly, isn't it,' asked the policeman. 'No, not me,' snapped Shankly. 'Him,' he said pointing to Hughes. 'Don't you recognise him? That man there is the future captain of England.' Hughes curled up in embarrassment.

Shankly had a way with young players. He was never one to discourage them or be authoritarian, even when they did not play for Liverpool. Derek Wynne, now director of the Institute for Popular Culture at Manchester Metropolitan University, but then a young apprentice on Port Vale's books, had a potentially embarrassing encounter with Shankly. Liverpool were the visitors to Port Vale for an FA Cup fourth round replay. The two sides had drawn 0-0 at Anfield a few days previously and the appearance of Liverpool, then heading for the title, attracted a near-record crowd to Vale Park.

Wynne's job as an apprentice that evening was to look after the visitors' dressing room. He was handed the key to their room and, as usual, told to turn on the taps of the enormous communal bath at half-time. The taps were regulated, so that after fifty minutes the water would be one inch from the top. As the Liverpool players trooped out of the dressing room at the interval he duly turned on the taps and locked the door behind him.

Wynne was due to return and unlock the dressing room about five minutes before the game ended. But in the 79th minute, Vale scored a dramatic equaliser and in the tense final moments all thoughts of turning off bath taps were forgotten. At full time, the two teams were still level and the game went into extra time. Wynne was now so carried away watching his colleagues in their desperate bid to beat Liverpool that he had forgotten all about his duties.

Unfortunately, Liverpool scored their usual late winner in extra time and Port Vale had lost. Wynne wandered disconsolately into the home dressing room to commiserate with his fellow players, without giving a thought to the bath. After a few minutes, there came a shouting and screaming. 'Where's Lightning, where's bloody Lightning? He's got the key to the dressing room.'

Wynne, who answered to the nickname of Lightning, then realised that he had the key to the dressing room. In the corridor outside, the Liverpool players were standing, shivering and complaining, waiting to get in. A red-faced Wynne appeared with the key and opened the door. But as he did so, he suddenly remembered the bath taps. The entire dressing room was flooded, twenty odd shoes were floating around, making their way lazily past sodden socks and underpants. Goalkeeper Tommy Lawrence was furious, screaming that his new crocodile shoes were ruined. Other players went round picking their soaking wet socks off the floor, muttering about crap clubs and crap grounds.

Poor Wynne was the butt of their humour as they cursed him. Lawrence was particularly upset about his expensive, new, shoes. Then in came Shankly to examine the damage. A terrified Wynne feared the worst. But instead Shankly put his arm around him. 'Ne'er mind laddie,' he said laughing at Lawrence. 'Worse things happen at sea.'

'He could so easily have destroyed me,' says Wynne today, 'but instead he saved me from the likes of Tommy Lawrence and Ron Yeats who looked ready to lynch me there and then.'

Another youngster, George Scott, was one of Shankly's first signings at Anfield. He was an Aberdonian who joined the club as a fifteen-year-old apprentice. Five years later, he had still not made any appearances and Shankly decided to offload him, back to Aberdeen. Scott was distraught and did not want to go. He went to see the manager. Shankly put an arm around him. 'Son, you're the twelfth best player in the world,' said Shankly. 'What do you mean boss?' asked Scott. 'Well, son,' explained Shankly. 'There's the Liverpool first team, then you, because you are the leading scorer in the reserves.' Scott walked away as tall and as proud as could be.

But it was just as difficult to relinquish his hold over the older players as it was to unearth and encourage youngsters. In May 1967, Blackpool offered £30,000 for Gordon Milne. The half back he had known since he was born was now 30. Shankly perhaps felt that he owed Blackpool one after having pinched Emlyn Hughes from them. £30,000 was a good fee, twice what they had paid for Milne, and half what they had paid for Hughes. A deal was struck.

During the summer of 1967, Shankly was to make two other signings; the second was perhaps his finest signing ever. The first was Tony Hateley, the tall, formidable Chelsea striker. At his previous club Aston Villa, Hateley had struck 68 goals in 127 outings. Hateley had had just one season at Chelsea but he never really settled and was now looking for a move back north. Shankly pounced, writing out a cheque for £96,000, which made Hateley the most expensive player in Liverpool's history. Shankly had signed him for his ability to score goals with his head. With Thompson and Callaghan able to fire in the crosses, Shankly reckoned Hateley would either score a bagful of goals for himself or lay them off for Roger Hunt. He began well, hitting a hat-trick in only his third game as Liverpool thrashed Newcastle 6-0 at Anfield.

The omens looked promising and the tabloids nicknamed Liverpool the H Bomb team but Hateley always seemed to be carrying an injury. Even though he scored 16 league goals, Shankly decided to let him go at the end of the season and in September 1968 Coventry stepped in with an £80,000 bid. Liverpool had changed their style slightly to accommodate Hateley, knocking long balls into the box, instead of persisting with their usual passing game. But if Hateley was less than successful, his other close-season signing would become a central cog in the club's success over the next 20 years.

Geoff Twentyman had left Anfield shortly before Shankly's arrival.

He had been with the club since December 1953, a £10,000 signing from Carlisle United. Shankly had known him at Carlisle and indeed the Twentymans had moved into the Shanklys' old house when he left the club. During the intervening years, Twentyman had gone on to Ballymena as player/manager before returning to Carlisle. He had then gone on to be player/manager at Morecambe, before taking over as manager at Penrith. Shankly was looking for a chief scout and the name of Twentyman cropped up.

'I got a call from him, right out of the blue,' says Twentyman. 'Would I come and work with him, be his chief scout. I jumped at the chance of a return to Anfield.' Over the next decade or so, Twentyman's eye for talent would be crucial to the signing of players such as Steve Heighway, Kevin Keegan, John Toshack, Jimmy Case, David Fairclough and many more. The first player he recommended to Shankly was Francis Lee, then playing with Bolton Wanderers.

'I recommended him to Bill in my first week at the club. I'd seen him play and thought, here's a great one for the future. Bill tried to sign him but nothing transpired. A couple of months later, he signed for Manchester City. What a signing he would have been.' With Francis Lee in their side, City went on to win the league championship that season.

Shankly trusted Twentyman implicitly. He supplied him with just a few simple instructions. Not only did each player have to possess obvious talent, but he wanted Twentyman to investigate every aspect of the player's life. 'Shankly wanted, above all, to know about the lad's private life, what he was like, did he go out drinking every night, what his home background was, and so on,' says Twentyman. 'He wanted to know if the lad had the heart to play for Liverpool. Shankly wanted players who loved the game and were passionate about it. He liked players with character and commitment.'

Shankly didn't want players who would crack under pressure or were simply in it for the money. They had to be committed to playing for Liverpool. 'Heart' was the word Shankly was fond of using. Shankly would occasionally go with Twentyman to see a player but as often as not he trusted his judgement although in later years Paisley proved to be even more trustworthy.

'Paisley never even saw Ian Rush play before we signed him,' says Twentyman. But Shankly liked to see a player if he could. 'We saw one player once. After about ten minutes, the player in question took a bit of a knock and rolled around like an actor. "That's enough for me," says Shankly, and we left. He just wasn't interested in that kind of a player. The lad had talent but Shankly spotted something was missing.'

Twentyman was also told to scour the lower divisions for potential recruits. 'Concentrate on the third and fourth divisions,' Shankly told him. 'We need players for the future as well as for now. Once we've got them, we can put them in the reserves and they can learn our ways there.'

Twentyman immediately began to set up a network of scouts around the country. By the end of the season, the system was paying dividends. Within a year, he had recruited Ray Clemence, Alec Lindsay and Larry Lloyd from the lower divisions. All three would go on to play for England as well as being vital components in Shankly's new Liverpool.

Ray Clemence was a young goalkeeper with Scunthorpe. He fitted the bill perfectly. A couple of years earlier, Shankly had recruited John Ogston from Aberdeen for £10,000 but, with Tommy Lawrence at his peak, Ogston made only one appearance. Ogston was never going to be a successor to Lawrence; he was only ever a cover goalkeeper. But with Lawrence getting older, it was becoming crucial to find a goalkeeper for the future. Clemence was young, had made a number of appearances with Scunthorpe and was cheap. In June 1967, he signed for Liverpool and went to learn his trade in the reserves, but it would be some years before he made his debut.

In March 1969, Alec Lindsay arrived from Bury, a fair-haired, craggy-looking half back for £67,000. He went straight into the reserves where he was converted into a full back but it would not be until the following season that he established himself in the first team.

When Shankly first saw him playing, he began to have doubts about him. But then Paisley suggested trying him at left back. Lindsay was a revelation. It wasn't long before Shankly was telling everyone that he had converted him into a left back. A month after signing Lindsay, Shankly recruited another bargain basement man, Larry Lloyd, who came from Bristol Rovers for £50,000. Lloyd was the perfect successor to Yeats: tall, powerful, the kind of defender who liked to organise those around him.

With Emlyn Hughes and Tony Hateley added quickly to the first team, Liverpool put up a spirited challenge for the title but in the end it rested between the two Manchester clubs with City sneaking the honour by two points. Liverpool finished third, three points behind the new champions.

In the FA Cup, Liverpool reached the quarter finals but made heavy weather of their progress. They drew 0-0 at Bournemouth in the third round, before winning 4-1 at Anfield, then drew 0-0 at Walsall before trouncing them 5-2 in the replay. In the fifth round, they were away at Tottenham, this time drawing 1-1 and winning the replay 2-1. In the sixth round, they were again on the move, travelling to West Bromwich Albion, where they drew 0-0. The replay at Anfield was also drawn and, in the second replay at Maine Road, Liverpool went down 2-1. They had played nine games in the Cup.

For the fourth year running, Liverpool were in Europe, though for the first time they found themselves in the Fairs Cup (later to be called the UEFA Cup). They opened with a tie against Sweden's Malmo, winning 2-0 in Sweden and 2-1 at Anfield. In the next round, they played the top German side TSV München and trounced them 8-0 at Anfield. The *Guardian*'s football writer was ecstatic. 'Not for a long time can any team have bestowed less pity on outclassed oponents,' he wrote, adding that no team in the world would have lived with Liverpool in that kind of form. In the second leg, Liverpool sprinted into an early lead, only to ease up and eventually lose 2-1.

In the third round, in late November, they visited Hungary, and were a trifle fortunate to escape with just a one-goal deficit. Few doubted that it was recoverable at Anfield. Unfortunately, Liverpool had miscalculated: Ferencvaros were an outstanding side and when they went a goal ahead in the 19th minute it left Liverpool searching for three goals. It was an impossible task. Ferencvaros mastered the icy, snowy conditions and wound up 1-0 winners, the first time Liverpool had been beaten at Anfield in European competition. The Hungarians went on to reach the final where they lost over two legs to Leeds United.

By the beginning of the 1968/69 season it was apparent to all that further recruits were needed. The first nine games of the season produced only 13 goals, although the results were far from disastrous. Ian St John and Roger Hunt were no longer the sharpshooters of the early sixties, while Tony Hateley, the man drafted in to provide an extra dimension, had forced too many changes on their usual style of play. Action was needed.

Shankly decided to revert to the old passing game and cut his losses with Hateley. Coventry City stepped in with an £80,000 offer and Hateley was on his way to Highfield Road. Shankly had already spotted the man he wanted as his replacement. He was Alun Evans, the promising Wolves youngster, who was promptly recruited for £100,000, a record-breaking fee for a teenager.

The Evans signing put Liverpool firmly at the head of the queue when it came to writing out cheques. The days when they hesitated over paying £30,000 for Jack Charlton were long-gone. They were now among the league's big spenders.

Sadly, Evans would never quite fulfil his potential, his confidence destroyed by a badly scarred face from a brawl in a Midlands' night club and his fitness interrupted by a severe cartilage problem. The incident in the night club 'possibly changed Alun's whole life,' claimed a sad Shankly years later.

Liverpool fans would see only a few snatches of his promise but, as soon as he stepped into the team, goals arrived – four in his first game, six in his next at Wolves, including two from Evans himself, and another four in his third outing as Liverpool swept to the top of the table. Although he was not always among the goals himself, he ended his first campaign in Liverpool colours with seven in 33 appearances.

Evans brought a whiff of youthful pace to the attack, always looking to carry the ball forward with his agile running. But he would always be remembered for the night he single-handedly destroyed Bayern Munich with as exciting a hat-trick as Anfield has ever seen. It was a glimpse of the reason Shankly had made him the most expensive youngster in football.

The season also marked the beginning of the end for Roger Hunt. Hunt had been ever-present since the season kicked off, but in 38 games he had managed only thirteen goals. Against Leicester City in a cup replay, Shankly took the momentous decision to pull Hunt off and send Bobby Graham on in his place. It was a time when substitutions were new to the game and most replacements were for injury reasons rather than tactical purposes. Liverpool had never really discussed tactical substitutions and, when Hunt was called off he was furious, convinced that he was being made a scapegoat.

As he left the pitch, he tore off his red shirt and hurled it at the dugout. At half-time, there was a furious row between Hunt and Shankly. Hunt decided to make his own way home. The rift was temporarily healed but the writing was on the wall. Hunt soon returned to the first team but in a couple of weeks was being substituted again, this time against Stoke City. It would not be long before he was cast aside altogether.

Apart from Alun Evans who had joined the club a few weeks into the new season, there were no other major signings. After their jittery opening, Liverpool were soon up among the leaders. The title race was always between two sides – Liverpool and Leeds. After five years of hovering among the favourites, Don Revie's side finally scaled the heights, clinching the title, a clear six points ahead of Liverpool in second spot with Everton five points behind them. United and City were nowhere – the mantle was about to switch to Merseyside again.

Sadly, there was no compensation for Liverpool in any other competitions. In Europe, they went out at the first hurdle, losing to Atletic Bilbao on the toss of a coin, while in the FA Cup they reached the fifth round before succumbing to Leicester City by a single goal in a replay at Anfield.

You would have put money on Liverpool reaching Wembley that season but it was not to be. There was nothing in the League Cup either, a competition scorned by Shankly. He never showed much interest in it and, in all his years, Liverpool never managed to progress beyond the fifth round. Usually, they were dismissed early on, a relief to Shankly who was keener to concentrate on the league or Europe. The League Cup was a diversion, neither lucrative nor necessary, its only compensation was that it allowed you to blood a few youngsters.

One youngster, who was blooded towards the end of the season as league honours disappeared over the horizon, was Brian Hall. Although he was born in Scotland, Hall had spent all his life in Lancashire. As a youngster, he'd had trials with a number of local clubs but none had taken up their options. Hall had drifted off to University but had not escaped Geoff Twentyman's highly efficient scouting net. Hall, like so many others would learn his trade in the reserves. This was the testing ground.

Even the occasional newly signed star would be obliged to spend some time in Central League football, discovering the 'Liverpool way'. Pass the ball, push forward, that was the Liverpool style. It didn't always come naturally to players and needed to be learnt. Joe Fagan spent most time with the reserves, teaching them the rudiments.

Even Brian Hall would have to spend the best part of three seasons in reserve football before he finally settled into the first team. Others such as Ted McDougall had their chance but, for one reason or another, never grasped it. In the case of McDougall, there was a lengthy queue of outstanding strikers ahead of him and McDougall was offloaded to York City for £5,500. Years later, he cost Manchester United £200,000.

The 1969/70 season was to be a watershed for Shankly's Liverpool. Although the writing had been on the wall for some time, it was read with some reluctance. By 1970, it was too clear for anyone to overlook. Liverpool began the season well; Shankly was in fine spirits as they won seven of their first nine matches, drawing the other two. But then their early enthusiasm began to wane. Perhaps it was the heavy pitches, perhaps it was just too much football. There was also a lack of motivation.

Most of the players had enjoyed unlimited success. League championships, an FA Cup triumph, a European final and international honours. They had done it all. But now they had lost their appetite. Whatever it was, ageing players like Lawrence, Yeats, Strong, St John and Hunt were about to find their places under threat.

Shankly used to say that his team picked itself. This was largely true. For seven years or so, it had barely changed, the occasional addition here, the odd tactical change there. The team had grown together, reaching full maturity in the mid-sixties but now they were in decline. Shankly, as ever, remained loyal but when Liverpool went down to an embarrassing defeat at Second Division Watford in the sixth round of the FA Cup, the time had finally come for wholesale changes.

'That was the crucial game,' wrote Shankly years later. 'After Watford, I knew I had to do my job and change my team ... It had to be done and if I didn't do it I was shirking my obligations. I could see that some of the players were going a bit. When you have had success it can be a difficult job to motivate yourself ... it was obvious that, while some players had an appetite for success, others hadn't and might do better elsewhere.'

Defeat was to herald the Night of the Long Knives. Shankly talked it over with Bob Paisley the following morning as the two sat slumped in the bootroom. It was easy to argue that Tommy Smith and Peter Thompson had been absent through injury and that their presence might have meant a different result. But that was the simple way out. Deep-down, the two men knew that decisions had to be made.

A week later, when Shankly named his eleven for a league encounter with Derby County at Anfield, the side was barely recognisable. Out went household names, Tommy Lawrence, Ron Yeats and Ian St John and in came a couple of young reserves Ray Clemence and Doug Livermore. Peter Thompson and Tommy Smith who had both missed the Watford game returned. Roger Hunt who was already being overlooked before the Watford disaster continued to miss out.

The side that lined up against Derby was significantly different. When Shankly pinned the team sheet on the noticeboard, it brought gasps. Clemence, Lawler, Wall, Strong, Smith, Hughes, Callaghan, Thompson, Evans, Livermore and Graham were the men charged with revitalising Liverpool.

Not surprisingly, the changes did not go down well with everyone. Although star names disappeared, the fact was that there had already been changes for the Watford game. Neither Thompson nor Smith had played with youngsters Wall, Ross and Graham drafted into the lineup. It was hardly surprising that Liverpool lost. A week later against Derby County, they were beaten again. Now was the time to hold your nerve. But predictably Shankly got a little nervous and back came Ron Yeats. For others, there was no reprise. The Watford game was to more or less spell the end of Ian St John's career at Anfield. He would remain a while longer but would play only two more games for the club. Tommy Lawrence played just once more, while Roger Hunt never pulled on a first-team shirt again. Ron Yeats played on for another season, gradually giving way to Larry Lloyd.

All season, Shankly had his scouting staff on red alert looking for new recruits. Top of his list was Peter Osgood, the mercurial Chelsea striker. In April 1969, Shankly finally decided to take the plunge offering the London club £100,000. Chelsea turned him down but Shankly was not to be denied. Nine months later, he returned to the chase having persuaded his directors to go to £150,000. It was a fee that would have broken a few records.

One or two directors quibbled at paying out so much, reminded how the Kop had dubbed him 'Osgood's no good'. But Shankly was determined. Unfortunately, Chelsea were equally determined to hold on to their man and politely turned Shankly down. After that, Shankly lost interest, reluctant to join an auction at silly prices. Osgood eventually wound up at Southampton a few years later for a massive £275,000.

Liverpool ended the 1969/70 season in fifth spot, fifteen points adrift of champions Everton, without ever putting up a serious challenge. It was another disheartening season in Europe as well, with Liverpool dismissed from the Fairs Cup in the second round by Portugal's Vitoria Setubal, after having put a record 14 goals past Dundalk in the opening round. At the end of the season, Shankly reflected on the number of players he had been forced to draft in. Twenty-three men had pulled on the colours that year, far more than had been usual during his period at Anfield. It spoke volumes. If he thought that his problems were over, he would be wrong. But at least they were part of the way to being solved.

The new season offered little respite. Shankly spent the summer carefully combing the market. In April 1970, he signed Jack Whitham, a regular goalscorer with Sheffield Wednesday who unfortunately spent much of his time at Hillsborough sidelined through injury. Yet his 31 goals in 71 league games suggested some promise and at £57,000 he was worth the risk. In the event, it never worked out. Injuries continued to dog him and he was never given an extended run.

Although Shankly would long be remembered for his inspired signings, there were just as many failures. Sammy Reid, Kevin Lewis, Jim Furnell, Phil Chisnall, John Ogston, Stuart Mason, Peter Wall, Dave Wilson, Tony Hateley, Jack Whitham, Trevor Storton, Frank Lane and Alan Waddle – all Shankly signings but none of them setting Merseyside alight. They would soon be forgotten. Shankly, like all managers, had his fair share of bad luck and misjudgements in the market.

But there would be two other important newcomers that season who would rank among his most astute acquisitions. The first was Steve Heighway, a university student, signed initially on amateur terms from Skelmersdale United early in 1970. Heighway was a winger, fast as a whippet and a flankman as much in the mould of Peter Thompson as it was possible to be. Heighway would soon burst on to the scene to become one of the most talked-about players of the season. The other recruit, signed in November 1970 from Cardiff City for a huge £110,000, was John Toshack. Like Hateley, Toshack was a striker and one of the best headers of a ball in the game. Both newcomers were to be vital additions to the side which was on the point of blossoming. Only one more recruit was now necessary. By the beginning of the following season, he would be in place.

Liverpool's progress in the league during the 1970/71 season was hampered by injury, readjustment and a glut of fixtures. Five draws in their opening seven fixtures set the trend. By the end of the season, they had drawn an astonishing ten games at Anfield and seven away and were never serious title challengers. They again ended the season in fifth spot with Arsenal nicking the title on a tense evening at White

Hart Lane. A few days later, the Gunners faced Liverpool at Wembley in the FA Cup final.

Liverpool were back in Europe for the seventh successive season under Bill Shankly. After their initial successes, the last few years had brought little but disappointment. The club seemed to have lost its way as it criss-crossed the continent. But in 1971, they rediscovered their old habits and went on to reach the semi-finals with some memorable performances.

In the opening tie, they defeated Ferencvaros, the Hungarians who had dumped them out of Europe a few seasons earlier. In the next round they faced another East European side, the Romanians Dynamo Bucharest. A 3-0 win at Anfield was enough to see them through to a third round tie with Hibernian.

At Easter Road, Liverpool won 1-0, thanks mainly to some old-fashioned wing play from Steve Heighway. At Anfield, the young Heighway came of age as he strode past defenders to score Liverpool's first. He was the toast of Merseyside as Liverpool stormed through to the quarter finals and a tie with Bayern Munich.

The clash with Bayern Munich was to be a battle of two emerging giants. Bayern with the likes of Beckenbauer, Maier, Schwarzenbeck, Breitner, Hoeness and Müller in their side would soon march on to become European champions as well as provide West Germany with the bulk of their World Cup-winning side. But on a warm spring evening at Anfield, Liverpool totally overpowered them with Alun Evans crowning an outstanding performance with three goals. Time and again, he swept downfield firing shot after shot at the German goal, to leave the Germans bewildered. The second leg was drawn one-apiece, and Liverpool were into the semi-finals.

Unfortunately, their opponents turned out to be Leeds United. Revie's side were just about the most experienced in the Football League, challenging for the title and boasting international class in every position. They proved too much for the inexperienced Liverpool, even at Anfield where Billy Bremner scored the only goal of the tie. Liverpool could take some credit for the goalless draw at Elland Road, but it only underlined yet again their lack of firepower upfront.

Since Ron Yeats had lifted the FA Cup in 1965, Liverpool had managed to reach the quarter finals on a couple of occasions but had never progressed any further. The curse of the Cup seemed to have returned but in 1971 they at last reached a second Wembley final under Bill Shankly.

They began the campaign by beating Aldershot 1-0 at Anfield and followed that with a comfortable 3-0 win over Swansea, again at Anfield. In the fifth round, they were drawn at home again and notched a third cup win, beating Southampton 1-0. Luck was with them again in the quarter finals when the draw pitted them against Tottenham, yet again at home. But after a goalless draw, it seemed that Liverpool's good luck was perhaps turning. But instead they journeyed to Tottenham and came away with a 1-0 victory to set up a semi-final against Everton at Old Trafford.

The neighbouring clubs had met once before in a semi-final, in 1950, when Liverpool won 2-0 at Maine Road, thanks primarily to a Bob Paisley goal. Liverpool then went on to face Arsenal in the final where they lost. In 1971, the outcome was to be almost identical. Prior to the game, Shankly was telling everyone, 'There is no way Liverpool can lose this match.' And he was right. At Old Trafford, Liverpool edged their neighbours aside, winning 2-1 and finding themselves on the road to Wembley to face Arsenal. In the week of the final, Arsenal clinched the championship and travelled the short distance across north London hopeful of a League and Cup double.

Shankly's new young side was at last taking shape. In goal, Ray Clemence was a fine prospect, and already an England Under-23 international who was knocking on the door for full England honours. Chris Lawler still held on to the right berth in defence, while Alec Lindsay had slotted in alongside him. Tommy Smith was still there, as forceful as ever and still only 26-years-old, with Larry Lloyd firmly established at centre half and described in one paper as 'one of the discoveries of the season'.

Emlyn Hughes had by then justified Shankly's prediction and become an England regular. Ian Callaghan was still around although he had missed a large part of the season through injury. Added to the attack were new boys John Toshack, Steve Heighway, and Brian Hall. Alun Evans was also named, the scorer of one of the semi-final goals. Only Lawler, Smith and Callaghan had played in the 1965 final, although a fourth, Peter Thompson, would come on as a substitute against Arsenal.

If the search for tickets in 1965 had been reckless, it was to be desperate in 1971. But when it came to handing out the tickets, you could always rely on Shankly being at his most generous. One Kopite remembers the occasion well. 'I'd got my ticket direct from Shankly because my wife worked with his daughter Jeanette and they were good friends,' recalls Brian Porter. 'I'd met him a few times and he knew I stood on the Kop and went everywhere to support the team. Well, the week of the Cup Final there was a photograph of some bloke in the *Liverpool Echo* who had just come out of prison. He'd served a very long sentence and when asked what he wanted to do most of all now that he was free had replied, "I want to go and see Liverpool at Wembley." But of course he didn't have a ticket.

'A couple of days later the same guy is in the *Echo* again and he's got a ticket. The ticket had arrived at the *Echo* from a mystery source with the message to pass it on to him. And there he was holding it up. Well, when I looked at the photo, I could see all the details on the ticket because the bloke was holding it up to his face and it was quite large. I got the shock of my life because it was the seat next to me. Now given that I had got my ticket directly from Shankly, you don't have to be a detective to work out where this bloke's ticket had come from.' Of course, nothing was ever admitted. But that was the Shankly style, one ticket quietly handed out here to a deserving cause, one ticket handed out there.

Liverpool writer Stan Hey was another who encountered the generosity of Shankly. 'I was working in a garage at the time in Derby Lane in Old Swan and the week of the Cup Final Shankly brought his car in for a wash and servicing. We were in awe of him and did a wonderful job on the car, washing and polishing it all up. It was an old brown Ford Corsair. Shankly came back later that day to collect the car and there it was, all gleaming. He was really pleased.

' "Well I suppose you'll all be going to the Cup Final," he says. "No," we replied, "we haven't got any tickets," and we carried on talking about Liverpool with him. Then off he goes. Two hours later, he's back and we thought, "Oh heck there's something wrong with the car." But no, he comes over and takes a wad of tickets out of his pocket and gives us one each. We were astonished. He had taken all that trouble to come back with tickets and gave them to us when just about everyone in Liverpool was desperate for a ticket.'

It was typical of Shankly. He would always recognise genuine Liverpool fans and his generosity towards them knew no bounds. 'Liverpool Football Club is about them,' he argued. 'They are the most knowledgeable crowd in the world, also the fairest.' In his years, the fans would clamour at his door, asking for tickets, an autograph or just wanting to shake his hand. He never complained although at times it tested Nessie's patience.

Shankly's only compromise was to pave over the front garden, so that he didn't have to keep replanting the patches on the lawn made bare by fans. 'Football was their life,' he once told Sue Lawley. 'They were more important than me because they were the ones who paid the money.' It was not a view common in football management in the nineties.

On Cup final day, TV's Kenneth Wolstenholme, in tipping Liverpool, praised Shankly on his 'bold decision to bring in young untried players'. Jimmy Hill was equally impressed by the new Liverpool noting, 'they had matured almost out of recognition'. Shankly was, as ever, prone to overstatement. 'We've got to Wembley with a team of boys. We've a pool of players that will last for ten years. And we've not come just for the fun – we've come to win the FA Cup.'

He was right on one count. But win it they did not. Liverpool with all their youngsters put up a spirited showing and, when Steve Heighway flew down the wing in the first minute of extra time to slot home the game's first goal, it looked odds-on a Liverpool victory.

Unfortunately they had not accounted for one of the season's other 'discoveries' – Charlie George – whose sprint down the left and fierce shot took the cup to Highbury. Earlier, Eddie Kelly had equalised Heighway's goal. There were sad Liverpool faces, none more so than Shankly. But it was a young side and they had performed bravely.

In truth, Liverpool were short of goalpower. They had the meanest defence in the league – only 24 goals conceded all season – but had managed only 42 goals upfront. Alun Evans was in decline after his various mishaps and John Toshack had yet to find a role for himself, desperately in need of a partner. Heighway was magnificent, but still developing, and never really a goalscorer. Fortunately, sitting up in the stands that warm afternoon, was a young lad just signed from Scunthorpe who would prove to be Shankly's finest-ever signing.

Kevin Keegan was born in Armthorpe, near Doncaster in Yorkshire, the son of a miner. That alone might have endeared him to Shankly but in addition he had a temperament that made up for any ability he might have lacked. Keegan was recommended to Shankly by Andy Beattie, his former team-mate at Preston North End and former boss at Huddersfield.

When Beattie was out of a job, Shankly put some work his way, asking him to do a spot of scouting for Liverpool in the Yorkshire area.

Almost immediately, Beattie was recommending Keegan to the club. He'd been watching him play for Scunthorpe for more than nine months on behalf of another club, but they had decided against his advice. So Beattie decided to pass his recommendation on to Shankly. Every time Shankly and Beattie chatted on the phone, Shankly was given the same message: 'Go watch this boy Keegan.' Eventually, Shankly told Geoff Twentyman to check him out.

'I went to see him,' says Twentyman. 'And I liked what I saw. So, I wrote up a good report and gave it to Bill.' Twentyman wasn't the only one to take a look at him. Other scouts were sniffing around Scunthorpe, but Twentyman insists that Shankly never actually went to see Keegan play. In the end, it took a £25,000 bid from Preston to awaken Shankly.

With Preston now in the market for the youngster, Shankly eventually agreed to give the lad a try and in May 1971 he was signed for £35,000. Shankly took to him from the start. Keegan bubbled with enthusiasm and commitment. They took him to the Cup Final where Liverpool lost to Arsenal and afterwards Shankly spotted him sitting around 'broken-hearted'. 'Christ,' thought Shankly, 'Here's a real character – and he's not even playing.' That kind of attitude appealed to Shankly.

Keegan trained hard when they returned to Anfield after the summer break and slowly began to impress. They even took him on their close-season tour. The tour however only underlined the problems of the previous season – a lack of goals. Shankly was despondent and began to wonder if he should dip into the transfer market again. He mulled it over with his staff. Ronnie Moran reported that Keegan had been doing particularly well.

Shankly wasn't convinced but agreed to play him in the first team for a practice match against the reserves. The first team scored a bagful of goals and Keegan was clearly giving Ian Ross a hard time. After the game, Shankly had a quite word with Ross. The Scottish defender was impressed by the newcomer. 'He's quick and you don't know what he's going to do next,' explained an exasperated Ross. 'He's a hell of a hard boy to tab.'

That was enough for Shankly. If the experienced Ross had problems with him, so would enough other defenders. A week later, Keegan was in the first team making his debut against Nottingham Forest at Anfield. In the 12th minute, he put Liverpool a goal up. Keegan had arrived.

16 A Lad Called Keegan

HE EARLY SEVENTIES were not particularly memorable years for the city of Liverpool. The optimism of the sixties had given way to a growing pessimism. The Beatles had long gone along with most other Merseyside bands. The Liverpool music scene was now history. Even Harold Wilson was out of office.

In fact, the city seemed to be racked with mounting problems. The rundown of the docks continued, while over in Birkenhead the Cammell Laird shipyard faced one crisis after another. Unemployment was steadily climbing and becoming a major issue for the first time since the thirties. It was only the start of what was to come.

But at least there was one saving grace for those who lived in the city and supported Liverpool. The fortunes of their football club were as bright as ever. After a long absence, the league championship would soon return to Anfield. Shankly would play his part, but the newcomer Keegan was to be the chief influence.

With Keegan drafted into their line-up, Liverpool made a forceful start to the 1971/72 season, winning four of their opening five games. The bubbly Keegan offered an extra option with his darting moves and simple enthusiasm. But then just as unexpectedly their form slumped. They won just one of their next seven games, losing three of them. The absence of Tommy Smith was a major factor while Keegan himself missed a few games.

Although the club returned to form, there was to be an even more barren period during the dark winter months. Over Christmas and the New Year, Liverpool went five games without a win, losing three of those, and all but forfeited any hopes of the league title. But you could never put a Bill Shankly side down and typically they put in an end-of-season spurt that brought only one more defeat, in the penultimate and most critical game of the season.

A win at Derby might have handed Liverpool the title. Instead, it was Derby who finished champions. But even then that result still left Liverpool with the faintest of chances.

In the final game of the season, Liverpool could still clinch the title if they won at Arsenal, and Leeds United were beaten. As it was, Leeds went down to Wolverhampton Wanderers, while Liverpool could only draw at Highbury on a night of blistering drama. With five minutes remaining, Toshack bundled the ball into the net from close quarters but the referee judged him offside.

Liverpool ended up in third spot, just one point below Derby County. Points thrown away earlier in the season proved decisive. But at least the new look Liverpool had demonstrated that they were genuine title challengers once more. And it would not be long before they proved their threat.

The success of the season had unquestionably been Kevin Keegan. Before 1972 was over, Keegan would have picked up the first of his 63 England caps. The gulf between Fourth Division football with Scunthorpe and European football with Liverpool presented no problems for him. Keegan was everything Shankly wanted in a player. He was enthusiastic, committed, and would play until he dropped. He had heart and this made him the final piece in the jigsaw of Shankly's new side. Keegan provided valuable options with his ability to beat players, pass accurately and hold on to the ball in tight situations. Indeed, it was almost impossible to shake him off the ball.

A deep affection soon developed between Shankly and his new superstar. 'He was like a father to me,' says Keegan. 'He taught me more about football than anyone, lessons that have held me in good stead since. He believed in me far more than I believed in myself. He made me a better player because I thought, if he believes in me then I must be good. He told me after three games that I would play for England within a year-and-a-half. Everything I achieved in football was down to him.'

There was little else to cheer during the 1971/72 season. On the domestic front Liverpool took early exits from both cup competitions, while in the European Cup-Winners Cup they found themselves facing Bayern Munich, the side they had destroyed a year earlier in the Fairs Cup. This time Bayern took sweet revenge on Shankly's side beating them 3-1 in Germany after a goalless draw at Anfield.

Before the game, Shankly had been his usual scathing self. 'Bayern Munich are not a football club,' he told the papers, 'they are a Christmas club,' adding, 'At Anfield both teams kicked towards the same goal.' For once, his boasting backfired. He would live to regret the remarks.

Bayern were an outstanding side about to embark on a run that would bring them three successive European Cups. It's doubtful if many took Shankly's remarks too seriously. It was all part of the propaganda war, convincing your own troops and supporters, that you were one better than the opposition. It's impossible to know whether Shankly himself really believed his own propaganda. If he did, then there were times when he made serious misjudgements.

After the Ajax game, he had been equally blunt, refusing to accept that Ajax might have been a good side, maybe even better than his Liverpool. Years later, he would still get into arguments with Dutch journalists over the insults he had hurled at the Dutch champions.

On another famous occasion, when Manchester United were the visitors, he began his team talk around the subbuteo table. 'They're rubbish,' he yelled, referring to three of their world-class players. 'One of them's got a dicky knee, one's too old and the other's a drunkard.' Then with a flick of the wrist he swept all eleven United players of the board. 'Rubbish'. It was all part of the ritual.

Keegan remembers a similar occasion when Liverpool played West Ham at Anfield. As usual, Shankly had gone out to meet the visiting team as they arrived. It was something of a ritual. He liked to see what shape they were in, who was limping and so on. He came back to the dressing room and sat down beside Keegan.

'Christ, son,' he said. 'I've just seen that Bobby Moore. What a wreck. He's got bags under his eyes, he's limping and he's got dandruff. He's been out to a night club again, son.' A short time before, the entire West Ham side had been caught red-handed in a Blackpool night club when they should have been tucked up in their beds. The story had hit the front pages.

'Suddenly from feeling a bit of pressure that I was up against the great Bobby Moore, I was playing against this old geezer with dandruff who'd been out all night and was limping,' says Keegan. 'Well, we beat them comprehensively,' he adds, 'but Bobby was brilliant. That day, he put on one of the best performances of anyone I've ever played against. When I came back into the dressing room, Shanks came over to me.

"Jesus Christ, son," he says, "That Bobby Moore, he's some player. You'll never play against anyone better than him." '

Ian Ross, who a year earlier had performed heroics marking the West German captain Franz Beckenbauer, found his true measure this time. It was to mark the beginning of the end of his Anfield career. The Glasgow-born Ross had never quite become a regular, always a utility player, ready to play wherever and whenever he was required.

Three months after the humiliation in Munich, he was sold to Aston Villa. He may have been the scapegoat but he was never bitter. Years later as manager at Huddersfield Town, he created his own bootroom, a shrine to the man he admired so much.

Alun Evans also came in for criticism following the Bayern Munich defeat. Evans had performed splendidly in the first leg and had even scored in Germany, but the combination of Keegan and Evans did not look to be the answer to Liverpool's continuing goalscoring problems. Toshack had so far been something of a disappointment, with only 13 goals that season. The side as a whole had managed only 64 in the league. Evans had made 104 appearances for the club but had scored only 33 goals. Toshack, for all his indifference, looked to be the better bet. And so, at the end of the season, Alun Evans joined Ian Ross on the road to Villa Park for £70,000, a sad reminder of the vagaries of football.

In their place came two other signings – Frank Lane a £15,000 reserve goalkeeper from Tranmere Rovers and Peter Cormack, a dashing midfielder from Nottingham Forest, priced at £110,000. Lane would make only one appearance for the club even though Shankly was fond of telling him that he would be a star of the future. On one occasion, he took Lane with the team to Chelsea.

'We're taking you along for an education, son,' he told him. 'You're going to see two of the finest goalkeepers in the world. There's Ray Clemence and then there's Peter Bonetti of Chelsea. Great keeper Bonetti, world class.'

That afternoon in the dressing room at Stamford Bridge prior to the game, Shankly began his team talk. 'Bonetti, absolute rubbish,' he began, 'Put in an early challenge on him boys, he can't take it. He's useless.' Lane sat in the corner of the dressing room wondering why on earth he had been brought on the trip to London if that was what Shankly really thought of Bonetti.

Peter Cormack however would quickly settle to become an artist in the Liverpool midfield, the supplier of passes as delicate as silk. Cormack was a much under-rated player, but in truth as vital almost as Keegan. He was recommended to Liverpool by Shankly's brother Bob, who had been manager at Hibernian when Cormack was playing in Scotland. Cormack was having problems at Forest and had never really settled. It became public knowledge and a transfer was inevitable.

Shankly called his brother. Bob told him that Cormack was a play-anywhere man and a more than useful player to have around. Bill had him watched and, as soon as the for sale sign went up, Shankly nipped in with a bid.

But the transfer talk in spring 1972 had been of Frank Worthington. The young Huddersfield Town striker was about to pull on an England shirt for the first time, albeit for the England Under-23s, to partner Liverpool's Kevin Keegan. It was an exciting prospect: the maverick, elegantly skilled, freebooting Worthington alongside the energetic but equally exciting Keegan.

The thought was enough to whet the appetite of any manager and Shankly was no exception. He needed little prompting to see the potential of such a partnership at Anfield. Shankly was soon on his way across the Pennines to secure a deal with his old club, although it would take a bid of £150,000 that would make Worthington the third most expensive striker in Britain.

All that was needed now was Worthington's signature on the contract. Unfortunately, he had just flown off with the England Under-23 party on a trip to Eastern Europe, leaving Shankly with a tiresome delay before he could parade his man. But Shankly did not envisage any problems.

Shankly had arranged for the Liverpool secretary Peter Robinson to meet Worthington immediately he got off a flight from Paris at Heathrow, along with Roy Lambert, the Huddersfield Town chief scout. Shankly was holed up in the nearby Aerial Hotel at Heathrow awaiting them. Worthington, Lambert and Robinson drove to the hotel where Shankly came down to greet them. Worthington remembers it well.

'Do yer wanna come and play for Liverpool?' growled Shankly. 'We need you, son.' Shankly told him that a fee with Huddersfield had been agreed and that he should come up to Liverpool the next morning to formalise the deal. Worthington was ecstatic and quickly agreed terms. The next day, as planned, they returned to Liverpool. 'As we drove past Goodison,' Worthington recalls, 'Shanks pointed a finger, "Take no notice, laddie," he said. "There's only two teams in Liverpool, Liverpool and Liverpool reserves." '

At Anfield, Worthington duly signed on the dotted line and then moved on to seal the deal with a medical. It was at this point that a problem occurred. Worthington had just experienced a hectic few weeks. He had already had preliminary transfer talks with Leicester City's Jimmy Bloomfield and had just made his debut for the England Under-23s against Poland and the Soviet Union, only to be met at the airport with more transfer talk, this time from the country's top club.

His father had also died recently and Worthington, even then, was not renowned for staying at home and going to bed early, well not by himself at any rate. All this turmoil would have been enough to send the blood and adrenalin pumping around anyone's body. Worthington was no exception. His blood pressure was unusually high. Despite a number of readings, it continued to remain at an unacceptable level.

The Liverpool doctor informed Shankly of the results, advising him that a week's rest might bring the reading down. Shankly was sympathetic and told Worthington to take a short holiday. 'Relax a little and we'll check you when you get back,' he advised.

Worthington had already experienced a few dizzy spells during his trip to Eastern Europe with England, but thinking nothing of it he went off for a short break to Majorca. While he was there, he experienced another dizzy spell, this time more serious, that ended up with him on his hotel bedroom floor. Picking himself up, he finally made it to a bed where he slept almost round the clock. Unfortunately, he then awoke and resumed his frantic lifestyle of womanising as if nothing had happened.

Back at Anfield a week later, the readings on the blood-pressure gauge were still sky-high. Shankly had little alternative. 'I'm sorry, son,' he told him, 'but as much as I want to, I can't sign you. I can't afford to lay out a record amount to bring in a player with a question mark hanging over his head.'

And so it was back to Leeds Road for Worthington. Huddersfield Town immediately booked him into a local hospital. Shankly was genuinely concerned, even sending flowers to Worthington's mother and phoning on a number of occasions to find out how he was doing. The tests at the hospital failed to uncover any serious abnormality. All Worthington needed was a good rest. Had Shankly waited another week, or conducted the medical before he went off to play with

England, then Worthington might well have become a Liverpool player.

Worthington was something of a 'Jack the lad' who might never have fitted into Shankly's idea of how a professional footballer should conduct his life. On the other hand, it might well have been that Shankly could have tempered Worthington's excesses, allowing the young man to realise his full potential. As it was, Worthington never quite lived up to all his promise.

Shankly had high hopes for the 1972/73 season. Having just failed to pinch the title the previous season, he could only see his young team maturing in the months ahead. They opened up well enough with four wins in their first five games but then lost at Leicester and Derby.

Cormack, after finding his feet with the reserves, was drafted into the side with Brian Hall reverting to spare man. They lost only one more game between then and the end of January. Leeds, as ever, and Arsenal were their chief rivals, but there was never really much doubt about where the championship trophy would wind up. At the end of the season, a goalless draw with Leicester at Anfield was sufficient for Liverpool to be acclaimed league champions for a record eighth time. It was also Shankly's third title, making him one of the most successful managers in the British game.

The *Liverpool Daily Post* called it 'Coronation Day'. Then as the team began their obligatory lap of honour, Shankly tore off his jacket to reveal a bright red shirt and red tie, and marched towards the Kop to take a solo bow. He stood there that day, playing to his audience. As he punched the air, the Kop responded with an enormous cheer and then chanted his name. It was Shankly at his finest, orchestrating the crowd.

But Phil Thompson remembers another incident from that afternoon. 'In the pandemonium that followed our lap of honour, a number of scarves had been thrown on to the pitch and a policeman had kicked one away. Shankly saw this and came running over and pushed the policeman away. "Don't be doing that," he said, "That's somebody's life. People have paid good money for that. Give it me here." And with that he picked up the scarf and wrapped it around his neck. To me, that summed up the affection he had for the people.'

'This title gave me greater pleasure than the previous two,' Shankly claimed, a smile as broad as the Mersey spreading across his face, 'simply because here we had a rebuilt side, some of them only two or three seasons in first-team football and they stayed the course like veterans.' Only Matt Busby could claim to have won more championships since the war. But there were more on the horizon. The city may have been plunged into economic gloom, but at Anfield the commentators were more interested in what lay behind the club's continuing fortunes.

By the seventies, the bootroom had become a focus of Liverpool's success. Yet there was nothing untoward or exceptional about it. It was simply an old cubby hole beneath the stand, not far from the dressing rooms. As the name suggested, it was where the players' boots and kit were stored. It measured about 12 feet by 12 feet, and was crammed with the various odds and ends of the football business.

Boots either hung from pegs on the walls or were stored on shelves, while other shelves groaned under the weight of various football books and diaries. There was always the odd titillating calendar adorning the walls, along with maybe an old team photo or a yellowing paper cutting. A fixture list was usually prominently pinned up and in the odd corner a football or two would be lying around. Upturned crates or a kit hamper provided the only seating. It was cramped, scruffy and untidy, a typical working room but it also made an ideal meeting place.

Shankly had his own office but after training, or a game, he preferred to congregate in the warmth of the bootroom with his principal lieutenants Paisley, Fagan, Bennett and later Moran. They'd make a cup of tea and sit down for a natter, with Shankly in his woolly cardigan, Bob Paisley in his slippers, Fagan and Moran still sweating in their track suits from a good morning's workout.

'So and so didn't look too bright this morning,' Paisley would mutter in his famed North-east vernacular. 'Probably out too late last night,' someone would suggest. 'Better have a word,' Shankly would add. Then he might ask about someone's injury. Paisley, the qualified physiotherapist, would give him a rundown on how the various injuries were and how treatment was progressing.

'Let's give him a run-out in the reserves,' Shankly would say, taking a sip of tea. Then they'd take out the big black books and write down the day's training routines. Each morning, they would record the weather, the various injuries to players and the training practices they had performed that day. In the months and years ahead, they would be able to refer back to their record.

The bootroom was nothing new to the Shankly era. It had always been there, always used as a kitroom. But during the Shankly years, it was to take on mythical proportions. Ronnie Moran remembers that while he was still playing 'there was never any big deal about the bootroom. It was just used for the kit and had no other significance.' But in time, as the pundits searched for an explanation for Liverpool's success, they hit upon the bootroom as a sort of Tardis with magical powers where new ideas and tactics were conjured up.

In reality, it was much the same as any other bootroom. There was nothing special about it, no brain-storming sessions, no magic potions, no wands. If there was any magic, it came simply from that small group who gathered within its four walls, headed of course by Shankly. What perhaps set them apart from other management teams was that they were as much a team as the eleven who pulled on a shirt each Saturday.

From the start, Shankly had demanded their loyalty threatening any-one who stepped out of line or was caught telling stories with the sack. They thought as one and acted as one, and they were just as passionate about Liverpool winning as any of those supporters who stood on the Kop each Saturday. There was never any bickering.

All that came out of the bootroom was plain common sense. And yet they had arrived at Anfield from diverse backgrounds. Moran and Pais-ley had both played for the club; Fagan was a scouser; Bennett and Shankly were Scots. Old Albert Shelley was part of the furniture.

By 1970, it had become a shrine. The players never went near it, instead steering a wide berth. It was sacrosanct, a sort of headmaster's study. 'It was definitely out of bounds most of the time, and if you were asked in then you knew there must be a problem to sort out,' remem-bers Phil Thompson.

The only time any of the players ever went there was to collect a pair of boots. Whenever they did go near, Ronnie Moran would usually bark at them which was probably the main reason for steering clear. Players were rarely invited over the threshold for a chat and, if you did go in, you always knocked on the door before entering.

In later years, visiting managers would be invited down for a drink. Although no-one in the bootroom was a great drinker, they would always unearth a bottle of something or other for their guest. He'd be seated on an upturned crate, a glass would be wiped clean and a drink poured. Then they would carefully glean as much information from their guest as they could.

'So and so didn't have much of a game today, got problems has he?'

Shankly might ask casually. Sometimes, Paisley might venture a question about an injury to one of their players. 'Looks a bad injury that one, think he'll be out all season?' And so on. It was never a planned interrogation. It was just that they were a canny bunch and their canniness was at the centre of all their footballing activities.

As ever Shankly was always in the hunt to strengthen his side and the bootroom was as good a place as any to mull over the possibilities. When good players became available, he would carefully consider the prospect. Most players were thrilled when it was reported that Liverpool were interested but one player who changed his mind about coming to Anfield that year was Lou Macari, the Celtic midfielder.

Macari was rated one of the most exciting Scottish players of the time. Shankly had no doubts that Macari was a man who could fit into the Anfield set-up. In January 1973, he put in a bid of £200,000. Celtic accepted and Macari looked set to be wearing the red of Liverpool. He came down to the club, met with Peter Robinson and was guest of honour one evening as Liverpool faced Burnley in a Cup replay.

Shankly even drove him part of the way and on the journey Macari was being given the hard sell by Shankly. 'Wonderful place Liverpool, wonderful people Liverpudlians, just like Glaswegians you know,' he was telling him. Unfortunately, fog had descended during the trip and Shankly managed to get them lost. He decided to wind down his window and ask someone the directions. 'Where are we, son?' he asked a passer-by. 'Liverpool,' came the reply. Shankly wound his window back up. 'See what I mean, Lou, great sense of humour.'

Shankly's plan was to use Macari upfront as well as in midfield, though his idea was clearly being interpreted as rejection of John Toshack who had largely failed to fulfil his substantial fee. But that night at Anfield, Toshack gave a rare performance, scoring twice. Macari watched from the stands and, after the game, met once more with Robinson and Shankly. He asked for more time to consider the move. Shankly agreed, unaware that others were about to tap Macari.

A few days later, Macari turned Liverpool down and signed instead for Manchester United. Almost certainly the terms offered by United were far better than the basic wage offered at Anfield. Macari's hesitation had alerted Tommy Docherty and the United manager moved quickly to sign his fellow Scot. But it was to be Macari's loss when Liverpool went on to win the title, while United headed for the relegation zone. The day after he signed for United, one of the Liverpool players dared to ask Shankly what had gone wrong. Shankly was dismissive. 'He couldn't play anyway,' he roared. 'I only wanted him for the reserves.'

In Europe, Liverpool were in the UEFA Cup again. They opened with a tricky tie, against the German side Eintracht Frankfurt, but a 2-0 win at Anfield was enough to set up victory. In the next round, they comfortably cruised past the Greek side AEK Athens, winning 6-1 on aggregate. Local boy Phil Boersma scored in both games and would end that season with four goals in Europe.

But Boersma, for all his promise, never became the goalscorer he first threatened to become. His form fluctuated as much as the weather: one moment brilliant, the next dismal. There was never any consistency and he was always a fringe player, although he did manage enough games that season to win a couple of medals. In December 1975, Bob Paisley sold him to Middlesbrough although some years later he would return to Liverpool as coach under manager Graeme Souness.

After their trip to Greece, Liverpool faced a second journey to Germany, this time through Checkpoint Charlie, to the East to face Dynamo Berlin. Smith was absent through injury and Keegan, as Shankly had warned, came in for some robust tackling. In the event, Liverpool were glad to escape with a goalless draw and nothing worse than a few bruises although Keegan was to miss the second leg at Anfield, still nursing the scars of his visit to Berlin.

Back at Anfield, Shankly decided to give another home-grown youngster his first opportunity in Europe. Phil Thompson had joined the club as an apprentice professional in February 1971. The spindly-legged Thompson had almost grown up on the Kop, and was brought to his first game by his mother to see Liverpool face Inter Milan in the European Cup semi-final. That night he'd been captivated by the passionate atmosphere. Now, seven years on, he was out there lining up with some of his childhood heroes. Thompson was to be an important addition to the side although his contribution would not really be significant until after Shankly had gone.

In fact, Thompson was in and out of the team all that season. Early in February, he was left out of the side to play Arsenal at Anfield. Liverpool lost 2-0 and on the Monday morning Thompson decided to go and ask Shankly why he had been left out. He knocked on the door and was invited in. 'Come in, sit down,' he said. 'Aye, young man, what is it you want?'

'Well,' says Thompson, 'I'm upset at being left out of the side on Saturday, I wanted to know why.'

'You're upset,' he snarled. 'Christ, son, you say you're upset because I left you out. Son, you should be thanking me. That side on Saturday was rubbish, absolute rubbish. You should thank me for leaving you out. One day you'll be captain of this club, playing for England, aye and maybe captain of England too. And then one day you'll realise and you'll thank me for leaving you out.'

Thompson was speechless. He stood up and walked out feeling ten feet tall. 'Thank you, thank you,' he said as he closed the door behind him.

Although Liverpool became recognised for their canny dealings in the lower divisions, Thompson was one of the few Liverpool-born players to make the grade through the club's youth system. Since Shankly's arrival, only Chris Lawler, Ian Callaghan, Roger Hunt, Gerry Byrne and Tommy Smith were home-grown players. What's more, Byrne and Hunt had previously made their debuts under Phil Taylor. There were plenty of others tried out by Shankly but few made the grade. Liverpool-born players, like Phil Boersma, Roy Evans, John McLaughlin, Doug Livermore and Steve Peplow, all came through the youth and reserve sides but, for one reason or another, fell by the wayside. Shankly's formula was to let other clubs discover the talent, before he nipped in to sign it up.

Incomers would then be farmed out to the reserves to learn their trade. The second team was almost an identikit Liverpool. They played the same system, learned the same passing game and were subject to the same disciplines. It was not uncommon for an expensive signing to arrive at Anfield and spend the next few months in the reserves.

Elsewhere, they would never have stood for it, demanding first team football immediately. But at Anfield Shankly captured their imagination and won over their patience. He'd tell them they'd been signed to win the title. 'Don't worry, son. Bide your time. You'll be there at the end of the season to pick up the medals,' he'd tell them. 'We don't have eleven players here, we have twenty.'

And it was true. Liverpool did have a substantially larger squad of players than any other club. It was Shankly who initiated the notion of the 'squad' and of having fifteen or more first-team players. Most seasons they were playing fifty or even sixty games and the club needed a large pool of players. He'd mix them around; some would play predominantly in the league, others would be saved for European games. And although the club never carried a big injury list, you always had to be prepared, have someone ready to step in just in case of injury.

There was never any relaxing. Every competition Liverpool entered, Shankly wanted to win with the possible exception of the League Cup. There was a saying at Anfield, 'First is first, second is nothing.' Shankly went about his business hell-bent on winning. And usually Liverpool were in contention for every trophy. That demanded a system that could cope with a high number of pressure games.

One bad week and the club could find itself out of Europe, out of domestic cup competitions and dropping league points. The pressure was always on. There was no time for relaxation. It kept players on edge, as well as making appalling demands on Shankly and the back-room staff. It was also a policy that was to continue at Anfield for many more years.

After beating Dynamo Berlin, Liverpool had just about had enough of German football but much to their astonishment they found themselves facing a third German side, Dynamo Dresden, in the quarter finals. Shankly was despondent: Dresden topped the East German league by a mile and the first game was at Anfield. It wouldn't be easy, though by now Liverpool were growing in confidence. In the first leg, they won 2-0 and then in one of their finest performances in Europe they even won the second leg. They were through to their fourth European semi-final.

Liverpool were developing into an effective European side. The mistakes of 1965 had been assimilated; their style had been perfected, and the logistics of European travel mastered. Careful preparation went into every aspect. Hotels were meticulously chosen and tested out in advance. They were always out of town, away from built-up areas and possible noisy fans. In the mid-sixties, Liverpool had travelled to the continent by scheduled flight. Now they chartered their own plane, flew out a day or so beforehand and returned immediately the game was over. They took no chances, even packing their own food and bottled water. Both Shankly and Paisley had a natural suspicion of 'foreigners' and their ways.

Invited to a banquet before one important European tie, Shankly warned his players not to touch a drop of drink or eat a morsel of their food. 'It could be spiked,' he told them in all seriousness. But usually on any trip, Shankly and the players were forced to eat the same meal.

It was always steak, chips and salad, followed by fresh fruit and cream. Wherever they went, whether it was London, New York, Paris or Newcastle, it was always the same.

Shankly had read somewhere that the famous American heavyweight boxer Joe Louis had trained on steak. If it was good enough for Joe Louis, then it was good enough for Liverpool. After that, it was always steak. God help a Liverpool footballer who might have been vegetarian. Phil Chisnall remembers going to the wedding of one of Shankly's daughters. 'I couldn't believe it,' he says, 'when they served the meal. It was steak, chips and salad, followed by fresh fruit and cream.'

Shankly had also drummed a European style into his players. 'Play the ball from the back,' he would tell them. Clemence would roll the ball out to one of his full backs who would then carry it upfield slowly. Next it would go to the midfield, then perhaps back to the defence, before going once more to the midfield or the flanks. The secret lay in passing, and holding possession. As soon as you lost possession, you were on the defensive.

It was a style that would be perfected even more skilfully under Bob Paisley. Players were taught to search for open spaces and then make runs into those spaces. It was the five-a-side game that helped perfect the technique. Quick, short, accurate passing, before running into space. Allied to all that was patience. Don't panic, don't get caught out by the counter-attack, don't be over-ambitious. 'It's a ninety minute game,' Shankly reminded them.

And with their fitness, it was often in the last few minutes that Liverpool were at their strongest as the opponent began to wilt. Over the years, so many vital goals were to come in the dying moments of a match as Liverpool pressed forward to find an equaliser or a winning goal. And with the Kop behind them, it was almost inevitable that they squeezed one from somewhere. And if they were winning, they would sit on their lead, happy to soak up the pressure without over-committing themselves.

It wasn't always pretty and it did have its critics. The Manchester United side of the mid-sixties played with far more gusto and flair; Leeds United tackled with more venom; Manchester City could pass the ball with considerable imagination. But it was Liverpool who won most trophies.

It was a style that was not always appreciated. 'Boring Liverpool' they were called at times. That hurt Shankly but it never deterred him.

And in the years ahead, as his style was refined, the club would go on to win four European Cups, proof enough that someone somewhere had got it right. Shankly liked to remind people that, when they came to Anfield, it was something special. A sign was erected in the player's tunnel. It read, 'This Is Anfield'. It was enough to frighten anyone. What's more, it was meant to!

It came as some relief that they should draw Tottenham Hotspur in the semi-final of the UEFA Cup. At least they did not have to travel too far and, with the north London club trailing Liverpool in the title chase by ten points and more, the odds were narrowly in Liverpool's favour. What's more, Spurs, then UEFA Cup holders, had not won at Anfield since March 1912.

As expected, Liverpool began the stronger, taking an early, if undeserved lead, in the 27th minute. The pressure from Liverpool continued but after 90 minutes they had failed to improve the scoreline. Tottenham left the field with smiles on their faces. But at least Shankly knew that Liverpool had already won at Tottenham that season and argued that there was no reason why they should not repeat that performance.

By the time the two clubs met again, Liverpool had been crowned champions of the Football League and were in confident mood even though this was their 64th match of the season. Confident they may have been but they were also showing signs of weariness. It was a hard night and not a night for defence. A one-goal lead was not enough and, four minutes after half-time, Martin Peters showed why as he levelled the scores. But Liverpool were always primed to attack and seven minutes later Keegan on a solo run drew Pat Jennings in the Spurs goal and squared a ball for Heighway to slip into an open goal.

It was a decisive away goal that left Spurs needing two more goals to win. One of them came in the 72nd minute but, try as they might Tottenham could not breach the Liverpool defence for a vital third time. Liverpool were through to their second European final.

Their opponents turned out to be yet another German side. This time it was Borussia Moenchengladbach, the fourth they had met in the competition. Borussia were a fine side who would give Liverpool some memorable games over the next few seasons. They boasted some of the great names of German international football, including Günter Netzer, Berti Vogts, Rainer Bonhof, and Josef Heynckes. Shankly rated them the best side in Europe. The two teams lined up on the Wednesday evening of 9 May with heavy rain and dark storm clouds breaking over Anfield. Shankly had made a controversial selection, deciding late on to leave John Toshack out of his line-up, plumping instead for Brian Hall.

Toshack was furious. All season, he had been in and out of the side, never able to secure his place. At times, his absences had been due to injury but he also suspected that Shankly was not altogether happy with his performances. Tonight however the gods were in his favour.

As the storm clouds broke, the heavy rain turned into a torrential downpour. It was impossible for players to keep their feet, even the referee was slipping and sliding, with the ball sticking in the glutinous mud. After 30 minutes, the Austrian referee had little alternative but to call the game off, much to the annoyance of Borussia who were coping well with Liverpool's tactics.

Fortunately, the half hour of play had provided enough clues for Shankly and his staff to undo Borussia. The game was rescheduled for the following evening. Back in the dressing room, Shankly announced to his players that he was sticking with the same line-up. Toshack was fuming. All evening, he had been brooding.

At this further setback, he decided to confront the manager. It was not a happy meeting. There was a stinging row between them with the Welshman storming out of Anfield, ready to slap in a transfer request. For a moment, it looked like the end of Toshack's career at Liverpool.

Shankly was left to mull it over. He never liked rows; he hated dropping players; he loathed confrontations. He may have looked like 'the tough little guy' but underneath he understood the passions of players and their aspirations. Shankly talked the situation over with Paisley in the bootroom. The more they chewed the cud, the more they realised the inadequacies of Borussia's defence. They had no tall men at the back and were reluctant to move out of the box.

'Toshack might just give them some problems,' suggested Paisley. Shankly looked at him stony-faced but was forced to agree that perhaps he had a point. Brian Hall was short and, in the 30 minutes of play, he had not been able to make much impact. Toshack, with all his height, might be able to knock a few balls down for the likes of Keegan.

'It's worth a try,' ventured Paisley. 'If it doesn't work we could always bring Brian on.' Shankly brooded on it and, later that night, he rang Toshack at home. 'Hello, son, are you in bed yet?' he asked. 'No boss, I've only just got home,' answered Toshack assuming that Shankly was on the phone to try and appease him. 'Well, get to your bed, there's a good chance you'll be playing tomorrow night.'

It was half an apology; the door was left open just enough to let in light, though there was still the chance that Shankly might retain Hall. But the more he thought about Paisley's suggestion, the more it seemed to make sense. There was also the fact that Toshack had something to prove.

And so the following evening, Shankly handed Toshack the number ten shirt. The rest was history. Toshack had an outstanding game. Time and again, he leapt above a flat-footed Borussia defence, feeding balls into the path of Keegan. Within 32 minutes, Keegan had put two of them into the back of the net. On the hour, Larry Lloyd, again climbing above the defence, headed in Keegan's corner to make it 3-0. Ray Clemence saved a penalty, that was to prove vital, and Liverpool were on their way to winning the UEFA Cup.

After the game, Shankly took the credit for reintroducing Toshack. 'Bringing back Big John was a masterstroke,' he told journalists. 'He destroyed them in the air.' Paisley and Toshack, overhearing his remark, smiled to themselves.

But the second leg was never going to be easy. By the time they arrived in Germany, Borussia had compensated for their lack of aerial power by bringing in tall defender Ulrich Surau. Toshack remained in the Liverpool line-up. But this time Shankly should have read the runes and left him on the sidelines. Lack of variation upfront almost proved a costly error.

As at Anfield, there was a torrential storm half an hour into the game and by half-time Liverpool were two goals down, and facing disaster. Sitting in the dugout, Shankly expected the worst. 'The way they were playing was unbelievable,' he wrote in his autobiography.

In the second half, it was every man to the pump as Liverpool faced a hurricane of attacks. But as the half wore on and the vital third goal failed to materialise, Borussia seemed to lose heart. They had given their all. In the end, Liverpool recaptured the midfield and although they had lost the game, they had won their first European trophy on aggregate, and had become the first English club to win both a European and a domestic trophy in the same season.

But this was no time for rest. New players had to be recruited. Shankly's philosophy had always been that you never rest on your laurels; you should always be improving your squad. Players should be signed when a club is doing well, not when its fortunes are on the wane, he argued.

As the season drew to a close, Alan Waddle, the Halifax Town striker was recruited for £40,000. Like any lower division signing, it was something of a gamble: in this case, a gamble that never paid off. Waddle was a powerhouse player and a fine header of the ball but he lacked vital finesse when it came to sneaking into goalscoring positions. He made just nine appearances for the club and was sold to Leicester City four years later for £45,000. At least, it proved Shankly's fallibility.

Over the years, Shankly would rightly be remembered for the likes of Keegan, Clemence and Heighway; but there were also Waddle, Whitham and Chisnall to remind everyone of the vagaries of the football business.

It had been a gruelling season for Shankly. Liverpool had played 66 games and the pressure of it all was beginning to tell. He was not getting any younger and, while he could cope with the intensity of the job, the constant dashing around, the long hours and dealing with the press were proving exhausting for a man of his age. He was almost 59 and even he had to admit that the years were creeping up on him.

Shankly's former secretary at Huddersfield Eddie Brennan went over to Anfield to see a game as his guest towards the end of the season. He returned to Huddersfield shocked. 'He was a different man. He wasn't the old Bill. I knew something was wrong. The enthusiasm seemed to have waned; he looked tired. I came back and I remember telling people he won't be there in a year's time.'

Nessie was also ill. All year, she had been unwell, in and out of hospital, and was finding it increasingly difficult to look after the home. Every morning, Bill would get up and make her breakfast, then leave the house at around 8.30 am. She wouldn't see him again until late in the evening.

As the season ended, she asked Bill to think about retirement. Maybe this was the time to go, she suggested, after winning a European trophy and the league. Liverpool had gone seven seasons without a trophy but they were now back to their winning ways. It was as good a time as any.

But Bill wouldn't hear of it. What would he do in retirement? There was no such word in his vocabulary. He wanted to win the FA Cup again, maybe the league as well. And this team was well capable of lifting the European Cup. When he refused, Nessie was upset and all thoughts of retirement were postponed. But at least it was now on the agenda.

17 The King Abdicates

THE 1973/74 SEASON was to be Shankly's last at Anfield. Nobody at Anfield could have guessed it and, to this day, the precise reasons for his departure remain confused, rather than mysterious. Months after the event, Shankly himself was probably just as unsure about why he had quit as anyone. There were no arguments, although with Shankly there was always a degree of suspicion when it came to directors.

Shankly was certainly weary, as he readily admits in his autobiography. The softer, rounded looks of his youth had all but disappeared. His face seemed longer, his jaw squarer, his brow more lined, though the hair was as cropped as ever. 'When I sat down with my tea and pies after the Cup Final,' he wrote, 'my mind was made up. If we had lost the final, I would have carried on, but I thought, "Well, we've won the Cup now and maybe it's a good time to go." I knew I was going to finish.'

Shankly had won everything possible except the European Cup and, with Liverpool now scheduled for a season in the Cup-Winners' Cup, it would be at least another year before he could have a further crack at that one elusive trophy. In 1973/74, Liverpool had failed miserably in Europe, going out in the second round. The question was: did Shankly want to spend another year trying to win the league title in order to have a further shot at the European Cup the following season? At the very least, that would be two more years. He was now almost 61-years-old, the time when most men are thinking of retiring. If he kept at it, hoping for another go at the European Cup, he would be 63 before he could contemplate retirement.

But deep-down there was another reason. 'We won the Cup, and the taxman came and took away all my bonuses,' he once told Liverpool journalist Ian Hargreaves. 'Then they came back and took away my league bonus too. It was heartbreaking doing all that work for nothing. I thought the club might have paid the tax for me but they wouldn't.'

He'd spent 14 years at Anfield, admired by the players and adored by the fans, yet he sometimes wondered if the directors cared that much for him. Throughout his footballing career, he'd never had much time for directors. They lived in a different world to him; swanky houses, bridge clubs, freemasonry and the rest. It was an anathema to Shankly. He was a simple man, still living in the same neat three-bedroomed, semi-detached house that he had moved into back in 1960, still driving a modest car.

In many ways, he was still a pre-war figure. Thirty years may have passed since the war ended, but Shankly's lifestyle was pretty much the same. He had money but he was not a wealthy man. He still nurtured the same small group of friends, many of them unconnected to football. He chatted to the neighbours, had a warm hullo for everyone, and did the kind of things most of us do at weekends, a spot of gardening and of course cleaning the cooker. When anyone knocked on the door asking for an autograph, they were usually invited in and given a cup of tea, irrespective of whether he knew them or not. Not the kind of thing today's multi-millionaire football managers do.

But by 1974, football had moved on. The players of the 1970s were on sky-high salaries, far more than he had ever earned in his life, living in mock-Georgian houses out in the suburbs, with huge bonuses and pay-offs from astronomical transfer fees. 'There are players with swimming pools and tennis courts who haven't even won one championship medal,' he once observed bitterly.

The game was slipping away from characters like Shankly. Busby felt much the same at Old Trafford. Like Shankly, he still lived in the same, simple semi-detached in Chorlton-cum-Hardy as he always had, although on his retirement he had been ushered upstairs as a director. That at least was recognition of his achievements.

Shankly wouldn't even get that. The more the game moved away from men like Shankly and Busby, the more difficult it became for them. Someone like Ron Yeats was better equipped to deal with the players' problems than Shankly ever was. Indeed, players had often gone to Yeats with their personal crises before they ever confronted Shankly. A new age had thrown up different problems, new trends, many of them alien to the older men.

It was the era of the young track-suited manager. Men like Shankly and Busby may not have been despised but they were not always valued. The track-suited manager, the former player of the sixties, grown fat on good wages, television punditry and continental tactics, was what everyone cried out for. Malcolm Allison, Gordon Lee, Tommy Docherty; these were the new managerial breed, young men who supposedly understood their players.

Shankly was a man of the people, proud of his roots, with few aspirations. Of course, he wanted to give as much as he could to his wife and family, but he never aspired to live out in the wilderness of the suburbs or to drive a posh car. That kind of status held no meaning for him. He lived and breathed football, and that was all that counted.

After winning the UEFA Cup in 1973, Shankly nursed ambitions of winning the European Cup the following season. Liverpool were clearly among the favourites and began their assault on Europe with a visit to Luxembourg to face Jeunesse Esch. It looked comfortable and perhaps Liverpool took it all a little too lightly. Whatever the reason, the bagful of goals they threatened never materialised and in the end they were lucky to avoid going to Anfield a goal or two behind. As it was, they drew 1-1. At Anfield a fortnight later, they showed little improvement. It even took an own goal to give Liverpool the lead and, although Toshack added a second, it was as one newspaper described 'a shamefaced victory'.

After their championship win, lethargy seemed to have settled in. Liverpool had lost two of their opening seven fixtures and drawn two. They then lost a couple more in October and were being written off as far as the championship was concerned. But more worrying was the prospect of facing Red Star Belgrade in the next round of the European Cup.

Red Star manager Miljan Miljanic waxed lyrically about Shankly's side calling them 'the team of our time,' adding that they were as 'outstanding as such famous clubs as Real Madrid and Ajax'.

It was a handsome compliment though it might well have been cunningly aimed at lulling Liverpool into a false sense of security. If it was, then Liverpool fell for it, going two goals behind early in the second half in Yugoslavia, though they were to be rescued by a late Chris Lawler goal which at least gave them some hope for the return leg. Nobody seemed to have any doubts that Liverpool could pull off another famous victory at Anfield. After all, as Shankly was always telling everyone, 'the Kop was worth a goal start'.

But this time there was to be no goal start for them. Instead, the goal went to Red Star and Liverpool were left to scale an impossible mountain. Chris Lawler gave them the faintest of hope in the 85th minute but it was all too late. There were some dramatic efforts with the ball cleared off the line on three occasions, but then with a minute remaining Red Star made it 2-1 from a free kick and Liverpool were out of Europe.

Shankly's dream had been shattered. He was deeply disappointed. It was a game Liverpool ought to have won. They had taken it all too casually, not helped by their sluggish start to the season. There were few excuses. Players had been injured but it had hardly been crucial. Liverpool were simply suffering a hangover from the previous season's exertions.

There was little point in Shankly raging around the dressing room although in truth that was never his style. He was always more likely to pace up and down outside in the corridor, holding his silence. If he ever heard anyone laughing inside the dressing room, then he would let rip. Defeat was painful for him and he could never understand why others didn't feel the same degree of pain.

The only consolation for Liverpool was that they would not lose many more games that season. After going down to Red Star, they would taste defeat only four more times that season in a total of 41 league and cup games. And yet despite their massive improvement in form it brought only the FA Cup to Anfield. Any other season and such form would have been enough to bring them the league title as well. But the prime honours went to Leeds United, five points ahead of Liverpool with Derby County trailing in third spot, a further nine points adrift. Liverpool pushed Leeds the whole way, but Revie's men lost only four games all season. There were still goalscoring problems with Liverpool. Top scorer was Keegan with a mere 12 goals, while Toshack, supposedly the chief striker, was way behind with a paltry five. In all, Liverpool netted just 52 goals.

John Toshack had rarely shown his true qualities under Shankly. They had argued, sometimes publicly, although never with any lingering bitterness. Toshack would eventually settle in the side and over the next few seasons work out his role as provider for Keegan but by then Shankly had departed.

That season, it was in the FA Cup that Liverpool excelled though they hardly began convincingly. There may have been a gulf of more than 80 league places between Liverpool and Doncaster Rovers, but at

Anfield it was the lower placed club who came away with the plaudits as they pulled off a sensational 2-2 draw, even leading until Keegan found an equaliser. In the replay at Doncaster, Liverpool made heavy weather of their task, eventually winning 2-0.

After emerging from that uneasy start, you began to get the feeling that maybe Liverpool's name was etched on the trophy. The fourth round proved almost identical; a goalless draw at Anfield against Shankly's former club Carlisle United, now in the Second Division, and then a 2-0 win at Carlisle. In the fifth round, Liverpool comfortably shunted Ipswich aside and in the quarter finals squeezed past Bristol City at Ashton Gate to set up a semi-final against Leicester City, a side that still haunted Liverpool.

It was no different this time. At Old Trafford in front of 60,000, the two old rivals shared the honours. A few days later, they met at Villa Park in front of another 55,000 plus crowd. This time, Liverpool were the better side, outplaying Leicester to win 3-1. Shankly was about to lead his team out for an FA Cup Final for the third time. Nobody could have guessed that it would also be the last.

Liverpool's opponents in the final were Newcastle United whose fanatical following rivalled Liverpool's. Wembley was turned into a cauldron of noise. With the formidable Malcolm MacDonald leading their attack and the redoubtable Bobby Moncur in defence, Newcastle were more than worthy opponents.

Before the match, MacDonald was boasting to the press and anyone else who would listen about what he was going to do to Liverpool. It was dangerous talk. Shankly made a point of repeating it to his players at every opportunity, knowing that it would only anger them more. He also made sure it was splashed across all the tabloids. After losing out in the league, Liverpool were doubly determined to carry some silverware back to Anfield.

The signs pointed to as close a contest as any in recent years, but instead it turned out to be as one-sided a final as anyone could remember. Liverpool won convincingly with Keegan a constant thorn in the Geordie's side. In one move, Liverpool strung twelve passes together before Keegan slammed the thirteenth into the back of the net. It was a scintillating display of passing, one of the finest Wembley had seen since the Hungarians knocked the stuffing out of English football in 1953, reckoned Shankly. If you were to end your career in football, then that was as good as any game on which to finish.

Malcolm MacDonald had turned out to be an anonymous figure, rarely getting a sniff of the ball and, when he did, the Liverpool defence tracked him relentlessly. But if MacDonald was anonymous, there were two other Newcastle players who did enough to impress the man sitting next to Shankly, Bob Paisley. It wasn't long before the new Liverpool manager had signed up Newcastle's Terry McDermott and Alan Kennedy, both of whom went on to give honourable service in Liverpool shirts.

After the game, Shankly stood, hands in pockets, on the sidelines. To his right, the packed masses of Liverpool supporters chanted his name. Eventually, he walked on to the pitch throwing an arm around Emlyn Hughes before ordering his side to take a lap of honour, making sure that they also paid tribute to the Newcastle fans.

Noticeably he did not join in himself. He simply wandered back to the dressing room although en route he was cornered by a pair of young Liverpool fans. The two lads paid homage, falling on their knees to kiss his shoes. Shankly laughed, telling them jokingly to give them a quick polish while they were down there. It was, as one paper suggested, the 'ultimate fan worship'.

'I've seen managers cheered off, chaired off and even knighted, but Bill Shankly is the first, inspiring such heights of worship that Liverpool fans flung themselves prostrate on Wembley's pitch to kiss his feet,' wrote Mike Langley in the *Sunday People*.

Outside the dressing room, Shankly shook hands with a disabled lad from Liverpool in a wheelchair, before helping him into the dressing room to meet the players. 'I'm happiest not for myself, the players or the staff but the multitudes,' he was telling everyone. 'I'm a people's man, a socialist. I'm sorry I couldn't go amongst them and speak to them. I'm happy that we have worked religiously, that we didn't cheat them and that we have something to take back to them tomorrow.' It summed up his philosophy perfectly. There was now something of the messiah about him, or at least that was how many people viewed him.

It worried Shankly, just as it had worried John Lennon when he innocently observed that the Beatles were almost as famous as Jesus Christ. Ian Hargreaves of the *Liverpool Echo* remembers asking Shankly if he would call at Alder Hey hospital one day to see a particularly ill child. 'He was reluctant to go,' says Hargreaves. 'Not because he didn't care but because he didn't want to raise expectations. I remember him saying to me "I'm no God. People seem to think I'm a miracle-maker." '

Throughout his Liverpool days, Shankly was actively involved with Alder Hey Children's Hospital. 'I remember he used to come home sometimes from the hospital,' says Nessie. 'He'd be so upset. "I don't want anything to eat," he'd say, and he'd just go off to the garden for a while. It really upset him. There was nothing he could do to help those poor children, and it hurt and worried him so much.'

'Football is not a matter of life and death; it's much more important than that,' he once said half-jokingly, although he fully realised the importance of football to many ordinary folk. In a way, it was at the nub of his conflict. Football had become too important, both to him and the fans. It would take a tragedy at Hillsborough to put it back into perspective. Suddenly, Shankly found himself raised to a deity; there were fans kissing his feet, trampling over his garden, the sick searching for hope. He had become almost too important, a legend in his own lifetime.

But what he did believe in was socialism. 'I am a socialist naturally because I am a coalminer. I believe in socialism but not to the extent that I'm bigoted.' he once said. It wasn't a refined form of socialism. There was nothing scientific or ideological about it, and he had probably never read a book or a pamphlet about socialism though he certainly understood the word 'capitalism'. It was simply that socialism happened to coincide with his own morality.

Shankly never cared much for politicians, they were 'two-faced, even three-faced', always trying to please one too many people. Nor was he much taken with the Labour government which he claimed had let them all down with some of their policies in the mid-seventies. But there could never be any doubting that on polling day he would be casting his vote for Labour.

Shankly's adherence to socialism could almost be taken for granted. His brand of politics was about compassion, sharing and the decency of working life. Its roots lay firmly in the mining communities back in Ayrshire, the same communities that had forged men like the first Labour leader Keir Hardie.

In later years, Shankly's politics had been refined in equally depressed areas such as Carlisle and Workington. 'A man's politics are himself,' he once observed. It was fundamental to him, like a living religion. He always called himself a religious man though on his own admission he was not a churchgoer. 'But that's not to say that I don't believe,' he would add cautiously.

Bill Shankly

He could almost have been a politician but he could never have been a party man, toeing a three-line whip, or abiding by conference policy. He was a political maverick, shunning authority, setting out his own rules and beliefs. After Liverpool had won the FA Cup in 1974, the team appeared at St George's Square in the city centre. Shankly spoke to the crowd of around 80,000 packed into the square. But he wasn't just talking football. He had a higher message for his audience.

'Since I've come here to Liverpool, to Anfield, I've drummed it into my players, time and again, that they are privileged to play for you. And if they didn't believe me then, they do now. I've drummed into them that they must be loyal, that they must never cheat you the public . . . The Kop's exclusive, an institution, and if you're a member of the Kop, you feel you're a member of a society, you've got thousands of friends around you and they're united and loyal . . .' It was the message of the fiery methodist preacher, the Labour politician, the angry trade union leader.

Shankly even took his politics on to the football field, preaching to his sides to play with a touch of socialism; which meant players helping each other out, complementing each other, being proud, and full of work and honour. But at the end of the day, you also had to stand up for yourself. He didn't take to slackers.

If players were not prepared to fight and challenge for the whole 90 minutes, then they were not his kind and consequently not the Liverpool kind. He talked of the pride in pulling on a red jersey and going out to greet the crowd for the first time. Similarly he hated malingerers and, especially anyone who was injured. In his book, you didn't get injured. If you were, he'd freeze you out. It didn't just happen at Anfield, it had happened wherever he managed.

After his retirement, Shankly hosted a chat show on Radio City. Among his guests was former Labour Prime Minister Harold Wilson. 'Wilson arrived with his entourage of minders, civil servants and police in tow. Wilson sat in awe of him,' remembers the show's producer Elton Welsby. 'It was astonishing to see this man, who held the highest office in the land, so in awe of a retired football manager.'

Shankly was in his element. 'Who do you think was the first social-ist?' Shankly asked. Wilson fumbled with his pipe, not quite sure of the answer. 'Er, Ramsay MacDonald?' he suggested hesitantly. 'Nah,' replied Shankly dismissively. 'Jesus Christ, son, Jesus Christ.' For Shankly, religion and socialism were one and the same thing.

Shankly had been a slave to football. Every spare moment had been spent in pursuit of footballing glory. He had travelled the length and breadth of Britain watching football matches, always on the look-out for a new star, always checking on some player or other. He was even reputed to have taken his wife Nessie to watch Rochdale playing on their wedding anniversary. 'Nae, it was nae Rochdale,' he growled, 'It was Rochdale reserves.'

He might have joked about it but he knew as well as anyone that his obsession had eaten into his homelife. Nessie had been the long-suffering wife though she had always put up with it in silence, accepting that this was the way it was. There were times when he should have been at home but had been away, and although the family was rightly proud of him they might also have liked to have spent more time with him. He once confessed that he and Nessie had only been out twice together since they had come to Liverpool. They had gone to the theatre once and also to a garden party. He wasn't proud of it. 'My family has suffered and I regret that,' he said. He meant it as well.

'We went downtown shopping once as a family,' remembers his daughter Jean, 'and we were mobbed. It was no pleasure.' After that, they preferred to leave Shankly at home, or if he needed to buy clothes, they would go somewhere other than Liverpool. 'It's true,' says Jean. 'We never went out as a family.' He was like a pop star. It made life difficult for them all.

Jean remembers being in hospital having a baby. 'I told him not to bother coming in because I knew what would happen. Well, I was sitting there one day and then I heard his unmistakable voice outside. There he was. Suddenly the entire ward emptied as every man rushed out to go and see him. I've never seen so many men move so quickly.' Family holidays never really existed. 'We'd go to Blackpool for a week,' says Nessie, 'to the Norbreck Hotel, and that was it.' Even when he was there, he found time for football. The Norbreck was full of Spanish and Italian waiters. It wouldn't be long before they were all out on the lawn playing football.

Shankly had nothing in the way of hobbies. His only interest outside football was the garden. He was no expert but he enjoyed mowing the lawn and doing some weeding. 'I'd plant flowers,' says Nessie, 'and he would be forever pulling them up, thinking they were weeds.' His only other activity around the house was cleaning the cooker. 'When Liverpool lost, he didn't come home sulking,' insists Nessie, 'but suddenly you'd hear a banging and a clanking from the kitchen and he'd be out there cleaning the cooker.'

Once Shankly had made his mind up to retire, it was simply a case of telling everyone. He'd been mulling it over in his mind since the season ended. Watching television with Nessie one evening in their lounge early that summer he casually told her that he had made a decision. He was going to retire. She was astonished but not wholly surprised. She had been ill the previous year and had asked him to retire, but he had said 'no' then.

A couple of days later, he asked John Smith for a meeting. 'It was like going to the electric chair,' he said. The directors could barely believe it. At first, they were inclined to think it was yet another Shankly threat. There had been so many in the past, especially in the early days. Every year, he would go along to Peter Robinson or someone on the board and tell them that he was going to quit. It was always a case of cheering him up, making him feel wanted, and they soon persuaded him to carry on. Give him time to cool down, they thought and he'll be back at the helm.

But there was also a feeling from some on the board that maybe this time it really was the right moment to let Shankly go. It had to happen sooner or later. He had had an abrasive relationship with the board. Peter Robinson had always acted as a buffer, soothing things down when they became heated or acting as a middle man. He'd always had a good honest relationship with Robinson, and they had never crossed swords during all their years. Tom Saunders was another he respected.

Shankly was a highly emotional man, torn between drama and devotion. There had been many blazing rows, though usually Shankly reserved his venom for pressmen. If they wrote something he strongly disagreed with, then he'd let them know, especially those he tended to trust. He expected loyalty in return, and was unable to comprehend that a journalist's job is not to enter into a binding contract of loyalty with the manager.

But he never bore a grudge or refused a journalist access to his thoughts or his players. 'Every journalist has done battle with him over and over again,' wrote Horace Yates of the *Liverpool Daily Post*, possibly the journalist closest to him, 'and yet at the very next meeting out would go his hand as though nothing had happened.'

There would be dressing room rows as well although it was usually left to one of his lieutenants, generally Fagan or Moran, to bawl out a player. Shankly would stand on the sidelines, pacing up and down the corridor. But just as he warmed to players like Hughes and Keegan, always shouting their virtues, he could just as easily take against players.

Like any other manager, he had his favourites. As long as you were playing well, you were certain to remain in his good books. But when things went wrong, the mood could change. Steve Heighway, for one, was terrified of him. 'We were all frightened,' he reckons. 'A lot of people see Shanks as being amusing and warm, and he was all those things, but I guarantee that 99% of all the players were frightened to death of him because he had that very abrasive, aggressive side to him as well.'

Just as Shankly could motivate a player and build him up into a footballing god he could also destroy someone. On one occasion, Heighway was reprimanded by Shankly during the half-time interval for blasting a shot over the bar when he should have passed to an unmarked teammate. 'I upped and told him he was being bloody stupid,' says Heighway. 'I felt so angry I was close to tears and Joe Fagan was quickly in to tell me to take it easy. Oddly enough, Shanks himself didn't mind my having reacted so fiercely. His words had touched me on the raw and I was still shaking with anger as I went out on the pitch for the second half.'

A Liverpool journalist also remembers travelling down to London on the train with Shankly. 'We sat in the restaurant car supping tea. Throughout the journey, he was telling me what a wonderful journalist I was, how I was always accurate, had insight and so on. I felt terrific. Then when we arrived at Euston, we noticed that Denis Law had been on the same train. Suddenly he was all over Law, they were hugging each other and so on. He introduced me to Law and then came out with some cruel comment. I was only young at the time and it knocked me flat. He could be very cruel, especially if you were young.'

There are many tales of Liverpool players being shunned when they were injured. Nor did it matter how good the player was. Denis Law claims Shankly did it with everyone. 'If I came out of the treatment room at the same time that Shanks was coming down the corridor, he would just walk right past me. It was incredible. Before the match, I'd been the greatest player in the game, but now I'd try to catch his eye and he'd just whistle and walk past staring at the ceiling.'

Even hard-man Tommy Smith was subjected to the cold stare when he was injured. Smith was never afraid to speak his mind and, on more than one occasion, he and Shankly ended up at each other's throats. But for all the arguing, once it was over, it was forgotten. 'He was the same at home,' says Nessie. 'He'd shout and then we'd forget about it. He never harboured a grudge.'

For Shankly, the game was about triers. Even if players had their off day – and even the best have the occasional lapse – Shankly expected them to at least try. It was when they didn't try that he would get angry and shun them. He and Paisley were triers, honest toilers who would never short-change anyone. If someone was paying for your services, you sweated, and gave of your best. The Kop always appreciated that. 'At least, he's trying,' fans would argue.

Maybe the parting of the ways was inevitable; maybe it was the best thing for Bill Shankly and for Liverpool Football Club. In hindsight, it made little difference to the way the club functioned. Shankly had established the structure and the practice; others simply (though it was never simple) took up where he had left off.

For some weeks, the board tried to persuade Shankly not to quit. The news hadn't yet leaked out of Anfield. Fortunately, it was summer and not too many journalists or players were around. But by early July it was clear that he was not going to change his mind.

Shankly made his announcement to the world on the morning of Friday 12 July 1974. That week, there had been whispers of a possible transfer deal bringing Arsenal's Ray Kennedy to Anfield. At the *Liverpool Echo*'s office that morning, the sports team were discussing the possibility of hanging a story around this piece of speculation when the phone rang.

Alex Goodman took the call. It was Peter Robinson, the Liverpool secretary. 'There's a press conference at Anfield at 12.15 today,' he told them. 'The board have a very special announcement to make. It is really important,' he stressed. 'It'll make front page news. Make sure you're there and don't be late.' 'Can you give us a hint what it might be about,' asked Goodman. 'No,' replied the ever-diplomatic Robinson. 'Is it to do with Ray Kennedy?' asked Goodman. 'No, it's nothing to do with any transfer deal,' answered Robinson. 'I can tell you no more.' When Goodman relayed the conversation to the others in the office, they were mystified. Goodman reported that there was an unusual tone about Robinson's voice. 'He sounded very official,' he said. 'It can only be one of two things,' suggested someone. 'Either they're about to sign someone really big like Mick Channon, or Shankly's resigning.' 'But he said that it was nothing to do with a transfer deal,' replied Goodman. 'That's it then,' replied the sports editor, 'Shankly's going.' But nobody really believed it for a minute.

In the VIP lounge at Anfield, the press corps was beginning to congregate. By 12 noon, there were 30 or 40 of them. Television cameras, microphones and lights were being erected. One by one, the club's directors wandered into the room and slowly took their places behind the long table that had been set out. There were a few smiles but generally it was solemn faces, just the odd nod here and there.

At 12 noon precisely, in marched Shankly looking tanned, relaxed and fighting fit. 'Hullo, boys,' he said to the pressmen, 'had a good holiday?' He was wearing a neatly cut herringbone suit, tangerine shirt and one of his famous ties. He turned to May the tea lady. 'Have we got time for a cup of tea May?' he asked. She nodded and poured him a cup. He then strolled over to the various reporters.

'Did ya see that World Cup?' he began. 'If some of that stuff had been played here at Anfield they'd have been hooted off the pitch.' The banter went back and forth as Shankly warmed to the subject of international football. Don Revie had just been appointed the new boss of England. 'Christ,' said Shankly, '48 and he's gone into semi-retirement.' After fourteen minutes of entertaining the press, Shankly glanced at his watch. 'Got to sit down now, boys.'

A television electrician switched on a light. 'Hold it, boys, Shankly joked, 'John Wayne hasn't arrived yet.' Everyone laughed. Then he sat down with chairman John Smith to his left and Jack Cross to his right. Further to his left was a tired looking club president Tom Williams, the man who had brought Shankly to Anfield.

John Smith began what was to be the most solemn press conference the club had ever held. It was also to provide the biggest shock Liverpudlians had known in years.

'It is with extreme reluctance,' began Smith his voice faltering slightly from time to time, 'that we have to announce that Bill Shankly manager of Liverpool Football Club has decided to retire. We have accepted his decision and want to place on record our great appreciation for the magnificent job he has done for us.' There was an audible gasp from the audience. Cameras flashed. Then Shankly spoke.

'This decision has been the most difficult thing in the world and, when I went to see the chairman to tell him, it was like walking to the electric chair. This is a decision that has not been taken lightly. It has been on my mind for twelve months, but my wife and I feel that we need a rest from the game so that we can charge up our batteries again.' More lights flashed as he spoke.

Within half an hour, the news had hit the streets of Liverpool. It was announced over the tannoy system at St John's market in the centre of town. Shoppers stopped in their tracks, and listened bewildered not knowing whether to believe it or not. Office workers sent staff on to the streets to buy the *Echo*; others searched for radios.

Tommy Smith dismissed it as nonsense. 'The close season's always too long for Shanks, never mind retirement,' he snapped. But it was true and it was there in black and white. 'Soccer Bombshell – Shankly Retires' was the only headline on the front page of the *Liverpool Echo*.

Nobody in Liverpool will forget the shock of hearing the announcement. Fans had expected him to go on forever. When Granada Television sent Tony Wilson and a film crew out on to the streets of Liverpool to gauge the public's reactions they found some fans who had not heard the news. They could scarcely believe it. It just wasn't true, they insisted. 'Shanks retire,' they asked astonished. 'Shanks'll never retire.' The very suggestion was ridiculous. That night in the pubs and clubs across Merseyside, there was only one topic of conversation. The King of the Kop had decided to abdicate.

As he quit Liverpool, Shankly was immediately asked by pressmen who he thought his successor might be. But he didn't want to get involved in that debate. In fact, he had offered a few names to the board but the surprise was that Bob Paisley's name was not among them. There were a couple of First Division managers, and one from another division. But Paisley did not feature in his suggestions. It was not until chairman John Smith asked him about Paisley that Shankly seriously considered him as a successor. 'Yes,' he said, 'I hadn't really thought about Bob. But yes.'

The *Echo* was soon suggesting Gordon Milne, Ron Yeats and Ian St John as possible successors, with Milne at the top of their list. Early the following week, Milne's name had been replaced by Paisley.

Perhaps Shankly's reluctance to suggest Paisley was because Paisley himself never seriously considered the job until it was offered him. To his credit, once he was in place, Paisley wisely decided that there was no point in changing things. Shankly had laid a good system down and all it needed was a little tinkering here and there when necessary. Anfield ran like a Rolls Royce engine.

At the end of the press conference, John Smith almost casually mentioned that Ray Kennedy, the Arsenal striker, was on his way to Merseyside and it was hoped that he would be signing for Liverpool later that day. By 3 pm, Shankly had settled the Kennedy signing leaving behind a worthy legacy. It was his parting gift.

'Do you fancy being a director,' someone asked him. 'Ah, no,' replied Shankly, 'not even if they paid me.' 'So how would he sum up his career?' 'Well, I was the best manager in Britain because I was never devious or cheated anyone. I'd break my wife's legs if I played against her, but I'd never cheat her.' 'Any regrets?' 'Aye, just one. Not winning the European Cup.'

And with that, it was all over. Shankly stood up, fighting back the tears. 'There'll not be many days like this, lads,' he said as he made his way out of the room. Tom Williams wept openly and unashamedly.

18 You'll Never Walk Alone

S IX WEEKS AFTER WALKING OUT OF ANFIELD, Shankly realised that he had made a dreadful mistake. He did not know what to do with himself. At first, it was a novelty. He could get out of bed whenever he wanted; he could sit and read the papers all morning. But that wasn't Shankly. He was always up early, always busy. He needed to be doing something and, above all, he needed to be talking football.

All his life, all he had ever wanted to do was talk football with people, whether they were managers, players or ordinary supporters. Now he was having to go in search of company. He had long been fond of telling people that the word retirement should be taken out of the dictionary. Now he was experiencing its full meaning.

Shankly had always led a simple life. Outside football, there was nothing except his family. He relaxed by doing a spot of gardening, though even that never amounted to much more than mowing the lawn and tidying around. Of an evening, he might watch television, especially if there was a good gangster movie on, or listen to his records. But it was a simple selection.

When he appeared on *Desert Island Discs* in 1965, his choice was predictable – 'My Love Is Like A Red, Red Rose', 'When The Saints Go Marching In', 'Danny Boy', 'Because', and of course 'You'll Never Walk Alone'. His book was *The Life of Robert Burns*. And his luxury item? What else, but a football.

The new season was about to kick off. In the papers, everyone was wondering how Liverpool would cope without him. The pundits were predicting that this was the end of the great Liverpool; like every team, they had had their day. Although Paisley had been appointed as his successor, everyone knew that Liverpool would never be the same without Shankly. Now they were about to go into decline. Shankly itched to be back at the helm. He was like a caged lion.

It gnawed at him not to be part of it. His daily routine had gone. He'd been down to Melwood on a few occasions, done a spot of training with the players and was now feeling refreshed. He'd even been at Melwood the Monday after he had quit, picking up as if nothing had happened, just keeping things going until they appointed his successor. He gathered the players together that morning and tried to explain his reasons for quitting.

But all he could muster were excuses. 'It was Nessie,' he said, 'a wonderful wife, she wanted me to retire, she hadn't been well and wanted me to spend more time at home with her.' It was all true, but it was only part of the story.

Weeks after quitting, Shankly decided to ring John Smith. They chatted for a few minutes then Shankly asked if he could come in and see him. 'Yes, of course,' said Smith wondering what it was all about. They met the following day at Anfield in the boardroom. Smith assumed that he simply wanted to talk some unfinished business, something to do with money.

After exchanging courtesies for ten minutes, Shankly reluctantly came to the point. Finally, he spluttered it out. 'I want to come back,' he said. Smith looked at him in astonishment. 'I've made a mistake. I should have sorted everything out, taken a rest. I was tired. But now I feel refreshed and ready for the new season.'

But it wasn't as easy as that. Smith needed time to think this one through. He didn't want to raise Shankly's hopes, nor did he wish to dash them so quickly. He needed to consult people although his own mind was firmly made up.

'Well, it's very difficult now, Bill,' Smith finally admitted. 'Bob's in charge and I don't think we can simply take it away from him. You've put us in a very tricky situation.' Smith promised to talk with his colleagues immediately and come back to Shankly. But there was never any doubt what Smith would decide. Paisley was in place and that was it.

The club were not about to suddenly cast Paisley aside after having persuaded him to take over the reins. The board had also spent considerable time trying to dissuade Shankly against retirement earlier in the summer. They had kept the matter quiet, while attempts were made to keep him at Anfield. But he himself had insisted on going.

Smith knew that it would not work either. Shankly was 60 and, even if he did return, how much longer would it be before he decided to retire again? No, a decision had been made, and the club had to stick by it. There was no going back for Shankly.

The news never leaked out and, even to this day, only a handful of people have ever been aware that Shankly might have returned to Anfield. Even his wife claims that she did not know about it. She remains sceptical. 'I think he would have told me,' she says. 'Once he had made up his mind about something, then that was it. He didn't usually change his mind.' But as Smith well understood, his return would have caused far more problems than it would have resolved. It was a case of 'The King is Dead; Long Live The King.'

Smith's decision didn't keep Shankly away from Anfield. He started by turning up occasionally, but, within a month or so, he was turning up every morning, getting into a routine. He'd train, laugh and joke with the players, talk about the game, their next opponent and so on. It was all very difficult. The players even continued to call him 'boss'.

At first, it was good to see him down at Melwood, but, as time wore on and Shankly kept showing up, it became embarrassing. At the back of everyone's mind was the situation at Old Trafford when Matt Busby had retired. Busby's continuing presence had made life unbearably difficult for new manager Wilf McGuinness and, in the end, had probably cost McGuinness his job when Busby was recalled to stop the slide. Paisley must have feared a similar predicament at Anfield, knowing that any mistakes, any failures would no doubt result in a chorus of demands for Shankly's return. Following a legend is difficult enough as it is, without the legend breathing down your neck.

Paisley was in an impossible position. He didn't want to offend Shankly, but his continuing presence was calling his own role into question. Shankly's charisma was as overpowering as ever. The players also needed to understand that the Shankly era was over and that Bob Paisley was now in charge. The situation drifted on for some time, but eventually Paisley was forced to have a word with him. He didn't want to but he was left with little alternative. Paisley had to do things his way.

Not surprisingly, Shankly was upset at his former number two telling him that his presence was an embarrassment. Paisley told him as gently as he could but it was still hurtful. Paisley insisted that he was still welcome at Melwood, and always would be, but that he simply had to understand things were different now. Sadly, in Shankly's eyes, Liverpool did not want him anymore. He felt that he was no longer welcome at Melwood. Shankly interpreted Paisley's message as a 'keep out' warning. He decided to take the hint.

Paisley even suggested that he might like to do some scouting for the club, to go up to Scotland and take a look at a few players. 'He could have taken Nessie up with him, looked around for players and got his expenses,' pointed out Paisley. 'I wanted to keep him involved but he got sickened off. It had got on top of him.'

There was undoubtedly a coolness between the two men after that. Rift is probably too strong a word, but there was a distance, especially when the season began and Shankly's absence seemed to make no difference to Liverpool's results. 'When I got away too well for him, he became a bit jealous and we didn't see much of him,' wrote Paisley in his book.

It had always been purely a working relationship and, when they were not working together, it was inevitable that tensions, even jealousies would surface – especially when Paisley proved that he could manage quite well without Shankly. The trophies were soon rolling in again. Years later, Shankly was invited to present Bob Paisley with the Manager of the Year award. 'You probably think I'm jealous at having to give this wonderful honour to Bob Paisley, Manager of the Year,' he began his speech. 'Well, you'd be damn right!' It was said with a laugh, but there was more than a grain of truth to it.

Nor did the club help the situation. Nobody was prepared to contemplate the obvious solution by offering a life presidency or a seat on the board to Shankly. A directorship would have flattered Shankly and probably kept him away from Melwood and out of the dressing room. There wasn't even a permanent seat in the director's box for him. At Old Trafford, Busby had a seat with his name engraved on it. Shankly however would never have asked for such a thing. He was too proud. If something wasn't offered, then he would not ask.

In truth, the board were frightened of Shankly. He was a powerful figure, both inside and outside the club. They feared the repercussions, worried that they would not be able to cope with his whims, that he might get out of control. They felt threatened. They reasoned he'd be interfering in transfer deals, suggesting team changes and so on. Such a role, they reckoned, would only consolidate Shankly's power and nobody felt equipped to challenge him.

The insecurity was probably mutual. Throughout his footballing days, whether as a player or in management, Shankly never felt comfortable in the presence of directors. There had been problems at Huddersfield and even at Liverpool, particularly in the early years. Shankly was not an educated man and simply felt uneasy in their company. He was not worldly-wise and all he knew about was football.

Directors, with their cigars and posh suits, were not his kind of people. He was far more at home with the ordinary fan, the Kopite. They were dockers, shipyard workers, bus drivers and the like. He could relate to them; they were from the same kind of background.

Shankly never had much social chat. He could talk about football but little else. Other managers, like Tommy Docherty or Malcolm Allison, despised directors just as much, and were no better educated than Shankly, but they had the confidence and brashness to get by. They mocked directors. Shankly felt both old-fashioned respect for them and scorn. In short, he preferred to avoid their company.

To be fair, the club did arrange for him to have a testimonial in 1975 at Anfield and a crowd of 40,000 turned up to see Liverpool play a Don Revie XI, bringing in £25,000. Shankly continued to watch games at Anfield but was never quite certain of his position. He would go in the director's box, but after the game would feel unwelcome in the boardroom. He'd visit the dressing room but didn't want to interfere too much. His solution was to simply ring up for a ticket and sit in the stands.

On one famous occasion against Coventry, he even went on the Kop. He probably felt more at home there, but he could never come fully to terms with Liverpool's continuing success. There would always be that nagging doubt that he had quit too early and that the glory could still have been his.

There were very few invitations to travel with the club to away games. Liverpool kept their distance. And when they did invite him to a match, to the UEFA Cup Final in Bruges, he was billeted in a separate hotel, along with the players' wives. He hated it and was deeply hurt not to be with the team.

Nonetheless, it still surprised everyone, when Shankly suddenly voiced his bitterness in print. His autobiography, published in 1976, was a revelation as his anger spilled on to the pages. 'It is scandalous and outrageous that I should have to write these things about the club I helped to build,' he wrote, after complaining about the club's reluctance to supply tickets, the failure to offer him a directorship and so forth.

But if he did not feel comfortable at Melwood, he was to find a welcome mat in the most unexpected of places – Everton. At Goodison, they regularly rolled the red carpet out for him. Perhaps they were just glad that they didn't have to face him any more. Whatever the reason, he was always made welcome at Goodison and began to watch Everton on a regular basis.

He even trained with them at Bellefield, a stone's throw from his house. It made sense. There was considerable respect for Shankly at Everton. The Blues legend, Alex Young 'the golden vision', had once been asked who was the greatest manager he had ever played with. 'Bill Shankly,' he replied.

Young had played for Shankly just once, in a testimonial for Dixie Dean in 1964. The game had been between a Liverpool Scotland XI and a Liverpool England XI. Shankly took charge of the Scotland side with Alex Young in his ranks. 'It was the only time I was inspired off the park at Goodison,' he says. 'I really admired Shankly. I would have loved to have played under him.'

Nobody at Goodison felt threatened by Shankly and equally he had nothing to prove. At the time, Mick Lyons, the former Everton captain used to take an Under-12s and Under-14s football session on a Sunday afternoon. Shankly would regularly turn up. 'He used to have his red track suit on, and he'd play with the kids,' remembers Lyons. 'They used to play about twenty-a-side and Shankly would be amongst them all playing. They'd play for about two hours. One day, he came in and said, "We had a great game today, we won 19-17." '

Other days, he would play five-a-side with friends at the Stanley Leisure Centre, then go for a cup of tea in the cafe opposite the Alder Hey hospital and hold court. His generosity continued unabated. Football commentator Elton Welsby remembers being with him on one trip in Europe, when they bumped into a couple of Liverpool fans with their girlfriends.

'The four of them had hitch-hiked, walked and busked their way across the continent to get to the game. They recounted their tale at length to Shankly. "How are yah goin tae get back?" he asked. They had no idea but weren't worried. Shankly reached into his back pocket, and brought out a wad of notes. I watched him count out £100 and hand it to them. It was enough to get them to Timbuktu.'

But he missed it all, so terribly. He was as active as ever. He went to nearby St Edwards College most days to help them out with their football training, and became active in various charities, especially the Royal Institute for the Blind and Alder Hey Hospital. 'We thought we would see more of him,' says his daughter Jean, 'but he seemed to be just as busy and happy.'

But at times he was lost. He just wanted to talk football. One journalist remembers going to Goodison to cover matches on a Saturday and hearing the voice of Shankly. 'I regret to say, I'd try and avoid him,' he says, 'I knew that, if I got into conversation, I'd never get away. All he would want to do was talk about the game. I had the job of covering the match and I couldn't afford the time.' He wasn't the only one who shunned Shankly in those later years.

Another journalist, Bob Greaves, kept bumping into him at grounds around the North West. Greaves noticed that Shankly would always vacate his seat with just a few minutes of the match remaining. Eventually he realised why. Shankly was leaving his seat in order to park himself close to the entrance to the directors' box, so that as soon as the whistle sounded he would be ideally placed to greet everyone as they came out. He wanted to be seen and to be recognised. And they would all have to pass him by. Invariably, they would shake his hand and chat to him. 'He craved an audience,' says Greaves.

On another occasion, Greaves remembers him standing by the directors' box entrance at Maine Road just as the final whistle sounded. As Greaves came by, Shankly stopped him, shook his hand and in a loud voice announced, 'Bob Greaves, Granada Television presenter supreme, one of the finest in the land, works on Granada Reports, along with Anna Ford, serene, beautiful voice, the nicest lady on television, and David Jones, amusing, scouser, does some of the funniest reports I've ever seen . . .'

By this time, there were some 200 or so standing around listening to his every word. 'It was an astonishing performance, a brilliant analysis of each presenter' says Greaves. 'But more importantly,' he adds, 'it was Shankly the stage performer, the man who needed an audience and who could play to an audience.' He was orchestrating everyone, just as he had with the Kop.

In April 1979, Shankly was invited to be a speaker at the Eastham Lodge Golf Club on the Wirral. Shankly was no golfer and normally he would not have bothered accepting such an invitation, but this one came from the club's President, his old friend Joe Mercer. Reluctantly, he accepted. Mercer then told the club's secretary George Higham, who was himself a director of Tranmere Rovers, to write and confirm everything. Higham did so, but on the morning of the dinner Shankly got in touch to say that he could not come. He gave some excuse but Higham tried to persuade him from crying off.

'I don't like golf, it's not my game,' argued Shankly. Finally he blurted out the truth. 'I don't like golf clubs, and I'm not very good at posh do's.' Higham did his best to put him at ease and eventually Shankly agreed to turn up. 'It was quite clear,' says Higham, 'that he was afraid and didn't think he would like it.'

In the event, Shankly had a memorable evening. 'When he stood up to speak, he had a great wodge of notes,' remembers Higham. 'He was very nervous and started reading his speech. But then he put it down and simply started talking to us and telling us tales and all the nervousness melted away.' Shankly spoke for almost two hours to a captivated audience.

But that evening also revealed something else. Higham, something of a football memorabilia collector, had managed to get hold of a programme for the 1938 FA Cup Final when Preston and Shankly had won the FA Cup. He had had it bound in red leather with a suitable inscription on the front cover. At the end of the evening, it was presented to an astonished Shankly. He could barely believe it. Like all footballers, he had either lost or given away his only copy of the programme and was thrilled to be receiving another.

'We just wanted to give him something nice,' says Higham. 'We knew he would never accept money, so I hit upon this idea.' Shankly choked back the tears and, in a rare moment, confessed to Higham later that 'I do all these events for people yet nobody ever thinks about what I would like.'

'He was very touched,' says Higham, 'but I always remember those words. I suddenly felt very sorry for him. People had been soaking him dry for years. And I think it hurt.'

But retirement had its compensations. Shankly had more time for the family. Every weekend, his two daughters Barbara and Jeanette would turn up along with his grandchildren. He delighted in playing with them. He even went on holiday, though not too often, to Glasgow. And of course there was more time to shake a few hands. 'I can always find time to talk to a kid or sign an autograph,' he said. In 1974, he was awarded the OBE and made the trip to Buckingham Palace with Nessie. It was a rare day out for them. It was another national honour, to add to his appearance years earlier on television's *This Is Your Life*.

Shankly also took a job with Radio City hosting his own chat show. It was enormously successful. Every week, he'd have someone new on the show. He'd suggest names and the programme's producer would try and book them. They never experienced any trouble in persuading people to come on the show. Peggy Mount, Freddie Starr, Lulu, even the Prime Minister Harold Wilson. They were all in awe of him. But it wasn't always a star name. Sometimes, he would just invite ordinary folk on, as long as they had something interesting to say, a good tale, a fascinating life.

Elton Welsby, then a commentator with Radio City, hired him as a co-commentator for the 1976 UEFA Cup Final in Bruges. Shankly had been billeted in a hotel with the players' wives. Welsby was staying in a hotel elsewhere. At 10 am on the morning of the game, Shankly called Welsby at his hotel. 'Ellie, my son,' he said. 'I think we ought to get to the ground early, soak up the atmosphere before tonight's big game. This is an auspicious occasion, you know.' 'Fine,' replied Welsby. 'When do you want me to pick you up?' 'Oh, in half an hour, son,' replied Shankly.

Welsby duly picked him up and by 11 am the two of them were in the stadium. They then had to while away the hours in an empty stadium until the 8 pm kick-off. 'He was lonely,' says Welsby. 'He didn't want to be stuck with the players' wives all day. He wanted to talk football, to be involved in the big occasion.'

Shankly also spent time at Tranmere Rovers, across the Mersey in Birkenhead, taking on a role as consultant in November 1974. Ron Yeats was manager at Tranmere then and John King was his number two. Tranmere were going through a particularly bad patch and were struggling near the bottom of Division Three.

The fans turned out in droves for Shankly's first match, as Tranmere beat Bobby Charlton's Preston North End 3-1. Shankly had been called in to lend some advice. He watched but said little. After six weeks and not much improvement, John King asked him what they should do. Should they change tactics, adopt a different style of play? What exactly did Shankly advise? Shankly looked him in the eye. 'You're making a fundamental error,' he told King. 'You're changing at Bromborough. You should change at Prenton Park.'

And that was Shankly's advice. Instead of changing at their ground, the team had been travelling directly to their training pitch at Bromborough and doing everything there. King and Yeats immediately instituted a new policy with the team changing at Prenton Park before travelling to Bromborough. It brought immediate results.

Unfortunately, the results did not last. By the end of the season, Yeats and Shankly had gone as Tranmere crashed into the Fourth Division. 'It was the greatest time of learning that I probably ever had,' admits John King. Wrexham also sought out Shankly's help. Every week, he'd ring them up for a chat just to find out how things were going.

He enjoyed his spell helping Tranmere, a friendly club, not unlike Workington or Carlisle. He'd turn up from time to time during the week and went to most matches. Occasionally, he sat on the bench. 'Who's that slow right winger?' he once asked Ron Yeats. 'That's Alan Duffy, boss,' replied Yeats, 'he's our PTA union rep.' 'Christ,' snapped Bill. 'Why are you paying him if he's on strike.'

Tranmere also invited Shankly to away games in the hope that some of his magic would rub off on the players. He was just the same as when he had been at Liverpool.

John King remembers sitting in the lounge of some hotel with Shankly and Yeats one Friday evening. The players had all gone off to bed. 'It was 10.30 pm. Shankly stood up and announced, "Right, lads, I'm off to bed now." He looked at Ron and me. "Good night," I said to him. But he just stood there hovering. Ron understood what was going on. "Come on, John," Ron says to me, pulling me up. So we got up and left the lounge. Outside, Ron says to me. "He expects us to go to bed at 10.30 pm as well you know. Come on, we'll go to our rooms and then sneak down later to finish our drinks." ' It was typical. Yeats and King might have been the managers but Shankly saw himself as the boss. Yeats even continued to call him 'boss'.

Within weeks of Shankly's arrival, Tranmere were giving a debut to a youngster called Steve Coppell. He was an old-fashioned winger, built like Tom Finney and with the devilment and pace of the former Preston man. Not surprisingly, Shankly took an instant liking to him. The more he saw of Coppell, the more he was impressed. He immediately got in touch with Liverpool.

'There's a lad here just like Finney,' he told them. 'You should come and see him. He's tremendous.' But his words of wisdom fell on deaf ears. Nobody was interested. Shankly was upset that his advice should be ignored.

In the end, he phoned Tommy Docherty at Manchester United. Docherty had been particularly kind to Shankly after his retirement. When he heard of Liverpool's treatment of Shankly, he had deliberately called to tell him that he was always welcome at Old Trafford. Shankly was touched by his kindness. When Docherty received his phone call, he immediately promised to have someone watch Coppell. Within the year, Coppell was a Manchester United player.

Over the years, Shankly had become renowned for his off-the-cuff remarks. Some were bizarre; others defied sense; some seemed to hit the nail on the head. His most famous remark that football was 'not a matter of life and death; it's much more important than that' caught the mood of many a fan. Sadly, the events at Hillsborough in 1989 really put football into perspective.

But some of Shankly's comments defied logic. 'Amazing grass, boys, it's green, professional grass,' he once told his players examining the turf at Anfield. It didn't make sense. Of course it was grass; of course it was green. But of course you knew just what he meant.

On one occasion, he was with Jim McGregor, the Everton trainer, jogging around Bellefield. McGregor told him how well he looked. 'Aye, I feel really well today,' replied Shankly. 'As a matter of fact, Jim, I wouldn't mind if I dropped dead right now.' McGregor looked at him quizzically. Shankly explained. 'Well, just imagine. I'd be in a coffin and they'd all walk past and say, "Look at Bill, doesn't he look well today. There lies a fit man!" '

Journalists collected and cherished his cracks. So did the players. They were rarely considered or planned; they simply spilled out. 'I remember we had just thrashed Fulham one day,' recalls Phil Chisnall. 'We could have scored ten, we were that good. A journalist asked Shankly what he thought about it. "Aye," he replied, "I thought Fulham were the best side we've played this season." On another occasion, he was asked if he had had a good Christmas. "Aye, no bad," he replied. "Four points out of six." '

Shortly after breakfast on the morning of Saturday 26 September 1981, Bill Shankly suffered a heart attack. He was immediately rushed to Broadgreen Hospital where his condition appeared to stabilise. There seemed to be no threat to his life though only his family were allowed to see him. Hundreds of cards poured into the hospital. But on the following Monday morning, his condition suddenly deteriorated. He was transferred into the intensive care unit but, at 12.30 am on Tuesday 29 September he suffered a cardiac arrest and was certified dead at 1.20 am. Nessie was by his side.

The news was scarcely believable. 'Shankly Is Dead' was the headline splashed across the front page on the *Liverpool Daily Post* that morning. Throughout the city, flags flew at half-mast. At Anfield, they called the day's training off and everybody hovered around the club not sure what to do, even though many of the players had never known Shankly.

Paisley, Fagan and Moran were in tears. Ron Yeats was heartbroken. 'He was like a second father to me,' he said. Over in Manchester, Matt Busby wept uncontrollably, unable to take any telephone calls from journalists. At the Labour Party annual conference in Brighton, delegates stood in silence to remember a man who had always been a socialist.

From across the world, the tributes poured in; from the great European clubs, from international stars, from all the former Liverpool players as well as those from Huddersfield, Carlisle, Grimsby, Preston and Workington. From Liverpool chairman John Smith came the simple but fitting tribute: 'In my opinion, he was the most outstanding and dynamic manager of the century.'

Everyone had a memory, a story to tell, some classic Shankly quip. But apart from his family, the pain was felt most by those who had never even met him, the ordinary football fans from Merseyside. Shankly had brought something to their lives, enriching them with his enthusiasm and love of the game. They would never forget him.

Shankly had seemed immortal. His entire life had been devoted to fitness. He'd jogged every day, never drank and had only smoked in his younger days. He was as fit as any man of his age. In those circumstances, to die at 68 was surely to die before your time.

Johnny Giles, the former Leeds United player, had a perceptive comment. 'I believe Bill Shankly died of a broken heart after he stopped managing Liverpool and saw them go on to even greater success without him,' he claimed, adding 'giving your whole life to a football club is a sad mistake.' There may have been more than a grain of truth in what he said.

Just over a week later on Friday 2 October, his funeral took place at St Mary's Church in West Derby, not far from his home. Outside the

Everton training ground near his house, all the Everton players and staff stood in respectful silence as the cortege began its journey.

The leaden skies that morning matched the mood of the thousands who lined the streets to see the funeral cortege pass by. At the church, the big men, John Toshack, Ron Yeats, Emlyn Hughes and Ray Clemence, carried his coffin, escorted by Kevin Keegan, Ian Callaghan and Ian St John.

Lots of his former players were there, along with his old friends Matt Busby, Tom Finney and Tommy Docherty. Almost every one of the 92 clubs in the Football League were represented. As the service ended, they played 'You'll Never Walk Alone' and Shankly was carried on his final journey through the streets of Anfield to the Priory Road Crematorium near the Liverpool ground.

TV presenter Sue Lawley once asked him how he would like to be remembered. 'Basically as an honest man,' he replied, 'in a game that is sometimes short on honesty. That I've put more into the game than I've taken out; that I haven't cheated anyone; that I've been working for people honestly all along the line, for people in Liverpool that go to Anfield. That I've been working for them to try and give them entertainment.'

In 1980, he attended the funeral of the former Everton centre forward Bill 'Dixie' Dean at St James' church in Birkenhead, a stone's throw from where Dean had been born and lived throughout his life. The two men had faced each other on many occasions. 'He was always a fair player,' Dean had once said of Shankly. Coming from Dean that was praise indeed. Joe Mercer read the lesson that morning but Shankly provided the most fitting comment. 'Today,' he said, 'there is no red and blue, no black and white, no protestants and catholics – just mourning for a great footballer.' Shankly would have felt proud and honoured to have the same epitaph.

There was a time when Liverpool almost forgot him. In the era of Graeme Souness, they cast aside many of the traditions. They ripped the heart out of the club, tearing the bootroom down to turn it into a press room. Then, worst of all, they pulled down the Kop, the very soul of Liverpool Football Club. But it all went badly wrong.

The club plunged from crisis to crisis. They signed misfits, they changed the training routine; they paid out vast salaries, almost went into debt, until they finally realised that the system laid down by Shankly marked their foundations.

Fortunately, the spirit of Shankly still stalks Anfield. It always will. On dark windswept nights, his steel toecaps can be heard echoing down the corridors, his shoes scuffing the concrete floor as he makes for the dressing room.

You can sense him lurking in the corner as the team make their last-minute preparations, his fist clenched, ready with a few words of encouragement. 'Come on, son,' he's telling them, slapping each one on the back as they prepare to leave the dressing room. 'They're rubbish that lot. They're not fit to tie your bootlaces.'

And as the players make their way out, he tidies things around a little. It's quiet in the dressing room now. He hangs up Roger Hunt's spare number ten shirt, sees that Kevin Keegan has some extra shin pads. Then out he goes, down the corridor, a smile here, a handshake there.

And as Shankly climbs the steps that lead out on to the pitch, he reaches up to touch the 'This Is Anfield' sign. In the distance, you can hear the Kop singing a final chorus of 'You'll Never Walk Alone'. As it finishes, he emerges on to the pitch, looks towards his beloved fans on the Kop and raises his arms in salute. The Kop responds, 'Shank-lee, Shank-lee, Shank-lee . . .'

Career Summary

Born: 2 September 1913, Glenbuck, Ayrshire

Playing Career:
Carlisle United
Joined July 1932.
Debut 31 December 1932 v Rochdale.
Sixteen league appearances, all in Third Division North.

Preston North End
Joined July 1933 for £500.
Debut 9 December 1933 v Hull City, Second Division.
First goal v Liverpool 2 February 1938.
1933/34 Runners up Second Division – promoted.
1936/37 FA Cup Finalists: Preston 1 Sunderland 3.
1937/38 FA Cup Winners: Preston 1 Huddersfield Town 0 (aet).
Final game v Sunderland 19 March 1949.
Total of 297 league appearances for Preston and thirteen league goals
including eight penalties.

International Career:
Five caps for Scotland
v England, April 1938
v Ireland, October 1938
v Wales, November 1938
v Hungary, December 1938
v England, April 1939

Seven wartime international caps for Scotland.

Wartime Football
1940/41 Northern Regional League Championship with Preston.
1940/41 League Cup Final winner with Preston.

Managerial Career:
Carlisle United
Joined March 1949.
1948/49 Fifteenth in Third Division North.
1949/50 Ninth in Third Division North.
1950/51 Third in Third Division North.

Grimsby
Joined July 1951.
1951/52 Second in Third Division North.
1952/53 Fifth in Third Division North.
1953/54 Resigned January 1954 after 26 games.

Workington
Appointed manager January 1954.
1953/54 Eighteenth in Third Division North.
1954/55 Eighth in Third Division North.
1955/56 Resigned November 1955.

Huddersfield Town
Appointed coach December 1955.
Appointed manager November 1956.
1956/57 Twelfth in Division Two.
1957/58 Ninth in Division Two.
1958/59 Fourteenth in Division Two.
1959/60 Resigned December 1959.

Liverpool
Appointed manager December 1959.
1959/60 Third in Division Two.
1960/61 Third in Division Two.
1961/62 Champions Division Two.
1962/63 Eighth in Division One.
   FA Cup semi-finalists.
1963/64 Champions Division One.
1964/65 Seventh in Division One.
   FA Cup winners: Liverpool 2 Leeds United 1 (aet).

European Cup semi-finalists.
1965/66 Champions Division One.
    European Cup-Winners Cup finalists:
        Liverpool 1 Borussia Dortmund 2 (aet).
1966/67 Fifth in Division One.
1967/68 Third in Division One.
1968/69 Second in Division One.
1969/70 Fifth in Division One.
1970/71 Fifth in Division One.
    FA Cup Finalists: Liverpool 1 Arsenal 2 (aet).
    UEFA Cup semi-finalists.
1971/72 Third in Division One.
1972/73 Champions Division One.
    UEFA Cup winners.
1973/74 Second in Division One.
    FA Cup winners: Liverpool 3 Newcastle United 0.

Retired July 1974

Awarded OBE 1974

Died: 29 September 1981

Bibliography

Among the many books and newspapers consulted are the following:

Newspapers

Athletic News
Sporting Chronicle
The Liverpool Echo
The Liverpool Daily Post
The Liverpool Footballer Echo
The Huddersfield Examiner
The People
The Association of Football Statisticians magazine
The Kop
XTRA Time
The Daily Mirror
The News of the World
The Carlisle Evening News and Star
The Daily Mail
The Daily Express

Books

Shankly: *Shankly* (1976)
Paisley: *An Autobiography* (1983)
Rogan: *The Football Managers* (1989)
Walsh: *Dixie Dean* (1977)
Rollin: *Soccer At War* (1985)
Young: *Football On Merseyside* (1963)
Doherty: *Spotlight On Football* (1947)

Bill Shankly

Thompson: *Shankly* (1994)
Dunphy: *A Strange Kind Of Glory* (1991)
Taylor and Ward: *Three Sides Of the Mersey* (1993)
Kelly: *Liverpool In Europe* (1992)
Kelly: *You'll Never Walk Alone* (1991)
Kelly: *The Kop, The End of an Era* (1993)
So Sad, So Very Sad, The League History of Workington
Ponting and Hale: *The Bootroom* (1994)
Marks: *Eddie's Golden Years Scrapbooks* (1986)
Law: *An Autobiography* (1979)
Triggs, Hepton and Woodhead: *Grimsby Town* (1989)
Pead: *Liverpool, A Complete Record* (1986)
Faulds and Tweedie: *The Cherrypickers* (1951)
Findlay: *Garcan 1631 to Muirkirk 1950* (1980)
Hodge: *Through the Parish of Muirkirk*
Huddersfield Town: *A Complete Record*

Miscellaneous

Football programmes and annual yearbooks of Liverpool FC,
Huddersfield Town FC, Workington Town FC, Carlisle United FC,
Grimsby Town FC, plus various Cup Final and international
programmes.